MR. GABE

A YOUNG BOY'S HOPE
THROUGH LIFE'S TRAUMA

HERSHEL MARISE

PAGE PUBLISHING
Conneaut Lake, PA

First originally published by Page Publishing 2022

ISBN 978-1-6624-7139-1 (pbk)
ISBN 978-1-6624-7140-7 (digital)

Printed in the United States of America

I dedicate this book to all of my children with hope and prayers that you use the challenges I have faced to learn from others' hardships. Have faith that your great Creator will guide you through all trauma and challenges that will come your way. Try to remember that trauma doesn't place you as a victim; it instead gives you pathways and opportunities to great learning.

Prologue

This is the story of the life of an ordinary man. I realize that others have had similar struggles occur in their lives, but I can only attest to life occurrences that have affected me. When I write about these occurrences, I'm not trying to say that these life experiences are any worse than what have happened in others' lives; what I am trying to explain in this story of my life is the way that these occurrences have affected me and my other siblings. In effect, I pray that this story will be a benefit to others that have also lived similar circumstances. The traumatic childhood a person goes through does not have to dictate the rest of their lives, no matter how terrible it might have been. They can and should come out of the trauma that has affected them and strive to make their lives a successful one.

My other siblings have also experienced these occurrences but in different physiological ways. Two as of this writing are deceased, have gone to another, higher spiritual existence. I am the second eldest in a family of six children, two of whom would be half-brothers, one by our father's second marriage and the other brother by our mother's second marriage. These siblings have had a life filled with different types of abuse. Some have had sexual abuse, drug abuse, and physical abuse by different members of the inner family or by distant relatives.

I realize that others in this world, as I have stated, have had similar circumstances, but I can only write about the knowledge I have about mine and that of my family. My wish is to do this in hopes that it will bring public awareness that there are real occurrences that happen without the public being aware of the horrors that might be occurring just a few feet away in the other apartment or right across the street.

Life in Ohio

❀

When I was very young, around three or four years of age, my family, which included my two sisters, Cynthia and Patricia, and Mom and Dad, lived in Columbus, Ohio.

My mother and father weren't very compatible, I think. Even though they were married and were supposed to be in love, or so I thought at that time, they didn't get along very well. What I can remember about the time we spent in Ohio isn't very pleasant. I have tried to analyze why they didn't get along as I thought back in my later years, and maybe after I tell the story, you, the reader, can make your own analogy.

Like in a typical family, in the beginning, my father went to work and my mother mostly stayed at home with me and my two sisters. Even though my mother was there with us, however, I felt she was distant and somewhat preoccupied. My father, on the other hand, was very fatherly and loved his children deeply. After he got home from work, he'd play games with us. There was such enthusiasm about him, and we loved the way he would run after us, playing, chasing, and grabbing us around our waist, lifting us high into the air and, of course, catching us on our way down. The thrill of our dad hoisting us high into the air always caused us to scream and laugh. Yes, what fond memories when I think about those times! When we had such a good and loving time with our dad.

We, my sisters and I, would, on more than one occasion, call from the backyard, "Mama, come and play with us! Please come play with us and Daddy!" I remember, most of the time, she would come to the back door with the telephone, talking to someone, and would just wave at us from the back porch while smiling, still talking on the phone. However, in all those times I can remember she would turn and go back into the house, still talking on the phone, but giving my dad a dirty and disgusted look.

That was when most of the arguments with my father and mother started.

She would be on the phone, talking, and I would notice, when my father came into the room, she would start to whisper to someone she was speaking to.

My father had asked her why she was on the phone so much. Why didn't she spend some time with him and the kids? She would get furious and start screaming at him. "I can talk to whomever and whenever I want to!" My mother would begin to call my dad bad names and start yelling really loud. I would notice some of the neighbors looking out the windows, and others would walk outside onto their porches to see what all the noise was about. All during the loud yelling, she would be talking to someone at the other end of the phone, saying, "Oh, don't worry about it, sweetheart. That's my ignorant old man trying to tell me I can't speak to whomever I want." All as she proceeded to walk into the house.

My father, when home with us, was a loving and kind father.

My memory of my father in that early childhood is mostly that his life was filled with worry and grief. I would see it sometimes in his eyes and the sad look on his face. He, of course, would try to hide it from us. There would be several times when he came home in the afternoon after work and saw us kids in the house by ourselves. There would be only my sister Pat looking after the three of us.

One time he asked, "Where's your mother? Why isn't she here?"

My sister Pat replied, "Daddy, she left earlier, saying that she would be back before you get home."

"Have you kids had anything to eat?" he asked, looking at us.

Pat answered, "Yes, Daddy. I made us all sandwiches with mustard and sugar early this morning."

"Okay, come with me."

We followed our daddy into the kitchen, where he made us dinner and playfully made a game out of preparing dinner, making us laugh as he told funny stories about him growing up on a farm in Tennessee.

On numerous occasions, in the early hours of the morning, while sleeping, I would be awakened by hearing a lot of commotion outside my bedroom window. Once, I got out of bed, tiptoeing to the window, and peeked out through the blinds, lifting them slightly so as not to be noticed. There was a lot of loud laughing and talking. I heard the familiar voice of my mother speaking to some man. I could not recognize his voice but knew that it was not my daddy's.

Suddenly, I heard footsteps walking across the front porch and heard the front door open. I hurriedly got back into bed, and after a brief period, a bad odor filled the house. This familiar odor that filled the room, I had learned to recognize later as beer.

Certain times in the evenings, I noticed that my dad would go outside into the backyard and just walk around. Whenever I looked around the rooms, trying to find him, I would eventually see him in the backyard, just strolling around, back and forth, and appearing to be talking to someone. But no one was there.

Once, I excitedly opened the back door and yelled down at him, "Hi, Daddy!" I hurried down all the steps from the back porch and ran toward him with my arms held high in the air, anticipating his picking me up and wrapping his arms around me, hugging me. I loved my dad so very much and missed him when he was gone to work all day.

He called back to me, "Go back inside. I will be in a little while. Go see what your sisters are doing!"

But I kept running toward him, and as I got near, he turned quickly around with his back toward me. I kept running and eventually ran into my dad, bumping him from behind.

He quickly turned around, reaching down, picking me up, and hugging me tightly, kissing me around the cheeks and neck, scratching me with his day-old beard.

"I thought I told you to stay in the house and see what your sisters were doing?" he asked.

"But, Daddy," I responded, "I want to be with you!"

"I know you do, son." He smiled at me, holding me tightly in his big strong arms.

While he held me, I could detect a slight quiver and break in his voice when he spoke. I held my arms against his chest, pushing back, and looked at him. My dad had tears streaming down his face, and his eyes were red.

I felt sad for my dad and wanted to cry.

"Daddy, what's wrong? Why are you crying?"

"Daddy is just tired from work, son," he told me, "and I've got problems with this bad air in this town. It hurts your daddy's eyes."

"But, Daddy!" I had a look of disbelief showing on my face.

"No, son, Daddy's all right. I'm just tired, okay?" he reassured me. "Let us talk about you starting school soon, son. Are you excited about meeting new friends?" As he spoke to me, I could see him wiping the tears from his eyes and cheeks with his hands, though still managing to smile at me.

I told him, "I guess so, Dad, but why do I have to go to school?"

"Because, son, everybody needs to go to school to be smart and to care for their families. I need for you to go to school also, son. I need for you to get a good education to get a good career so you won't have to work as hard as your dad does or get as dirty as I do. When you have a good career, you'll be able to care for your family. You will need to provide for your family and love them like I love all of you," he told me.

"Daddy?" I asked, not because I did not know the answer but because I wanted to hear my dad say the words. "You do love us, don't you?"

"Oh yes, son, I love you all so very much." He looked at me with tears streaming down his cheeks. "Don't you ever think that your dad doesn't love you!" As he spoke those precious words to me, he embraced me tightly and held me in his arms.

"But, Daddy, why are you crying? And why are you so sad most of the time when you're home?"

"Son, I'm not sad, and you don't need to concern yourself with things like that," he said. "Now, let's talk about going to school, okay?

Have you got all your school clothes ready for your first day of school tomorrow?"

I nodded.

"Now, go back inside with your sisters and I'll be in there shortly." He turned me around and patted me on the backside gently, sending me on my way toward the back door.

I looked around at my dad, pouting, and it must have looked like my lower lip was dragging the ground. "Daddy, when is Mommy coming home?" I asked.

"She'll be home in a little while, son."

Most of the time, as I remember, living in Ohio, some of the circumstances seemed very vague, because I was very young. Hence, it's hard for me to remember my father and mother ever being very loving toward each other. They were mostly arguing and fighting. I'm sure there were times that they did love each other, but those times are so hard to visualize in my mind now.

When my dad was home, our mother would find some excuse to go somewhere by herself. We would all try to go with her because we didn't want her to leave and we didn't know when she would be back, but she would tell us, "No, you kids stay here and wait for your dad. He'll be home shortly. You don't have to chase after me every time I go out the door." Most times I would grab onto my mom's leg, crying, "Please, Mom, I want to go with you. Take me with you!" I would look around at my sister Pat, who would usually be sitting on the couch, holding Cynthia. I would look and plead for her to help me and get our mother to take us with her. My mother would look over at Pat sitting on the couch. "Come over here and get your brother." She would then grab me by the arm and pull me off her leg, dropping me to the floor. I remember just lying there, crying, as she went out the door, and my sister Pat coming over, grabbing me by the arms and pulling me over toward the couch.

Whenever my dad would come home and my mother wasn't there, he would always ask us, "Where is your mother? And how long has she been gone? How long have you kids been here by yourself?" He would have an angry look on his face as he asked us about our mother. Though my dad would be angry, when he got home and saw that we were alone, he would always make excuses for her and say she must be out shopping or visiting friends. However, when my mother was home, she would either be on the telephone or out near the street, talking to different men that would frequently stop near our house and blow their horns. Mama would run from the house to the curb, laughing as she did, only stopping when she got to the car. She would reach her arms into the door of the car, hugging this man and kissing him on the cheek, all the while laughing at the top of her lungs.

I'd stand on the front porch of the house, watching her and this strange man laughing and talking, all while my sister Pat whispered for me to come inside before Mama got mad.

"Mama," I asked her once from the front porch, "are you going anywhere? Can I go?"

"Get back in the house!" she shouted. "Pat, get out there and get your brother right now!"

My sister came out on the porch, grabbed me by the arm, and pulled me into the house, telling me, "Come on, Bubba!" That was the name she called me when we were small.

There was one man that came by the house quite often. My mother would get in his car, and they would sit there for what seemed like hours. On many occasions, they would leave and be gone for hours at a time, right up until my dad would come home from work. When we'd hear the car motor starting and see it begin to pull away, we'd run outside, yelling at him and our mama, "Mama, where are you going? Please take us with you!" We would run alongside the car as it traveled down the street, pleading with her to not leave us and to take us with her.

"No!" She would then start to curse at us. "You two, go back inside and watch your sister Cynthia until I get back! I won't be long. Now, go back inside like I said!" She would look around through the back window, laughing as the car sped faster away from us. She would then lean closer to the man, putting her arm around his shoulder, all while kissing his cheek and ear.

Of course, we'd run after her and the car until we got tired of crying and yelling for her to stop, but she'd just look out the back window, pointing at us and laughing.

Eventually, we would stop staring at the car speeding away with our mother inside and then walk back to our house. As we did, we would notice the neighbors out on their porches, having apparently heard what had occurred with all our yelling and crying. They would come out with concern to see what was wrong.

Our neighbors had seen this sort of thing too many times before, with our mother driving off with some other man that they knew was not our father. Sometimes they would ask, "Is anything wrong, children? Can we help you? Do you want to come in and wait here until your dad gets home?" My sister Pat would grab my hand, and she would tell them, "No, ma'am, we will be okay." And we'd continue walking toward the house as fast as we could.

They would be standing there, looking at us and talking among themselves. We did not want to cause any trouble for our mother in the neighborhood, or with our dad.

Once, when we got back to the house from running after our mother, we heard our baby sister, Cynthia, crying and screaming from inside. My sister Pat hurried up the stairs, onto the front porch, and tried to open the door, but it wouldn't budge.

She looked around at me, and I asked her, "What's wrong?"

"The door's locked. I can't get in!" she shouted. "Oh, Bubba!" she said. "We're locked out, and Cynthia is in there all alone. She's crying!"

I screamed at her to keep pushing. "We've got to get in there to Cynthia! Mom is going to be mad at us for not taking care of her while she's not home."

"I'm trying to get it open," she said, "but it won't!"

She took my hand, and we hurriedly walked around the house, climbing the back stairs and onto the back door, but it was also locked. We hurried back down the stairs, walking around the house, looking at all the windows to see if any were open. We found one window partially opened, but it was too high for either of us to climb up and reach.

"I know! I have an idea. You wait here!" Pat yelled. She ran around the house and eventually returned dragging a large ladder behind her. "Bubba, come here, help me! Please!"

I rushed over to where she was, and we both struggled to pull the ladder near the wall where the window was. We could hear Cynthia crying from the open window, and we both began to cry while still struggling to get the ladder up against the house. We pushed to lift it and finally hefted the ladder with all our strength up the wall, then lost our grip and heard one of the windowpanes break. We both looked at each other, trying to wipe the tears from our eyes. My sister climbed the ladder, looking back at me, telling me to stay right there and hold the ladder.

"I'm going inside to get Cynthia. When I get inside, I'll yell, and then you can come around to the front door and I'll open it and let you in."

When she got to the top of the ladder, she began pushing on the partially open window, but it would not move. She looked down at me, crying loudly, "Bubba, it won't open!"

She pushed and pushed, and eventually, she got it to open. She climbed inside, and I could hear the crushing sound of her body falling to the floor. She could be heard running and crying through the house toward the room where Cynthia was also crying hysterically.

I was still holding on to the ladder and crying but finally realized it was okay to let go.

I heard my sister Pat yelling at me to come around to the front door, which was where she had told me to meet her. Before I could get around to the front door, I heard her yelling, "Bubba, where are you?"

I came around the corner of the house and ran onto the front porch still crying. "Here I am!"

"Okay," she said, "come inside and help me with Cynthia. She won't stop crying."

It was beginning to get dark outside as we shut the front door and went into our parents' room, trying to comfort Cynthia. We emptied her bottle and put some fresh milk in it, then checked her diaper and changed it the best Pat knew how. Cynthia eventually stopped crying, and we both sat down on the floor at the foot of our parents' bed while holding Cynthia lying across both our legs.

"Pat," I asked, "what about the broken window? What are we going to do?"

"We'll just have to tell Mama and Daddy what happened if they ask, okay?"

"I wish Mom would come back home. I'm getting scared. When will Daddy get home?"

Pat replied, "Daddy will be home late as usual because he's at work. Mama hopefully will be home before he gets home, just as she does all the other times when she goes away with that man."

Eventually, we all three fell asleep at the foot of the bed, on the floor.

Suddenly, sometime during the night, I was suddenly awakened by a loud crying and screaming. Mama had gotten home and was hitting Pat with her fists repeatedly as she held a handful of her hair in her hand.

My mother had a bad smell on her breath and apparently was mad because she thought Pat had not changed Cynthia's diaper even though we both knew that she had. Sometimes, when my mother went out and stayed away for a while, she'd come home and have a bad smell on her breath, and the odor would linger throughout the night and on into the next day. As she had been so many times before, she was so angry and started hitting and yelling at me and Pat. We could not understand why we were getting hit or why she was screaming at us. She directed most of her anger toward Pat and hit and slapped her, asking her why she didn't do what someone else was told to do.

It was not entirely Mama's fault, though. She didn't mean to hit or yell at us; she was just mad at something or someone else when she got back home. We should have gotten up and changed Cynthia again before she got home. We tried to do everything she told us to do before she left, but sometimes I think we forgot some things she had told us to do.

She wanted the house to be cleaned when our daddy got home because she told us she had to leave on business and we needed to have it cleaned for her. I think she did not want Daddy to know she had been gone on business.

I began to cry, asking my mother to stop hitting and slapping my sister. She had her by the hair and was hitting her and slapping her repeatedly about her head and viciously throwing her around the room. My mother looked over at me and told me, "Shut up, because you're next, you little ——!" She used a curse word that I would not repeat. I was screaming and crying, and our baby sister, Cynthia, was screaming also at the top of her lungs.

My mother, while holding Pat by a handful of her hair, was slapping her back and forth across the face. I think she would have hurt her badly if Cynthia had not caught her attention with her continuous loud crying. Pat fell to the floor as my mother released her tight grip on her and let her fall to the floor. I think maybe her arm had gotten tired, but again she picked her up by the hair and slapped her again with such viciousness that I just knew my sister had to be hurt seriously. I was praying that my sister would either run away or just stay on the floor when she again fell, but Mama picked her up again, grabbing her around the neck, choking her, yelling, "You little [she called her another bad name]! You'll do what I say next time!" And then she went toward the closet, opening the door, shoving Pat inside as she kicked her with her feet.

I could see and hear her falling to the floor, crying because of an injury that I knew later came from her nose and lip. Pat scooted with her backside on the floor to the back of the closet, into a corner, bringing her legs up to her chest, and turned away from us.

My mother called me over to her. "Come here, you little [expletive]!"

As I struggled to my feet, trembling, I walk toward her, and as I did, she grabbed me by the hair and pushed me inside the closet with Pat. "Get in there with your sister until I tell you both when you can come out!" I hurried inside as Pat reached out and grabbed me, both of us holding each other, trying to not cry out loud. My mother then slammed the door shut with us inside. I heard the lock turn and then click.

It was dark inside the closet, with a faint light coming from beneath the door of the adjacent bedroom.

A few minutes later, the closet door opened again, and my mother stood there, holding our baby sister, Cynthia, by the arm; she just dangled there. "Here, take your sister!" Mama yelled, and Pat reached up, grabbing Cynthia as she dangled from my mother's arm right at the instant my mother let her go. "Here's a diaper. Get her cleaned up. She's a mess!" Then she slammed the door shut again.

I saw that she put something at the bottom of the door to keep the light from coming in.

I heard the door lock again, and I and my sister Pat just sat there in the dark, crying, holding each other and trying to comfort baby Cynthia. The closet floor was bare hardwood, but we managed to all three cuddle one another. Eventually, we all fell asleep.

This was not the first time our mother had put us in the closet, and eventually, we started to find it to be some sort of sanctuary for us.

During the night or early in the morning, we were awakened by the closet door opening. We both looked up to see my daddy reaching down, talking gently to me and Pat to get up. I noticed my dad's eyes fill with tears as he went down to his knees and held us on the floor. "Everything is going to be all right," he told us. "Daddy's going to see to that."

"Daddy, where is Mom?" I asked. "She didn't feel well last night," I told him.

"She is asleep in the living room, on the couch. Come with me," he said.

We followed him to Mom and Daddy's bed, where he laid us down, pulling the covers over all of us. He kissed us both, Pat and me, on top of our heads and told us all to go to sleep.

"But, Daddy, where are you going?" I asked with a tremble in my voice.

"I'll be back in a minute. I just must wash up before I come to bed. You two just go to sleep," he responded as he walked away, looking around at me and Pat. "I'm not going to leave you. I'm going to have my two precious angels sleep with their dad tonight."

I must have fallen asleep, because soon I could feel the weight of my dad as he lay down and pulled me, Pat, and Cynthia into his arms. I felt safe falling asleep, knowing everything was going to be okay.

I do vaguely remember overhearing a conversation that my grandfather had with our daddy. This occurred on one of the visits that they had before we moved to Tennessee. "And a little hard farmwork wouldn't hurt them either!" he said with a defiant laugh.

This scary man that spoke with such harshness was my grandfather. He wore what appeared to be an old gangster-type brimmed hat, and as he pushed himself back in his seat, he raised his arm in the air, pointing his finger at my dad. "I don't know why you did not listen to me and Mama when we told you that you would get yourself into a lot of trouble if you came up here. These women up here are nothing but prostitutes! They are not like a good young Southern girl—they do what you tell them, and if they don't, you can always whip them if they get out of line. Your mother always stayed in line, except one time, when she did not have supper on the table when I came in from the field. But after I switched her bottom good, she had to sleep out in the smokehouse that night. I could hear her blubbering most of the night until I went out and opened the door and threw a bucket of cold water on her. She shut up after that!" He reared back and chuckled. "I guess because I did turn the overhead light on for her and told her it would go off if she did not shut up. It does get dark out in the country, and you know we did not have a city light out on one of those poles like you have up here."

He continued, "You know, the good book says that a woman should obey their husbands. That's probably why that jezebel you're married to left, because she wasn't raised with hickory switches across her backside! If you had taken her on one of those coon hunting trips we used to go on and tied her to a good, sweet gum tree and left for a few hours, she then would have learned to do what she was told and not talk back! If she had gotten beaten a few times, you and the kids wouldn't have had this problem, would you?"

My dad then spoke up in a loud, angry voice. "Listen to me. You're not going to treat my kids like you treated us, or do to them the things you did to my sister!" He glared over at my uncle William as he said the last part. "These are my kids, and I'll raise them with all the love and kindness that I can give. If there were any other way, I would not be asking you for this help."

Uncle William attempted to calm the situation down and spoke up. "Are you going to wake the kids up?"

"Well," my grandfather said, then cursed, "they should've been awake an hour ago. It's five thirty now and going on six o'clock. It is time they woke up. I can tell you now they are not going to sleep all day when I get them back home."

"Dad," my father called, speaking up, "they're just children."

"Well, let me tell you again, you know I was clearing land when I was seven with an ax and a team of mules at daylight until after dark. I know a little farmwork won't hurt any of them," Grandpa responded.

"Let me tell you again," Dad said, pointing his finger at Grandpa, "if there were any other way, I'd keep them all here with me." I noticed my father holding a serious stare over to where my grandfather was seated. "I don't want any of my children abused or mistreated in any way, do you hear me? They are your grandchildren, and *my* children, no matter how you feel about their mother," he continued. "I expect you to treat them with loving-kindness."

"How do you know they're my grandchildren with the jezebel of a wife that you have? Those young'uns could belong to half the state of Ohio, as far as I know!"

Hearing those comments that my grandfather made to my dad caused my mind to drift back into deep thought. Certain instances in my dad and mom's relationship resurfaced in my subconscious mind.

Most of the time during my life thus far, I had been successful in keeping these horrible, traumatic thoughts of these events out of my mind. Such tragic events, even to this day, still surface from time to time; it is what happens at the moment that might trigger these thoughts.

One time, my dad came home from work early one afternoon. I and my two sisters, before he arrived, had been taken by our mother downstairs into the basement, which led off from the kitchen. The basement had a cold concrete slab as the floor; it was cold and dark, with only a couple of windows to give light during the daytime. The basement also had a playpen that our baby sister, Cynthia, was often placed in when our mom had to go out on "business." We were locked down there and told to stay there and watch Cynthia until she returned. There were numerous toys scattered around and throughout the floor. If it got really quiet, we could hear something scurry around on the floor and climb up the walls. We looked over at Cynthia's crib and noticed a furry large dark rat perched up on the railing. The rat was looking down into the crib toward Cynthia, who was nursing on a bottle of milk. She also had wet milk that had dried up on her face and made a wet, soaked spot on the cold plastic mattress. My sister Pat and I then started clapping real loud and started yelling at the rat to make it leave from its perch. It reluctantly ran off into a corner, where some coal was piled up, used for heating during the wintertime. We were often brought down there by our mom when she had man friends visiting. Sometimes we'd stay down there for hours and be brought back up just before our father came home.

On another day, while our mom had a man visiting, I overheard what sounded like my dad's car driving onto the driveway. Suddenly, I heard conversation coming from the kitchen and a lot of moving around and noise. I heard my mom yell out, "That husband of mine is here! What is he doing home this early?" She paused a bit. "Well, that's okay," she then said. "Just sit down there, Harley, and drink your coffee."

When I had heard the voices upstairs, I quietly began to ease up the stairs. As I crept up step by step toward the top of the stairs, my sister Pat yelled up at me, "Bubba, get back down here before you get in trouble!"

"Daddy's home," I told her. "I heard him when he drove up. Please, Pat, get Cynthia out of the crib and come up here. I don't like it down here with those big rats! Daddy, when he discovers us down here, he will come let us out and let us come up."

"Bubba, no! You better wait! If Mama catches you, it will cause her to be really mad!" Pat said with a horrified look that she seemed to show whenever she spoke about Mama getting mad.

I looked down at her and told her, "I'm not going to do anything. I'm just waiting here and listening for Daddy's voice." I knew he came into the house because I heard the car pull up and knew that was him walking across the porch.

Cynthia began to whine in her crib as Pat hurried down the step from where she had gotten up, looking up at me to say, "Now, look what you've done!" She went over to the crib and struggled to pick Cynthia up over the crib's railings. She held her in her arms, rocking her back and forth in an attempt to comfort and keep her quiet.

I heard the front door open and slam shut. Then I heard my daddy's voice call out, "Jeanette, where are you? I'm home!"

"Here in the kitchen, having coffee with Harley," she answered back.

"Harley! Who in the world is Harley? And what's he doing in my house drinking coffee with my wife while I'm not at home?" I heard and could actually see my dad's footsteps as he passed the basement door and cast a shadow under the frame and entered the kitchen.

"He's a friend of mine and my mom's. And don't you come in here raising a fuss with me!"

I peeked through the crack in the basement door into the kitchen and saw my dad standing across from this man, Harley. He was pointing his finger at him, telling him, "It's time for you to get yourself up and get out of my house!"

"Wait a minute," the man said. "I didn't come here to cause any trouble. I didn't know Jeanette was married! And I've known her and her mother for years! We had a few beers together down at the Owls club, and some good times playing shuffleboard."

My dad took a step toward this man named Harley, speaking in anger and with a quiver in his voice. "Well, you know it now!" he said. "And I'm not going to tell you again. There is the door!" Dad pointed toward the back door, which led down to steps to the backyard.

My mother spoke up. "Who in this world do you think you are, telling me who I can have in my house?"

21

"It's okay, Jeanette," Harley spoke up, holding the palm of his hand up toward my mother's face. "I've got things to do, anyway."

My dad took another step toward Harley, shouting, "Let's go!"

"Okay, relax," Harley said, looking very irritably back at my dad. "I'm going!" And we heard footsteps walking to the back door.

The back door opened, and my dad yelled as the man named Harley left, "I don't want to see you back over here again, ever!" And he slammed the door shut.

Footsteps were then heard hurrying down the back steps.

"Jeanette, what in this world do you think you're doing? And what kind of fool do you think I am? He might be an old friend of yours and your mom's, but if you think you're going to make me believe that's all there is to the relationship, you're crazy! You don't have a man in another one's house while your husband is away working! What do you think the neighbors are thinking?" Daddy asked her.

"I don't care what you believe," she shouted back, cursing Daddy, "or what the neighbors think! And why aren't you at work like you're supposed to be?"

"I'm off for my lunch hour," Dad answered. "Don't you have any common decency about you at all? To have a man up in our home while I'm not here? Don't you have any respect for me or our children?"

"How can anyone have any respect for a piece of trash like you?" she said. "Anyway, I haven't done anything wrong. We were just having coffee and talking about old times!"

"Maybe you haven't done anything today because I probably interrupted your little get-together. What am I supposed to think when I come home with my wife and a strange man alone in our home?"

"I really don't care what you think!" my mom said. "And I will do as I please and when I please! Why don't you just get out of here and go back to work?" My mother was pacing back and forth in the kitchen, furious at my dad, apparently, for making that man, Harley, leave.

"I'll go when I get good and ready. And I'm not finished talking to you yet!"

"Well, I'm finished talking to you, so leave me the —— alone!" my mother yelled at the top of her lungs. I could see spit spray from her mouth as she continued to hurl obscenities at my dad.

My dad tried to reason with my mother. He took on the attitude that the argument was his fault and he was the one that should have taken a different approach with her. "Please, honey, why don't you just come over here and calm down? Sit down and let's talk."

As I peered through the crack in the cellar door, I saw my mother grab a cup of hot coffee from the counter and throw it at my dad. Coffee went flying all over the kitchen, and the cup struck my dad on his head, right above his nose and forehead. My mother ran across the room and started swinging her fist at my dad as he attempted to defend himself. She was swinging her fist and kicking at him as he pleaded with her, saying, "Now, Jeanette, calm down. Stop all this, please! Don't you realize just how much I love you?"

My dad had his arms up in the air, trying to defend himself, and continued trying to reason with Mama to please stop. During the struggle, suddenly, my mother raised her knee and struck my dad between his legs. He grabbed himself, groaning, while my mother shoved him up against the door, breaking the glass window. She grabbed the doorknob and struggled to open it as he fell against it.

She finally opened the door and reached down, took her shoe off, grabbed my dad by the arm while pulling, and then shoved him out onto the back stairs. She began to beat him continuously about the head and face with her shoe. He fell on the top of the stairs' platform as she continued to hit my daddy on his body and head.

She cussed him and spit on him as he lay there. My mother continued kicking at my dad and hitting him with her shoe. And he continually tried to defend himself as liquid began to flow from his face and head. My dad had his hands up, defending himself, and was scooting backward to the edge of the stairs. The back porch platform was on the second floor, which led downstairs to the backyard.

My mother started kicking my dad, which caused him to lose his balance while he attempted to defend himself and fell down the staircase. He rolled and tumbled down the stairs, and I could hear his bones crumple on each step as he went down.

He finally came to rest on the ground at the bottom, and I heard him groan out in pain. I yelled after daddy and rushed out of the basement, going to where my mother was standing on the back porch. I could hear my sister Pat yelling my name in the background. "Bubba, come here!" she said as she cried hysterically.

Mama was pointing her finger down at Daddy and was laughing as though she had heard a joke. "Now, you!" Then she called my daddy a very bad name. "Get up and get out of here before I call the cops and have you locked up for hitting me!"

I rushed up to my mother, grabbing her by the pant leg, screaming and crying, "Please, Mama, help Daddy. He's hurt!" I looked down the stairs toward my dad, who was sprawled out on the ground at the bottom of the stairs. My mother just stood there laughing as she glared down at Daddy. I let go of her pant leg and hurriedly started down the stairs, crying, looking back at her. "Mama," I said, "you hurt Daddy! Please, Mama, help Daddy! Please, Mama!"

She looked down at my tearstained face and shouted, "What are you doing out of the basement, anyway? I didn't tell you to come out! Where are your two sisters?"

"They're still in the basement, Mama." I told her this because I did not want her to get mad at Pat and start hitting her. I pleaded again, "Mama, please come help me!" as I continued down the stairs toward my daddy.

"You get back up here right now!" she yelled.

I stopped suddenly, looking back toward her. "Please, Mama, Daddy's hurt!"

"I don't care! Get back up here!" I reluctantly climbed back up the stairs, looking back and forth from her to Daddy and crying until I reached her. She then grabbed me by the top of my head, gathering a handful of my hair, and slapped me really hard.

"Mama, please!" I cried and pleaded, looking up at her. "I'm sorry! What's wrong? I just wanted to help Daddy. Please, let's help him!"

"Oh, shut up! He is not hurt," Mama said. "And even if he is, that's what he deserves!" She grabbed me by the hair and pulled me up step by agonizing step until we reached the top. "Now, get back in the house!" She proceeded to shove me toward the back door.

My mama, moments later, went inside, then I again slipped back outside and shouted down at the bottom of the stairs, "Daddy!" I could hear my dad groaning, then I cried down toward him, asking him, "Daddy, are you okay?"

"Yes, son," he managed to groan out. "I'll be all right. Don't worry, Daddy's okay." I noticed my dad attempting to get up. He then fell back down on his back and could be heard crying out in pain.

"Daddy, you are hurt! What do you want me to do?"

"Son, go tell your mother to call the ambulance. I'll need to go to the hospital," Daddy told me. "I am hurt a little bit." But when he looked up at me, he forced an agonized smile on his face. He even managed to give a little forced chuckle.

My mother had gone into the house, and I went after her to get her to help my daddy. I began yelling throughout the house, "Mama, Mama! Daddy wants you to call the doctor!" I began rushing through the house, going from room to room, looking for her, but I couldn't find her anywhere. I went to the cellar door and looked down and saw Patricia halfway up the staircase, holding Cynthia in her arms. "Sissy! Daddy fell down the stairs, and he's hurt bad. He wants Mama to call the hospital for help, but I can't find her!"

"I think she's already left," Pat said. "I heard the front door open and close a few minutes before I heard you running through the house."

I ran toward the front door, looking out, hoping to see my mother.

Pat walked to the other side of the living room, laying Cynthia down in her crib. I rushed toward the back door and was joined by Pat. We both hurried down the back staircase toward Daddy. Patricia grabbed his head, picked it up, and began to cry and embrace him.

"It's okay, baby girl. Daddy will be fine." Then, looking over at me, he asked, "Did your mother call the hospital, son?"

"We couldn't find Mama. I think she left again."

"Patricia, you stay here with me," Daddy said, then looked over at me. "Son, you go next door to the neighbors and tell them I had an accident and fell down the back stairs. Go to Mr. Johnson's house—I think he's home—and tell him I need for him to call for help."

"Okay, Daddy, I'll be right back." And I started to run toward Mr. Johnson's house across the street. I ran to Mr. Johnson's front porch and began to yell out, "Please! Help my daddy! He's hurt!" Screaming and crying, I knocked on every door and peered through all the windows around the front porch as I continually cried out for help. But nobody answered. I frantically ran around the house on the outside, banging on each window and peering inside as I had on the front porch, banging and crying for help.

Suddenly, I looked across the street; and standing in a doorway, looking in my direction, was the old widow Mrs. Ruby. Running off the porch and across the street, I began to cry out, shouting and crying so loud I knew the whole neighborhood could have heard me. "Please help us!" I ran up onto her porch and almost ran into the old lady, who grabbed me by the shoulders.

She held me tight, shaking me, and asked me, "Boy, what's wrong with you? Why all the crying and shouting so?"

"Please help us," I said, trying to catch my breath. "My daddy fell down the back porch stairs, and he's hurt bad!"

"All right, boy. I know where you live. God knows I've seen you before," she said in what sounded to be a rude, sarcastic tone. "You go back home and I'll call for help for your dad."

I ran back down the street toward our house and circled it toward our backyard. I was running as fast as I could and crying so hard my eyes were blurred with tears. In an attempt to hurry back to my daddy and sister, I ran so fast I stumbled and fell face-first onto the concrete walkway leading to the back of our house.

I hurriedly picked myself up and noticed I had injured myself; I had apparently busted my lip open and skinned my chin. I kept running, anyway, until I reached the back of our house. I was not concerned with myself or the injury that dripped blood down onto my shirt or the pain I was feeling; I knew I just had to get back to my dad and help him.

"Daddy," I said, trying to catch my breath, "the woman across the street said she would call for help."

"Okay, son, so let's see what you've done to yourself. What has happened?"

"I was in a hurry to get back, and I fell on the sidewalk out front. I'm okay, Daddy." I looked at him and my sister Pat still sitting on the ground.

"Oh, son!" Dad cried as he reached out and pulled me toward him. "Your lip is all busted, and you must be hurting. You've also skinned up your hands when you fell."

I looked up at him from his lap and, with tears streaming down my face, told him, "I'm okay. I'll be all right. I'm afraid for you, Daddy. You're the one that's hurt. And Mama isn't here. I don't know where she is. Why didn't she stay and help us, Daddy? Where did she go?"

My dad pulled me closer to him and tried to raise himself up on his elbow, causing him to show intense pain on his face. He reached out with his other arm, putting it around Pat and pulling her closer. "Son, now you stop that fussing. I need for you to be a big boy for your dad." He hugged us both, telling us that everything was going to be all right. I could tell my dad was in excruciating pain, and I could see his whole body was drenched in sweat.

I could also feel and see his body trembling, could see the pain in his eyes as he lay there grimacing in pain but trying to reassure both Pat and me that everything was going to be all right. "Daddy is going to make sure of that," he said. "Just wait and see. Daddy will take care of everything. Don't you two worry so much. And try to stop that crying, okay?" He looked over at Pat, asking her, "Where's your sister, Cynthia?"

Suddenly, Pat looked at Daddy, then looked at me, and quickly jumped up, running toward the house, saying, "She's in the house! I left her in the house…"

I came out of my daydream and back into reality and could hear my dad, grandfather, and uncle William still talking in the

27

kitchen. I could hear them discussing moving me and my two sisters to Tennessee.

I don't like it when my memory goes back to certain traumatic events that have occurred in my life. I'd much rather keep traumatic thoughts out of my mind and in the past, where they belong. There are so many times I can remember violent confrontations between my mother and father, and others, during my early childhood and again later in my teen years.

I felt Pat stirring next to me on the bed. Raising her head, she asked, "Bubba, what are you doing?"

"Daddy's in the kitchen with two men, and they are talking. I think they were talking about me, you, and Cynthia going to live with Grandpa in Tennessee, wherever that is."

Pat suddenly jerked up on her elbows. "Where's Cynthia?"

"I think she's with Daddy or in the bedroom. I haven't heard her since I've been awake." I looked over at Pat, asking her, "Are we going to Tennessee to live with Grandpa? I don't think I like him. He sounds really mean, and he scares me. He said something about us working on a farm and said it would be good for us."

"I don't know, Bubba. I'm sure Mama or Daddy will make sure we'll be all right."

"Maybe Mama and Daddy will go with us and we can move into a new house and a new town. Then maybe Mama won't have so many man friends come and cause problems. I really hope so!" I said.

My memory of my early years in Ohio isn't very clear on certain instances that occurred, but in my later years, I did realize that it must have been because of the traumatic effect it had on my impressionable young mind. I believe that your mind has a defense mechanism that guards itself by eliminating from or shoving back in your subconscious certain events that might do you harm emotionally. Now, as I look back on certain things in my childhood, it doesn't seem like they are, in fact, reality, but I also realize that for me to remember these occurrences, they must be an embedded part of my subconscious. To emphasize, I truly do not think anyone could have dreamed up these occurrences unless they are, in fact, a part of one's reality.

As best as I can remember, it was in the fall of the late 1950s. Our father had sent for his dad, our grandfather, and his brother, Uncle William. My dad had packed suitcases for me and my two sisters, Pat and Cynthia. Our mother had left our home in Ohio and had not returned. We didn't know where she had gone and didn't know when or if she would be coming back. My dad had been taking care of us for some time, doing the best he could on his own. During this time, my dad would have somebody come in and watch us while he worked. I know it had got to be a big strain on him trying to work and worrying about three kids at home. The worry and strain about where his wife our mother had gone had to be more than any man could have taken. We could see him come home from work day after day trying to force a smile upon his face, just to soothe his children.

When he came home one day, he asked if we would like to go out for ice cream and a movie. We were all excited and jumped up and down, clapping our hands together, yelling, "Yes, Daddy, yes!" He said, "Okay," and told me and Pat to change clothes and get Cynthia dressed. After we changed clothes, we got into the car with our dad. We were very excited about getting out of the house and going for ice cream and a movie. As we all drove through the city with all the traffic and city lights, my thoughts tried to imagine where in all the tall buildings and city streets Mama could be. I was so excited. I was sitting up front with my dad, and we were going to get ice cream. I was sitting up, trying to be a big man like my dad, but having a hard time seeing over the dash of our big Buick car.

I looked over at my dad while he was driving and asked, "Where is Mama? When will she come back home?" I must have had a sad look on my face but was also trying to hide it due to the excitement of being out with our dad. I did not want to spoil anything that might make my dad sad during this special time going to the movies.

"I don't know, son, but I'm sure she'll be home any day now," Dad said. "Now, sit back and just watch the traffic, and let's have a good time tonight, okay?"

"Daddy, I miss Mommy and love Mommy. Why did she leave us? Doesn't she love us anymore?"

"Of course she does, son, and I don't want to hear you talk like that ever again!"

I felt my sister's hand on my shoulder from the back seat, and turning around to look at her, I noticed she put her finger up to her lips and shook her head back and forth in a motion for me to not talk about Mommy.

My dad pulled into a drive-in Dairy Queen. He ordered all of us ice cream, and we sat there, enjoying it. Daddy shifted in his seat, turning toward me, and began to look at me and then at my two sisters, who were seated in the back seat. I could tell he was troubled by the look on his face. I had seen that look before. When he began to speak, I noticed there was a slight quiver in his voice and knew that he was saddened by what he was about to say to us. I could see his eyes begin to tear up. I hated to see my dad so sad, and we kids could always say or do something to make him happy.

"Kids," he said, "all three of you know that Daddy loves you with all my heart. Kids, it breaks my heart to be telling you this, but I want you all to know that the most important things in my life were a home and family. But right now, since your mother isn't home and Daddy is finding it hard to work and pay the bills without your mother being here to help…" My dad looked over at me with his deep-blue eyes filling with tears; he was struggling to fight back emotions as he asked me, "You know your dad loves you very much, don't you?"

"Yes, Daddy."

Pat rose up from the back seat and began to cry, asking Daddy, "What's wrong? Why are you so sad?"

He wiped tears from his eyes and reached around in the back seat, putting his arm around Pat, and bent over toward me, putting his arm around both of us now. My sister Pat was hugging my dad and kissing him on the cheek, crying as she said, "Daddy, everything is going to be okay. Mom is coming back home. You'll see." She looked over at me, smiling, tears streaming down her cheeks.

My dad stopped embracing us both and wiped his eyes with the back of his hand, saying, "I've called your uncle William and your grandfather and asked if you three could go down to Tennessee for a while and stay with them. It will only be for short while, and after I straighten things out here, Daddy will come down and join you."

I and my sister Pat looked at each other as we continued to cry. We both stared back at our dad as we both simultaneously pleaded, "No, Daddy, we don't want to leave without you!"

"No, Daddy!" I said. "Mama will be back soon and we'll be okay, and we can be a family again!"

"Please, Daddy, we must stay together. I know that she will be back soon, just like she always does. I just know she will!" Pat screamed. "Please, Daddy, me and Bubba will take care of the house, and I can watch Cynthia until you get home! We won't fuss at each other ever again!" And she reached over toward me and hugged and kissed me on the cheek, looking at me with tears streaming down her cheeks. "Will we, Bubba?" she asked, forcing a smile from her tearstained eyes.

Dad said, "Okay, just calm down, you two."

Cynthia began to cry, sensing that something was very wrong. Pat reached around and picked her up from where she had been lying on the back seat.

"Everything is going to be fine," Dad went on, "but right now, until your mother comes home, I just don't know what else to do. All your relatives live in Tennessee, and I need their help with you children right now. You kids know I don't want to be separated from Daddy's angels, but Daddy needs their help right now."

After we finished our ice cream, we arrived at the movies and watched a horror movie, *House on Haunted Hill*. Still to this day, I remember that movie—it was so scary, starring Vincent Price. We all three set on either side of our dad, with Cynthia on his lap. For most of the movie, I remember Pat and I just sat there frightened, with our heads buried in our dad's side, covering our eyes. After the movies, while driving home, we all sat up front with Daddy and cuddled next to one another, not because it was cold outside, but because the movie was so scary.

When we got home, Daddy picked Cynthia up and we all fol-lowed him into the house. As we did, my thoughts were of me hoping and praying that when we got inside, I would see Mama standing there, and then we could all stay together.

A few weeks after our movie outing, I had been playing outside in the backyard and went inside to get a drink of water. I had not noticed at first that my dad was in the living room and was apparently on the phone, talking. As I stood in the kitchen, I overheard him speaking to someone that I found out later to be my dad's brother, our uncle William from Tennessee. I heard him say that he could not take care of us on his own. I also heard my dad telling Uncle William, "As I told you over the phone, William, if Dad could take the kids with him and Mama, I'll straighten things out here and try to be in Tennessee in a few weeks to get them. I'll send Dad some money each week for the kids because he has agreed to let them stay with him and Mama until I can get down there."

"Yes, Robert," I could hear the other voice say. "I told you I'll take them to Dad's, and I will keep in touch with him to make sure that they will be all right."

My memory of my early years in Ohio is very vague and clouded about certain instances that occurred. I do believe that I can only remember them because of the very nature of the trauma that was involved. In later years of my life, I started to wonder what effect these traumatic life experiences that occurred in my early childhood would have on my young and impressionable mind. As the years passed, I was assured by God's spiritual presence and that he was protecting me and had always been there with me through all those traumatic life circumstances. The mind must protect itself by eliminating from or shoving back into the subconscious certain events that might do you harm emotionally. With these events, if the mind does not protect itself from certain trauma, I believe they might turn into physical problems and/or manifest into addictions, which some of my siblings had succumbed to in their later lives. Certain situations in my life have caused some memories of the past to resurface from time to time. Some of these thoughts do not seem like reality. However, I don't think it's possible for anyone to have dreamed up such occurrences unless they are, in fact, part of their reality.

My earliest remembrance of my grandfather on my dad's side of the family is when I was very young. It is hard for me to remember the exact age, but I think I might have been around five or six years of age. This early remembrance occurred when he and my dad's brother, my uncle William, both came to Ohio to, as was my understanding, take me and my two sisters, Cynthia and Pat, back with them to Tennessee. My dad and mom were having marital problems that would sometimes turn violent.

I remember, the day we left Ohio, neither my mom nor my dad was home. Our grandfather and uncle William were taking suitcases out of our house to the car. All three of us children—I, Pat, and Cynthia—were seated in the living room on the couch, watching them go in and out of the house. Our dad had spoken to all of us before, telling us of the possibility of them coming to take us to Tennessee. I had not, however, in my young mind realized that this would or could happen. Grandfather, who was the father of my dad, had always been a scary-looking man and had a mean expression on his face and talked with a loud, deep, garbled voice. His face most of the time would get beet red. This was noticeable when he was either yelling at us or he had been drinking. He reminded me of the pictures I remembered of Lucifer, the horned devil. They both, Grandfather and Uncle William, kept moving boxes of our clothes in and out of the house through the front door. Some boxes, they decided, did not need to go and were just left in the house.

Uncle William wiped his forehead, looking back and forth at us and Grandpa. "I think that's all of it. These kids didn't have very much. I think a box of clothes for each of them. What should we do about these toys over here that the kids have piled up in these plastic bags?"

"No!" Grandfather raised his voice. "I'm not going to haul that garbage all the way back home! They don't need anything junk like that, anyway. They'll be too busy working, helping me and Mama, to be wasting their time with a bunch of ignorant toys. I don't see why anybody would waste their hard-earned money on garbage like that, anyway!"

Uncle William was a large man, larger than my dad or grandpa. But even though he was a big man, he was kind and didn't scare me when he talked, as my grandfather did.

Both stood inside the doorway, looking over at the three of us seated on the couch. Uncle William looked over at us sitting on the couch and asked, "You kids ready? We've got a long way to go, and we need to get started."

"What about Mama and Daddy? Are they going too?" Pat asked.

"No, your mama and daddy aren't going," Grandfather said. "Just you young'uns." My grandfather glared over at Pat and pointed his large crooked finger at her, yelling, "Shut up, you little witch, and get your sister, brother, and yourself in the car!"

"I want to see my mama and daddy before we leave," Pat told him and started crying. "He'll be home from work soon. I just know he will."

"No, we're not going to wait. I have already spoken to your dad, and he said to take you young'uns to live with me and Mama for a while. Your mama's no good, anyway, and if it were up to that jezebel, she would have you doing the same as she is. We've got a long way to go, and I'm not going to waste another hour, so shut your nasty mouth and get in the car! I won't tell you again!" my grandfather said as he proceeded to walk over to where my sister was standing.

"Yes, Grandpa," she said, then jumped up and grabbed me by the arm. Pat carried Cynthia as we walked to the front door quickly, going around my grandfather.

The three of us were all cuddled up and frightened in the back seat of Uncle William's car. I and Pat started to look at each other and whisper back and forth. We had hoped Daddy would show up and take us all out of this car while telling us everything was okay and he and Mama had worked everything out. I stretched my neck, looking out of all the windows, searching for my daddy, just knowing he would be here soon.

On the back seat with us were plastic bags that couldn't be loaded into the trunk. We were huddled to one side behind Uncle William. It was beginning to get dark outside, and I whispered to Uncle William if I could go to the bathroom as we were about to leave. I tried to quietly ask him while Grandpa was out of the car, fastening a rope to the trunk to hold it shut. I wanted to do anything I could to stop us from leaving, in the hopes of having Daddy come home in time. Uncle William told me, with a smile upon his face, "If you must go, I guess we could wait just another minute."

When he opened the back door and reached inside to help me out, suddenly my grandpa yelled, "William, where are you going with that boy?"

Startled with Grandpa's sudden yelling, my uncle turned, sternly looking at him, and said, "Little Hershel said he must go to the bathroom, and I was taking him inside."

"No! He should have thought about that earlier. You know they are just wasting our time. If he must go, he will just have to go right here outside the car, on the street. I'm not wasting another minute with this nonsense!"

Uncle William looked down at me, and with a frustrated look on my face, I told him that I could hold it for a while. I did not want to use the bathroom out in the open and in front of the neighbors, who might see me. I also did not want to leave my sisters out in the car with mean and evil-looking Grandpa.

After what seemed like an eternity, Uncle William began to drive the car down the street and both Pat and I quickly turned around in our seats, staring out the back windows while still hoping at the last minute that Daddy would suddenly show up, stopping the car, and take us back home with him.

Uncle William was driving this large car, and I looked over, noticing my grandfather smoking a pipe. He clenched the pipe between his teeth, blowing out white clouds of smoke. I could see and hear him sucking the spit that dripped from between his teeth and the pipe. Some of the spit would drip down and slide off his whiskers to his dirty chin. When he spoke to Uncle William, he filled the car with smoke, and I almost got sick from the terrible, pungent odor. I was seated in the middle of the back seat with my sisters. Pat was next to the door, and Cynthia had her head on her lap. Cynthia had her feet lying across and touching me. Both were asleep, with Pat leaning on some clothing items next to the door. I sat there listening to my uncle William and grandfather talking. I couldn't quite understand or hear what they were saying. I rose up, looking around the outside of the car, trying to see different things and keep my mind off the reality of what was taking place in our lives as we traveled.

I did not know at this time in my life that this would be the beginning of just another emotional trauma that our lives would experience.

It was dark outside, and all I could see or hear were the other cars and trucks coming toward us, with their bright lights blinding me.

I sat there for what seemed like hours, looking all around the car and at my two sisters, who had fallen asleep next to me. Thoughts of the events during the day and throughout the last several months had taken a toll on me emotionally, and I wished I could sleep as my sisters did. I kept looking outside, with my head against the window, at all the traffic and houses on the side of the road. Sitting there in the dark, I had a frightening thought of what our future was going to hold for us. I knew that I felt terrified of my grandfather, and sometimes I felt my stomach hurt as if a large needle was being stabbed inside of me through my navel.

It was my understanding, from overhearing the conversation my dad had had with Grandfather, that we were going to stay with him out in the country on a farm. From time to time, as we traveled, I listened to the sound of the traffic whizzing by, and I would feel myself drift off to sleep. Then suddenly, I felt myself jerk awake, with my body seeming to be shaking all over. My heart felt like it was beating out of my chest, and I was sweating profusely, soaking up my shirt. In my exhausted state of mind, I had forgotten where I was, but then I realized, from looking around at my sisters sleeping, that we were with my uncle and grandfather, going to Tennessee.

I must have fallen asleep, as I had done throughout the night, because suddenly I felt a horrific, hot, burning feeling across my face. My entire body was launched, first backward, then forward, as I landed onto the floorboard of the car. My eyes jerked themselves open wide, but my vision was blurred by whatever had struck me. My face burned as though it had been struck with a scalding iron. I

looked into my grandfather's eyes and was confronted with his shouting and spitting in my face as he yelled. I could see Pat to my right
holding Cynthia in her lap. She had a terrified look on her face and
was curled up as close as she could to the car's door. She held Cynthia
tightly and away from the direction where Grandpa was sitting as
she shielded her from any possible harm. Pat was just sitting there,
staring, terrified at my grandfather yelling at me. Cynthia was crying
and screaming, jerking and moving around, trying to get out of Pat's
lap and away from the direction of the yelling.

Cynthia was crying and asking, "Mama…Mama…Daddy…
Daddy!" She had suddenly woken up and was now looking for Mama
and Daddy. She was just a baby and had not been away from them
for long since she was born. I did not know at first what had happened and was now thinking that Cynthia had somehow aggravated
Grandpa and he was taking his frustrations out on me. I thought I
was slapped because I was the closest to him.

My grandfather slapped me again and was turned around in
his seat, leaning over, yelling at me. I could smell his awful, putrid,
urinal-type, smelly breath as he continued to yell. He raised his hand
and slapped me again across the face again, yelling, "I told you to
leave that young'uns alone and stop teasing her. I don't want to put
up with her crying all the way back home!" I cried out not only to
stop him from slapping me but also to tell him that I had not done
anything to Cynthia and had, in fact, been asleep.

I was crying and rubbing my face, trying to soothe the hot sting,
and my left ear had a loud ringing inside. "Yes, sir," I said.

Then, suddenly and with such viciousness, he turned back
around, facing me. My grandfather reached back with his hand and
grabbed me by the top of my hair, pulled me up to his face, yelling
as loud as he could, "I told you not to say a word! Now shut up!" He
forcefully slammed me back into my seat.

I was crying and felt emotionally devastated that my grandfather was doing this to me. I was trying to hold my breath as much as
I possibly could to calm myself and not let out any crying.

"Now, don't lie to me, boy!" Then he slapped me hard again and grabbed my ear with his hand and was pulling me toward him, jerking my head around as I felt a loud pop inside my head.

Uncle William reached across and put his right hand on my grandfather's shoulder. "Dad, I think little Hershel is telling the truth because when I looked around at him a few minutes ago to check on them and see how they were, I could see that he was sound asleep. I think you need to try to get some sleep and stop drinking that Busch beer. You have been on these kids since you laid eyes on them!"

"Well, I just can't stand nonsense, and they need to stop being so unruly. I have cotton in the fields and need to get back before they get eaten up by the weeds. And you better believe that these young'uns are going to pay through hard work for their room and board! I'll have them getting up bright and early and out to those fields before the sun comes up!"

"Yes, I know, Dad," Uncle William said, "but you know they are small kids and they can only do so much."

My grandpa just snorted through his nose at Uncle William and began to relight his pipe, turning toward the front again.

"I just want all three of you young'uns to stop whatever you're doing to upset your grandpa and just sit there," Uncle William said. "I don't want to hear another sound from any of you." And he rubbed the top of my head, looking at me briefly, then back to the road, and smiled as though to calm me down from crying. Looking over at Pat and Cynthia, he also smiled and, with a calm demeanor, laid his large hand upon her shoulder, saying, "You kids try to go back to sleep." This gentle personality, I had noticed also from our dad.

Every now and then along the way, we would stop for gas and Grandpa would allow us to get out of the car to use the bathroom. Uncle William was quiet most of the time, but when he spoke, it was in a deep voice. He was a large man and seemed like a giant but had a gentle way about him, especially to us. Later in my grown life, I would relate him to the character Hoss Cartwright of the Western TV show *Bonanza*. When he spoke, he treated us with kindness.

My grandfather, on the other hand, I thought he would fight the devil himself and kick him out of the bad place if he could. I believe he could take over Satan's place—that was how mean and scary I thought my grandfather to be.

Whenever he spoke, he would do so abruptly, jerking his hand toward us, always frightening us. Sometimes, when we were sitting quietly, he would suddenly bring his rough large hand over toward one of our legs, grabbing it, squeezing it as hard as he could. We jerked around, trying to break free, screaming at him to let us go. He would hold on, squeezing as hard as he could, looking at us while laughing, saying, "What's wrong, boy? Why are you jumping around so much? Be still." Whenever he'd grab baby Cynthia's leg that way, I would feel so sorry for her and would plead and cry to Grandpa, "Please let her go. You're hurting her!" Cynthia would be jerking around, trying to break free of his grasp on her thigh, crying at the top of her lungs. Some of the time, she couldn't hold her kidneys and would pee all over herself, wetting her clothes.

As I have said previously, my grandfather was an evil man, and I did not understand why anyone could be so evil or want to continually terrify his own grandchildren. The spirit that possessed my grandfather had to be one of Lucifer, the devil, or his angels from the bad place down below. This evil spirit that I believed possessed my grandfather seemed to terrify all three of us. Whenever he spoke, it sent chills up my spine, and the different changes in his moods were not of the normal character moods that we all have; it was as though there was a different person that possessed and controlled him. My grandfather seemed to have a hatred for all three of us but, maybe more so toward my two sisters than me. After he struck me in the car, I have never forgotten it or, I believe, ever recovered from that experience or was ever the same again.

I had just met my grandfather for the first time in my life when he and our uncle William came to Ohio. Now, I was being taken away from my mom and dad by this terrifying man that I had been told was my grandfather. Then being suddenly physically attacked by him while I was asleep and being accused of something that I thought to be a minor thing that I hadn't done.

Throughout the rest of my life, even to this day, that traumatic experience has never left me, and the emotional damage is still embedded in my subconscious mind. It would have been horrifying if it had been a stranger, but this man had been my grandfather. This, I believe, made the memories that much worse emotionally. And it was to be followed by more extreme physical and emotional abuse throughout the time that we lived on the farm with him.

Uncle William pulled off the main highway and onto the large parking lot of what appeared to be a truck stop. "Okay, you kids, we're going to stop here for a while. If you need to go to the bathroom, you had better go now, because once we get started again, I'm not going to stop for a while." Uncle William and Grandpa got out of the car and walked toward the front entrance of the truck stop, leaving us sitting there.

I looked around at Pat, asking her, "Sissy, let's go to the bathroom. We got to hurry and catch up with Grandpa and Uncle William." We all three got out, holding Cynthia by the hand between us, and hurried toward the entrance.

I looked around and noticed large semitrucks parked throughout the parking lot, with their motors running and exhaust fumes billowing up to the sky.

Grandpa turned and looked at us, raising his hand toward the building. "Okay, you young'uns, if you're going to use the bathroom, better go ahead, because we'll be leaving soon."

"Grandpa!" Pat yelled out, trying to catch him before he went inside the building. "Where is the bathroom?"

"Well, young'un, it's not out here in the parking lot." And he continued to walk away. I noticed he turned again toward us and had a disgusted look on his face.

Uncle William spoke as he went inside. "Kids, ask one of the waitresses where the bathrooms are."

We tried walking quickly toward the front entrance, where Grandpa and Uncle William disappeared. Several men and ladies were coming out the front door, and we couldn't get by them. When we finally got inside, it opened into a large room filled with smoke and a lot of noise from all the people inside, some standing, with some sitting, but all talking to one another.

There was a lady walking toward us with a large tray in her hand. "Ma'am?" Pat quickly reached out and tapped her arm and asked, "Ma'am, could you tell us where the restrooms are?"

"Why, sure, sugar. There, over there against that wall, men's on the left, women's or little girls' on the right," she said as she looked down at us with her big smile. "Well, come on, sweetie, let me show you." And she took Pat by the hand. "Come on with me." She then led us to the other side of the room. "Okay, kids," she said with a big smile on her face, "here they are. And let me know if you need any more help, okay, sweetie?" She patted me on the head and reached down, squeezing Pat on the side of her cheek.

We looked at each other, then looked around the room, noticing a lot of people staring at us and smiling, whispering to each other. "Pat, I think you and Cynthia go in there and I'll go in here, and when I get out, I promise I'll meet you right here, okay?" I said. "Now, promise me, if you get out first, you will wait right here, okay?"

"Okay, Bubba, I promise. Me and Cynthia, if we get through first, we'll wait for you here. And if you get through first, you wait here for us too, okay?" Pat asked.

When I walked inside the bathroom, I noticed some men were inside, standing up against the wall, using the bathroom. "I guess you need this, don't you?" A man held a booth door open for me to go inside. "You're still a little guy, aren't you? You won't be able to reach anything but this toilet in here." The door slammed shut behind me, and I heard his steps walking away.

After I had finished in the restroom, I went outside and stood to the side of the restroom door, where I had agreed to wait for Pat and Cynthia. While I waited, men and women walked past me, smiling and looking down at me, some speaking and patting me on the head. "How are you, young man?" one of them asked. "Are you waiting for your mom and dad?"

"I'm waiting for my two sisters," I said, pointing toward the restroom door. I was a shy child and was afraid of being in this strange place. All these strange people did not make me feel any better, and I hoped that my sisters would hurry and get out of the bathroom. This was the first time I could remember ever being away from my mother or father. I tried to stay out of the way and backed into a corner so that I would not attract attention to myself, and hopefully, they would stop asking me questions. It seemed like I waited forever for Pat, but I was relieved when she came through the door, holding Cynthia by the hand.

"Oh, Pat!" I said, sounding relieved. "I'm so glad you're here! I was beginning to wonder if you and Cynthia were still in there or you came out before I did and left. There were all these people that were talking to me and asking me questions. I told them I was waiting for my sisters, who were in there." I pointed at the restroom.

"No, Bubba," Pat said. "I've told you we'd meet right here out-side the restrooms when we got finished."

"Yes, I know, but it scared me, and it seemed like I was waiting a long time for you."

Pat reached out and took me by the arm, and with Cynthia on the other side, she said, "Come on, let's try to find Uncle William and Grandpa. They've probably finished getting gas by now and might be looking for us."

The thought did enter my mind that we might have been left behind in this strange place. Because of the previous experience with Grandpa, I did not know if he would get mad and decide to leave us just to teach us some sort of punishment. We had not had anything to eat since we left, and the aroma of the restaurant food was making my stomach growl.

We walked back through the restaurant area and went out on the other side, looking around the parking lot, but didn't see Uncle William's car or Grandpa. We walked around in front of the build-ing, searching everywhere, then went around to the other side, still looking, and finally saw the car. There were several entrances to the restaurant, and we had gotten confused about what door we had used when we arrived. We'd thought maybe Grandpa and Uncle William were already in the car, waiting for us. I was thankful that we at least just found the car and did not want to leave it again for fear that they would come back and we would really miss them and be left in this strange place.

When we got to the car, they weren't there yet. I felt a sense of relief, but that my grandfather was not there waiting for us made me think he would be mad again. "They'll probably be here in a few minutes," I said. We went to the car doors and tried to open each one, but all of them were locked. "Pat," I said, "we can't get the doors open. "What are we going to do now?"

"I don't know," she said. "Let's get out of this parking lot and go over there." She pointed to a sidewalk next to some stairs. There was a glass door that led inside and up some stairs to the second floor of the truck stop. We all three went inside and sat down on the bottom step and waited. Not knowing what else we could do, we just sat there and looked out the glass door toward our car, waiting for Grandpa and Uncle William to walk up.

As we sat waiting, suddenly, a door at the top of the stairs opened, and we heard a man's and a woman's voices laughing as they mumbled to each other. "I'll see you in a couple of weeks, baby. I'll have a run up this way about the fifteenth of the month, so keep that day open for me, okay, baby?"

"If you're sure you'll be through this way on the fifteenth and you've got the cash, sweetheart, I'll keep that day open for you. You know my time is valuable, and you know how precious my gorgeous body is. And I might add *priceless*. Haha!" They both laughed.

"Oh! I'll be here, honey, even if I've got to drive up here on my own time!" Laughing, the man grabbed her with one of his hands in the back of her head and pulled her close, kissing her. At the same time, I could see him grabbing her by her behind and squeezing it several times with these large hands. As they kissed, one of the woman's legs was high in the air and wrapped around his back. She braced herself with her other leg, leaning back against the door.

They stopped kissing, and the man turned around and started to walk down the stairs but noticed they had been seen by us. The man started to laugh, looking at us and then looking back at the lady.

"Hey, Barbara, whose kids are these? Is there something you're not telling me?" he asked as he leaned back and bellowed out a loud laugh.

She looked around the man, glaring at us at the bottom of the stairs. "Hey, you kids, what in the world are you doing down there and in front of my door?"

"We're waiting for Grandpa and our uncle William to get back from inside the truck stop."

"Well, you can't wait there. It's bad for my business to have three kids hanging around the entrance to my place!"

We hurried outside, trying desperately to get away from the lady and the man, forcing our way through the glass door and toward the car, in hopes that Uncle William and Grandpa would be there. When we got close to the car, Uncle William, with a puzzled look on his face, asked, "Where have you young'uns been? We have been waiting inside the restaurant for you." He was trying to open the driver's side door and saw that it was locked, and after checking all the other doors, he acted aggravated. "All the doors are locked," he said, looking over at Grandpa. "I thought you were going to leave some of the doors unlocked in case the kids got separated and came back to the car?"

"Well, I thought I did," Grandpa said. "Anyway, here is the key." Which he took from his pocket. "Let's get in the car and get started. We still have a long way to go until we get to Ripley, Tennessee." All at once, Grandpa reared back in his seat and let out a big belch, sounding something like "I eeeeat!" as he patted his large stomach.

Uncle William looked over at Grandpa and said, "I'm going back inside to get these kids something to eat. I know they got to be hungry."

"Oh! No!" Grandpa yelled toward him. "They should've come in while they had a chance, instead of sitting out here."

"It won't take but a minute," Uncle William said. "I'll be right back. They can eat while we're traveling."

"They had their chance to get something to eat," Grandpa said as he reached toward the glove box. "I got a few packs of the crackers in here that I take when I go fishing, and that should be enough for them. Right now, let's get on the road! We've wasted enough time coming up here to get these young'uns, anyway. I've got a lot of work to do when I get back home and need to hitch up old Blue and

Mable. They're good mules, and I know that they miss their work. Mama is supposed to be feeding and watering them, and if she knows what is good for her, she had better be doing what she was told to do!"

We all got into the car just as Cynthia started crying. Uncle William kept walking toward the front of the restaurant. We knew that she had to be hungry because my stomach was also growling. I knew I would be okay, but Cynthia was a toddler and had just started walking, and I didn't think she understood how to be patient and/or do without. We hadn't eaten since we left Daddy and Mama, which had been most of the night.

After we settled into the car, Grandpa turned around in his seat, glaring with that evil expression we had seen too many times before. "You kids should've come inside when you had the chance when your uncle William and I were eating. Now you want to sit back there and start complaining again. You just want everybody to start feeling sorry for you, don't you?" he said. "Well, I'm not going to put up with it!" He took the crackers and, reaching around, threw one pack at us, which struck me in the face. And then he threw another pack at Pat, then at Cynthia, hitting them both in the chest and face.

Pat cried out, and while holding Cynthia in her arms, she pleaded, "Grandpa, please, I'm sorry, but she's just hungry, Grandpa! We haven't eaten since we left."

My grandfather's face turned beet red as he glared at us in the back seat. "You young'uns, you're starting trouble already. And we haven't even gotten halfway home yet! Now, sit back!" And he slammed the palm of his left hand in her chest, shoving her back into the seat. Her head snapped back, causing her to reach up, grabbing her chest. Cynthia had been sitting in her lap, and the sudden slap caused her to fall to the floorboard of the car, hitting her mouth. Cynthia raised her head up, screaming and crying, staring toward Grandpa with horrifying emotional hurt. She had liquid streaming down from her mouth.

I tried to reach down and help her up, as did Pat, but Grandpa yelled out, "Leave that young'un alone! If she can't get up by herself, throw her a blanket down there and leave her on the floor."

Cynthia struggled around on the floorboard, crying, while Pat and I sat there, looking at her and crying, as well, but mostly for our little sister than for ourselves. I noticed Pat placing one of her legs and reaching down toward Cynthia, helping her partially up where she could grab the edge of the seat. Cynthia then started pulling herself up the rest of the way.

"Grandpa, she's bleeding and hurt. Please let me help her. Please!" I said.

He suddenly swung around with his hand, trying to slap me as he had just done to Pat, but could not reach me. "I told you what to do, and I won't say it again! You young'uns will do as you are told! Eat those crackers and shut up, before I take them away from you! I usually save those and some Vienna sausages for my fishing trips, so you better be glad you have that, as much time and expense you kids have been!"

"Grandpa…" I was frightened still but spoke up to hopefully calm him from getting angrier at Pat. "We didn't know where you were and were afraid that we had lost you, so we came back to the car and waited. Then you were not here, and the doors were locked, so we had to go back inside that door." I pointed over toward it. "And wait."

"You young'uns, I told you that I got work to do and animals to feed when I get back to Ripley!"

Pat looked at me and then back toward Grandpa. She reached under Cynthia's arms, pulling her back onto her lap from the floorboard of the car. Pat pulled Cynthia up close to her while trying to comfort her so she would stop crying. Pat surrounded Cynthia with her arms not only, I believe, to comfort her but also to possibly shield her from any more of Grandpa's slaps with those large hands. We were both trying to stop crying and hold back our tears, staring wide-eyed and terrified at Grandpa and wiping our eyes and faces with our hands. Why was he so angry at us? What had we done for him to be so hateful toward us? We tried to be still and quiet, sucking back whatever saliva or mucus that was dripping from our noses. We wanted to please our grandpa and do whatever it took so he would stop getting angry at us. This was the same type of anger that our mother had shown toward us, and whatever bad things we were doing, we needed to stop and learn to be good kids.

I started sliding over next to Pat as Grandpa looked around and noticed what I was doing.

"Now, you get your little skinny behind back over there where you were. You're not a little sissy girl, are you?"

I scooted back across the seat, looking at Grandpa with my pleading, tired, tearstained eyes.

Uncle William returned to the car a few minutes later and sat down, looking around at us, and noticed that we had been crying. "What's wrong with you young'uns?" he asked, looking concerned. Both Pat and I just sat there, looking at Uncle William, but were afraid to answer him. We sat there looking at our uncle with eyes that pleaded for help, and then back at Grandpa, sniffling, trying to stop crying.

Grandpa looked over at Uncle William, pointing his finger back at Cynthia, and answered him, "Oh, that youngest one there fell off the other one's lap and hit the floorboard. I guess when she fell on the floor, she cut her lip. She'll be all right now. She has got to toughen up, anyway, and her sister will take care of her. These young'uns have got to be more careful, anyway, and stop being clumsy." He turned around and looked at us with that evil expression, as if to say, "Don't any of you say a word!" Then Grandpa continued, "Okay, Bill, let's get on the road!" And he let out a big belch. The words sounded as though they came from the pit of his stomach. "I guess when one of them cries, they all must cry." He turned sideways, looking back at us with another mean, evil expression. His eyes seemed to have a glassy, glazed-over look about them. His eyes and beet red face terrified me and Pat when we saw them. He glanced back over toward Uncle William, and I could see deep-red veins at this angle in his eyes.

"Here, kids." Uncle William reached over the seat toward us and handed us a sack of the great aroma that I could recognize to be hamburgers.

Grandpa reached back over the seat and grabbed the sack. "I'll just keep those up here until these young'uns stop being so unruly and disobedient. They all three started this nonsense when we left

Ohio, and they won't get anything until they stop all that crying. They couldn't be that hungry, anyway. This is what happens when you take a young'un up north. They think of so many stupid ways of how to raise a young'un. Just look at their mama, Jeanette, Bill," he said. "There is a good example of why we should have killed all of them during the war. And if I had been around at that time, things would have been a lot different!" He set the sack down between him and Uncle William.

I was so hungry and knew that Pat also could smell the enticing aroma of the hamburgers. My stomach started growling, and I looked over at Pat with my eyes widening and whispered, "It smells so good. I'm so hungry!"

"I know, Bubba. Just try to be quiet. I'm hungry too, and so is Cynthia."

We started driving down the road, and after a while, I noticed Uncle William looking over at Grandpa. Grandpa had fallen asleep with his head leaning back onto the seat and was snoring loud. Uncle William looked toward the back seat, and seeing that we were still awake, he grabbed the bag from the front floorboard and handed it back to us.

He had a smile on his face as he watched us both scrambling with our hands inside the bag. The hamburgers were wrapped in paper, and we were careful not to make any noise taking the paper off so as not to wake Grandpa. As we got each our hamburgers, I don't know why, but I looked over at Pat, and she at me. We had tears starting to well up in our eyes, and while we both enjoyed eating, we began to cry. I tried to be quiet but couldn't stop crying, and my tears were falling into my hamburger. I slid over next to Pat, leaning my head on her arm as we ate, while she pinched off little pieces and fed Cynthia.

On the Farm with My Grandparents

A couple of days had gone by since we had last seen our dad and mom, and it did seem to take what felt like forever to arrive at our grandparents' home.

Grandpa's house was in a very rural country setting outside the small town of Ripley, Tennessee, which was in the southwestern part of the state. Several large trees surrounded the house, which shaded the house, as I remember during the blistering heat of the hot summer days. There was an exceptionally large tree just a few feet from the porch, which was on the right side of the house. This was truly in the country, which I had only seen in books by then. As far as I could see on either side of the highway, there were fields lined in rows with planted crops. This was a strange and different setting from the city and neighborhood existence that we had always been accustomed to. In Ohio, we were used to seeing a lot of streets, and the houses were mostly two-story dwellings that were clustered in neighborhoods. The noises of the traffic and fire trucks traveling through the streets could always be heard all hours of the day and throughout the night. This country home was without any other family houses around, and this thought frightened me: to be this far out in the country alone with our grandfather. There were several other buildings in the adjacent area, but away from the house.

To the right side of the house and into a big field were two large barns, one larger than the other. A large barn and sheds also had large hogs and cows close to them. All these other buildings were surrounded by barbed wire fences. I also noticed chicken that ran freely throughout the property. The house had a porch that went almost all the way around it on the left side. It was located just off an old high-way that, by today's standards, would be considered a country back road. Later during my stay with Grandpa, we would use this highway to catch rides and go into Ripley to sell purple-hull peas on the court square. My grandfather raised pigs, raised chickens, and had a couple of mules that would plow the fields. He would hook up these two mules to a steel plow every morning before going to the field. I'd go with him to the barn and watch him struggle with these two mules as he hooked them up to the plow. When they got fastened to the plow, he would yell and use some type of language that they seem-ingly understood, because they jerked their heads up and their ears went back, and Grandpa had to almost run trying to keep up with them as they headed toward the fields to plow. These mules would pull this plow in front of my grandfather as he stumbled, trying to guide it through the dirt as the piles of dirt curled up then over and lie on top of the ground. Sometimes he would get furious at these mules when he thought they were doing something wrong. He used the leather strap that ran from the mules, draped over his shoulders, and savagely beat them. They would be so afraid of my grandpa and throw their head back, with their eyes wide open, trying to get away from the sting of the strap as it popped on their sweat-drenched hips and back. At the end of the day, they would have injuries and sweat dripping down their bodies and onto their hooves.

This change in scenery was quite an overwhelming shock to me and my sisters; we had no idea what was in our future while staying with our grandparents. We had already been terrified on the way down from Ohio because of the way Grandfather acted toward us. We started walking slowly toward the front porch of his house and noticed that on it were two ladies sitting. They were looking in our direction, and I noticed they had two large buckets on the porch between their feet. They were, as I was to find out, shelling peas.

Then I heard my grandpa's voice. "Hey, Mama, what's for sup-per tonight? I'm hungry." Which was the way he pronounced *hun-gry*. "Mama, these are Roberts's kids. It's been a while since we've seen them. They were just small young'uns when Robert left here and went chasing that jezebel woman Jeanette." He reached over and grabbed a handful of my hair and shook it, hurting me. "This boy is Hershel. He's grown a little, hasn't he? This girl over here is Patricia. Remember her, don't you? She calls her brother Bubba. Don't know why, but she does."

Our grandmother, whom he was speaking to, grabbed two handfuls of peas that she had in her lap and threw them in a bucket that was a few feet away, close to the edge of the porch, and stood up. She wiped her hands on her apron, which was wrapped around her waist, and stood there looking back and forth at the three of us. A big smile filled her face, and I could see her mouth seemed to be full of something. She raised two fingers to her mouth and leaned to one side, then suddenly spit something brown out of her mouth off the porch. I noticed this brown spit landing on the back of one of the chickens walking near the porch. She then wiped her mouth with her hand, smearing the liquid on her sleeve.

"Well, you young'uns have really grown a little bit since your grandmother saw you last," she said. "Hershel, you are the spitting image of your dad, such a fine, handsome boy!" I felt that the words she just spoke were so different from her spitting from the porch. Apparently, this vile habit was just another everyday occurrence people did here. "And these two girls, aren't they pretty, Pa?" I heard my grandpa grumbling something under his breath as he stepped up onto the porch, going past her and into the house, and slammed the screen door behind him. "You young'uns probably don't remember your grandma, do yaw? You were just babies when your dad and mom moved way up north." She looked over at Pat, smiling. "I know what your name is, young'uns. Your name is Patricia, and this little young'un is Cynthia." She reached down to pat her on the head, then put her arms around the three of us. "That lady on the porch is your great-grandmother." Turning sideways, she pointed at her. "She's been sick lately. She's got sugar bad. That's what the doctors call diabetes."

Grandpa came back outside and stood there looking down off the porch at Grandma hugging us. She looked back over her shoulder, looking at Grandpa, and asked him, "How are Robert and Jeanette doing?" Grandpa didn't speak to her; he just shrugged his shoulders, gave her a disgusted look, then turned around and walked back inside the house, again slamming the door behind him.

Grandma looked at Uncle William and asked him, "How are Robert and Jeanette doing? I wish they had not run off up north and instead stayed around here like I asked them. I believe things would have been better for them if they'd stayed around home, where your brother Robert is familiar with everything. I can't understand what people see up there in that godforsaken place, anyway."

"Mama, I believe he's not doing too well," Uncle William said. "And I agree with you, Mama! I don't know why he had to go off up yonder, anyway, to find him a wife."

"William?" Grandma spoke. "He did not find her up yonder. Son, you know when all this came about, don't you? You remember when he was driving that purple-hull pea truck from Covington to Memphis? That was when he made the mistake, like a lot of those truckers do, of stopping at one of those honky-tonks out on Highway 51 south of Memphis. That was where he met Jeanette, in one of those filthy juke joints. Her family had moved to Memphis from Indiana."

"There is plenty of nice Southern girls right here at home," William said. "He's sure having a lot of problem with that woman."

"Son," Grandma told him as she looked sweetly down at us, "we just must trust in the Lord that they will be shown the way out of this mess that they have gotten themselves into, but it will be up to us to help these young'uns." Our grandmother walked over to where we stood and embraced the three of us with her frail arms. "You young'uns come on inside and let Grandma see if I can find a biscuit and some sorghum molasses."

We followed Grandma through the house, noticing that the first room had a large bed placed against the wall. A TV and a few other furnishings also made it look like a living room. She walked into another room that had a large table that was covered with a tablecloth colorfully designed with flowers. Against the wall, behind the table, was a long bench that reminded me of church pews.

I noticed that the personalities of my grandparents were very different. Grandma had the spirit of a loving Christian woman. Even the farm animals, when she walked around the yard, would flock to her. Her face seemed to glow as though she had the Holy Spirit inside of her. Looking back to that time in my life, I thank our heavenly Father that she was a kind, loving, and spiritual grandmother. If she had had the cruel and evil personality as Grandpa did, I do not think that I or my two sisters could have survived.

Walking into another room, I could see an old iron stove that burned wood, and this would be the way Grandma prepared many, numerous delicious country meals. Reaching up, she raised the cupboard on the top of the stove. "Now, let me see if I can find a biscuit for each of you young'uns. It won't be long until I start supper, so a biscuit should not spoil any one of you young'uns' appetite." She spun around with three biscuits in her open hands and smiled, giving each of us a biscuit. "Here you go," she said. "Now, go outside onto the porch and sit down while Grandma starts to prepare supper before your grandpa gets his whiskers in a knot!" All three of us went outside as she had told us.

Grandpa was sitting on a wooden chair at the edge of the porch, smoking a pipe. The chair he sat on was different from any other I had ever seen and appeared to be made from tree limbs. The seat was weaved together with straw. We all three were smiling and were thrilled to be enjoying our biscuits, but our smile was soon destroyed as we looked toward Grandpa. Ravenously, due to hunger, we continued to eat our biscuits and were enjoying what I thought was the best bread I had ever tasted.

Grandpa's harsh voice suddenly echoed throughout the house and surrounding countryside. "Heh! Boy, come over here!" With my mouth full of the delicious biscuit, he must have startled me, because I almost choked but did manage to gulp it all down. Cautiously, I left my sisters' side and slowly walked toward my grandpa. When I had gotten close enough, he struck his arm out and grabbed me on the shoulder, clamping his crooked, arthritic fingers close to my neck. "Boy, where did you young'uns get those biscuits? We don't eat around here until it is mealtime!" He grabbed me with such force that the biscuit that I had been eating was knocked from my right hand and onto the porch, rolling off onto the dirty and dusty ground.

The biscuit, at first, was suddenly surrounded by what seemed like a dozen chickens coming from all areas of the yard. They were quickly and momentarily pecking at the biscuit, then suddenly, two large hound dogs attacked the chickens, trying to get also to where the biscuit had fallen and scattering the flock of chickens throughout the yard in all directions. Some jumped high into the air, flapping their wings, while all the others continued to scatter safely, or so they thought, into other areas of the surrounding yard. Both dogs began to growl and fight each other until the weaker and smaller dog eventually gave up and ran away but still managed to slip away with a piece of biscuit.

My grandpa's grip was so strong I grimaced in pain down on my knees to the porch and begged him to please let me go. "Grandma gave us each a biscuit and told us to come out onto the porch and eat them. Please, Grandpa!" I pleaded in pain, begging him to please let me go.

He kept his grip on my shoulder, then yelled out, "Heh! Mama, come out here! Did you give these young'uns these biscuits? You know we don't eat unless it's mealtime!"

I was still crying and pleading with Grandpa. "Grandma gave them to us!" I repeated.

I heard Grandma calling through the house, "Yes, Daddy, I gave those young'uns one biscuit apiece. I didn't know when the last time they had anything to eat was. I know how you and Bill are when it comes to stopping when you're traveling. Daddy, now, you behave yourself!" Grandma said. "This one time I didn't think would hurt anything." She looked through the partially opened screen door and saw that he had a grip on my left shoulder. Grandma yelled at him, "Papa, you let that boy go! And can't you see that you are hurting him?"

I attempted to turn my head and look toward her with my head crooked sideways while trying to ease the pain that had my whole left side numb. "Please, Grandma," I pleaded to her, "help me! And please tell Grandpa you gave us the biscuits!"

"Oh, shut up, boy! Neither Grandma nor the Almighty himself can help you if you have lied to me!" His grip went even tighter on my shoulder.

"Now, Daddy, you let that boy go. He's your grandson! I told you that I gave those three young'uns those biscuits."

Grandpa suddenly released his grip on my shoulder, and with a shove from his arm, I fell backward on my behind near my sister's feet. Pat grabbed me by the arm and pulled me close against her while she held Cynthia with her other arm. The three of us walked quickly around the porch and away from Grandpa, to where his mother and our granny were seated in her wheelchair. All of us, frightened and huddled together, sat down on the steps that faced the road. Granny was my grandpa's mother, and I noticed that she was not capable of any conversation that made any sort of sense. Our granny had succumbed to what I would later know as Alzheimer's disease. She had reverted mentally back into a childhood stage of existence. She was also without both her legs, and I was told that she had lost them due to diabetes. We felt compassion for her, especially when she was not able to control herself verbally or of her bodily functions, which caused a terrible odor. Her body and clothing stayed in this soiled condition sometimes all day, without anyone cleaning her.

In the days that followed, our lives would change dramatically. Each morning we were awakened by my grandfather and his loud yelling. "You young'uns get up out of those beds! We have fieldwork to do, and the chores must be finished!" Each morning the aroma of Grandma's cooking filled the entire house.

The first morning, Pat whispered to me, "Bubba, we don't have a bathroom in this house."

"I'll go ask Grandma where the bathroom is," I told her.

I found Grandma cooking in the kitchen and asked where the bathroom was. She reared back and laughed, then brought me over to the kitchen door and, pointing toward a small building in the backyard, said, "Honey, that is the only toilet we have." Going back to where I left Pat, I told her what Grandma said, that it was the small building outside in the backyard. I followed her as she led Cynthia by the hand out toward the small wooden shed. The inside was scary and had spiderwebs spread all around the ceilings. Looking down toward the back of the homemade toilet, I noticed it had a thick slab of wood that had two holes cut out in it, which was where we were to sit and apparently use the bathroom. I looked at Pat as we both stared back at each other with a puzzled look on our faces. We could smell the sickening, foul odor coming from the holes, and as we looked down through them, we could see that this was some type of bathroom. This outside toilet, however, was only used for eliminating body functions and not for bathing, because it was not connected to any type of water supply. This was one of the many differences from what we were accustomed to in the city.

Also, on the outside, there was a pump where we were to get the water to drink and bathe. Water first had to be heated on the woodstove in the kitchen and then poured into a large circular steel tub before bathing. There were times, especially during the winter months, when I and my sisters would have to bathe in the same water. Bath would have to be hurriedly taken due to the water getting cold after it was heated from the woodstove.

These were the lifestyles that we had only heard or read about in books of the early pioneers.

Our grandma cooked from a steel stove that had to be filled with wood even in the hot summer months. Grandpa did not believe or want to waste his hard-earned money on these modern contraptions, as he called them, saying that they would only spoil Grandma.

After the first awful experience of using the outhouse bathroom, we walked back to the house and up onto the porch. Grandpa came through the screen door and dropped a metal bucket onto the porch in front of us. "Hershel, take that bucket over to that pump and fill it. Don't get any trash in the water, and bring it back into the kitchen for your grandma. We got a lot of work to do." And he looked over our head toward the vastness of the fields nearby.

"Grandpa," I asked, "how do you get the water from that pump?"

"Put the bucket under that spout, and see that handle at the other end? You pump it up and down, and sooner or later, water will start pouring out of that spout. Don't stop pumping that handle until the bucket is filled, or you will have to start over again, and then get it back to the house."

I did as my grandpa told me, but when the bucket was filled with water, it was too heavy and I could not carry it. Each time that I tried, the water splashed out all over the ground. Taking the bucket back to the pump, I filled it a second time, then looked up, frustrated, and noticed that Pat had been watching me. I pleaded with her to come help me. She looked around behind her to see if Grandpa was watching, then ran off the porch toward me to help.

"The bucket is too heavy when it's full. Please help me before Grandpa hurts and yells at me again!"

She looked around. "Bubba, I'll grab the handle on this side and you grab the handle on that other side." We both walked toward the porch and swung it together up onto it, splashing some of the water out.

Grandma looked out and saw how we were struggling and splashing some of the water out. "You young'uns get inside and let me have that bucket." She picked it up with ease, carrying it inside.

My grandma was the best cook in the world, and it's still amazing to me how she could arrange to fill the entire dinner table with so much delicious food. Grandma, as I said earlier, did not have an electric stove, and all the meals had to be cooked on a stove that was heated with wood. This same stove also kept the house warm in the winter, along with one other woodstove in my grandparents' bedroom.

Each morning after breakfast, which included gravy and biscuits, we all met on the front porch. Grandpa would be sharpening the steel hoes that we used in the fields to chop weeds from between the cotton stalks. In the morning, we would get up while it was still dark outside. There would be dew on the grass, and most cold mornings, we needed to dress in extra clothes. In the early morning and after the sun came up, it started to get warm, and some of the outer clothes needed to be taken off. Our grandpa told us on most mornings that he was going to take two to three rows and we were to stay ahead of him and chop the weeds from between one row of cotton stalks. He told us that we should be able to stay ahead of him and not let him catch up to us. "I'm not going to put up with a lazy young'un, so don't let me catch up with either of you." He then bent over and grabbed a large stalk of johnsongrass out of the ground by the roots and shook the dirt from it. "This will make a good believer out of either of you and a good switching for both of you, so if you know what's good for you, don't let me catch you!"

I knew what johnsongrass would do to us if he was to hit us with it. I had pulled on a stalk before, and the sharp edges had sliced my hand wide open. Grandma had put some spit that was filled with snuff along with a little tobacco juice from her mouth on the cut and then wrapped it with an old rag. She assured me that it would form a God-given, natural medicine from both juice combinations and heal any wound.

Days in the cotton fields were long, very dusty, and sometimes extremely hot. During certain parts of the year, it was time to cultivate the fields of all the weeds, which would suck out all the nutrients from the cotton if not taken out. In the early part of the year, Grandpa would go out to one of the barns and harness the two mules together then plow up the soil and later plant the crops. Toward the fall of the same year, it would be time to pick the cotton. The cotton was picked by pulling a large cotton sack with straps that wrapped around your shoulder and then dragging the bag behind up the rows until it was filled full of cotton. During the fall was when all the crops would be harvested, and the landowner, Mr. Burns, would meet with my grandpa and discuss the shares of profit that would be divided between them. When the cotton was ready to be picked, Mr. Burns would meet again with my grandfather to decide how many workers he thought he would need to get the cotton harvested and sent to the gin. This time of year, large trucks would arrive at the cotton fields filled with Negro workers, which was what Black people were called at this time in my life. My grandpa had another name for them that I do not care to mention because of the severity of the language he used. My grandpa, after each person filled their sacks with cotton, would then weigh the cotton on a scale that looked like a large steel hook that hung from the back of the cotton trailer. The sacks of cotton would be emptied into the trailer and, when the trailer was filled to overflowing, hauled away to the gin. We looked forward to going to school because that gave us the chance to not have to go to the cotton fields. Grandpa thought it was foolish to send us off to school when there was work to be done and crops to be harvested from all the fields. He just had a third-grade education and knew how to read a small amount and figure numbers, as he called it.

The farmhouse was adjacent to a small creek that ran through a large section of one of the cotton fields. I remember one year, there was a severe thunderstorm that flooded the creek, causing it to over-flow its banks. All the fields were filled with water, and most of the cotton that year was destroyed and had to be replanted. The rain-water kept rising and eventually reached the house. We were stuck in the house and could not go anywhere because the house was sur-rounded by floodwater. The flood reached the porch, and all were worried that it would eventually get inside the house. My grandpa called me from inside the house as I was looking across the field at a sea of water in all directions.

"Hershel, come here!" he said.

I quickly went inside and located my grandpa, answering, "Yes, sir."

"Here," he said, "put on these overalls." The overalls were blue jeans that had suspenders attached to each shoulder. "I am going to need you to go under the house and get all those chickens off the foundation before they drown."

"But, Grandpa, I can't swim. I'll drown!" I said.

"Shut up, boy! You won't drown. The water is not that high yet. I'll tie this rope on your belt loop so I will always know where you are. Anyway, those chickens are what feeds us, and we can't afford to let any one of them drown. Those chickens provide us with those eggs you and your sister eat. And where do you think that chicken comes from that your grandma cooks for you young'uns?" he said. "Now, do as you're told!" And he raised his rough open hand toward my head.

"Yes, sir!" I said, backing away.

"After you get those trousers on, I want you to come out onto the porch, and I'll tell you what to do next."

I pulled on the oversize trousers, which were double the size of my small body, and hurried outside to join Grandpa.

"Now, come over here, boy, and listen to me," he said as he tied the rope to a loop on my trousers. "I don't want any of those chickens to drown. Now, get down off the porch in that water and work your way under the porch to the foundations. That is where all the chickens probably are perched."

I was frightened that I might drown, as I noticed the swiftness of the water that swirled around the porch. My greatest fear, though, was what would happen if I did not do exactly as my grandpa had said.

I first sat down on the porch and was frightened more than I had ever been in my life, but as I said, more so for what Grandpa would do if I did not save his chickens from drowning than if I actually drowned myself.

"Okay, boy."

I felt my grandpa foot-push me the rest of the way off the porch. I felt the swiftness of the water's current and attempted to stand but lost my balance and went under the water. I quickly gained my footing and grabbed for the porch, lifting myself back onto my feet. I looked up to see that my grandpa was laughing, and he told me, "Boy, you stop that nonsense and listen to me! I want you to slide yourself under this porch, and when you get under, I want you to use the rafters to ease your way to the foundation of the house." I eased myself down and under the porch with just enough air space to keep my head above the water. "Now, you get going before the chickens drown or the water gets any higher!"

"Grandpa," I pleaded, looking up through the cracks of the porch at him in horror, "what if the water gets too high under here and fills all the spaces? How I will breathe? What if I can't get back to the porch in time before the water rises?"

"Boy, you do as you're told. I have this rope tied to this post, and the rain is slacking. You had better make your way to those chickens before they all drown. Now go, boy!"

"Okay, Grandpa." I slanted my head sideways to stay above the muddy water as I slowly crept my way under the house. I reached through the muddy water to whatever rafters I could find and slowly eased myself along. I could see above my head through the cracks in the porch and house that my grandpa was still there, just in case I needed him. I felt a sense of relief that if something terrible occurred, I could depend on my grandpa to help me and pull me back to the porch. I thought for sure that my grandpa would save me.

Little by little I crawled through the mud, with one hand holding on to the rafters above my head and the other feeling along the muddy ground below. Finally, I reached one of the many concrete foundations of our old farmhouse. The chickens were, as my grandpa said, perched on the foundation but were pacing back and forth in a frantic behavior. I heard footsteps walking through the house and heard my grandpa's voice speak.

"You see those chickens, boy?"

"Yes, sir," I said. "They are all here as you said, Grandpa."

"Now, try to get two at a time, one in each hand, and maybe we can save them all. But keep their head above the water and bring them back to the porch!"

"Yes, sir, I'll try!"

Grandpa responded, "No, you won't try! You will do exactly as you are told and get all those chickens back onto this porch! Do you understand me, boy?"

"Yes, sir!" I said and quickly reached toward one of the hens, feeling a sharp peck on my hand. "Owe!" I looked and could see that the large red rooster Grandpa had named Big Red had pecked my hand. He had pecked so hard, in fact, that my hand began to bleed a bright liquid that ran down my arm into my sleeve. "Grandpa," I said, "this red rooster has bitten me!"

"Keep your hands away from his beak and his claws! He is probably frightened by the rising water. You have got to sneak up on him and grab him around his feet, then he won't be able to bite you!" Then he laughed.

I noticed the large rooster was still pacing back and forth, watching me as I crawled around in this muddy water. The water had risen, and just my head and some of my shoulders were out of the water. The other hens were just sitting on the foundation, but I could tell that they were frightened, as was I, of the swirling, rising water. I do believe that all of them, except that stupid rooster, were hoping that I would be able to save them from certain death.

Suddenly, I thought Grandpa turned on a bright light from above in the house to help me see everything, then I heard a voice whisper close to my ear, saying, "You'll be all right, my child. I'm here to help you, and no harm will come to you."

I looked up through the flooring and yelled out to Grandpa, "Thanks, Grandpa! I'm not afraid now that I know that you are there and told me nothing will harm me!"

"What are you talking about, boy? I haven't said anything to you! Now, get those chickens out from under the house!"

"Yes, sir, Grandpa! Thanks for the light. It was dark under here!"

"Boy, you stop that foolishness! There is no light, only the candles that Mama has lit! Because of the storm, the electricity went out hours ago. We have been using these dim oil lamps also for light."

If that wasn't Grandpa that spoke to me, then where did that soft, comforting voice come from? And who was it? Maybe because I was extremely frightened and was just hearing things; yes, maybe just my imagination!

When Big Red wasn't looking and was turned away, I slowly reached under one of the hens and grabbed its feet, holding it up above the rising water. It started to flap around and wave its wing all around, which caused a torrent of muddy water to fill my mouth and soak my entire face.

"Grandpa, I have a big one, and I'm coming out with it now!" With one hand, I held on to the frantic chicken, and with the other I tried to keep my head above the water, working my way out from beneath the house. Eventually, I reached the edge of the porch, coming out from beneath the house, and swung the chicken up onto it. Quickly I let go and threw it onto the porch, where it scurried into one of the corners at the far end. The chicken looked around at me, seemingly happy to be safely out of the water. "There, Grandpa!" I looked up, smiling with great joy, hoping that I had pleased him, but did not see my grandpa. "Grandpa, where are you? I got one of the chickens up onto the porch as you told me."

"Well, boy, keep at it now. You still have a lot more of them to get! Go back under there and get all the others!" I heard his voice coming from inside the house. I knew that I had made my grandpa happy because I was saving the chickens from drowning in the rising water.

One by one, going from one foundation to the next, I eventually brought all the chickens out from under the house and sat each onto the porch. I waited until all the other chickens were rescued before I attempted to catch Big Red, the rooster. He was pacing back and forth on the flat level of the concrete foundation as I crawled cautiously toward him. He seemed to be bothered by the rising water, which had reached the highest point of the foundation before going over the top. The rising water could have forced him off the foundation and into the water to drown. The water was rising to the point that the top of my head was against the floorboard of the house, and I defiantly needed to hurry to save him.

Cautiously, and frightened, I eased through the mud beneath my feet to where I could reach out and almost touch Big Red. He was still pacing back and forth and bobbing his head up and down, looking directly into my eyes in defiance. I talked to him, saying, "Now, Big Red, I'm just trying to help you. And you don't want to bite me again, do you?" Suddenly, with my right hand, I waved in front of him to distract him, then I quickly brought my left hand out of the water and safely grabbed those dangerous legs, but away from those claws that were attached to his feet. I held on tight as he flopped around in the water and desperately tried to free himself from my tight grip. I had seen this rooster fight other roosters and knew that if he had those sharp claws make contact with my skin, they could rip me open or possibly put an eye out. There had been a few times during barnyard fights with other roosters where Big Red killed the others, and then he'd stand over them as if in defiance, rearing his head back, and give out a screech-like yell. This was my grandpa's favorite rooster, and I thought it might be because of its vicious, evil nature.

I stopped to think that it might be possible that they both might have something in common, and then I felt guilty that I thought such a thing about my grandpa.

"What's all that commotion under there?" Grandpa asked.

"Grandpa, I got ahold of Big Red, and he sure is giving me a fit!"

"Now, boy, try to get him out of there before he drowns the both of you!" Grandpa chuckled.

Holding on tight to his feet, I hurriedly tried to make my way through the muddy water and pulled myself along by the floor rafters until finally, I lifted Big Red, throwing him up onto the porch. Getting to his feet, he suddenly took a vicious forward stance, with his head bowed down and his backside up, then raced toward me at the edge of the porch. If not because I had been in the water, I don't doubt that he would have spurred me with those daggerlike claws, pecked me with his knifelike beak. I backed away from the porch while Grandpa waved him away.

"Thank you, Grandpa! He was really trying to get me, wasn't he?" I asked. I looked up at him, smiling, proud of what I thought I had accomplished. "Grandpa, that is all the chickens. I saved them, even that mean Big Red. I don't know why he was trying to bite me. I was just trying to save him from drowning." I wiped the mud from my head, face, and nostrils and was proud that I had hopefully pleased my grandpa.

"Now, boy," my grandpa said, "those chickens would have probably been all right and have made it out of there. The creek has flooded many times before, and we haven't lost very many of them so far. If the water had gotten up to the foundation, they would have floated out from under there, and then we could have picked them out of the water and set them on the porch, as we had in the past."

My smile suddenly turned to one of disappointment and puzzlement about what he had just told me. "But, Grandpa, why did you want me to go under there if the chickens could have made it out and not drowned?"

"Boy!" Grandpa's face turned beet red and his eyes were glazed over, as I had seen them do before when he became angry. "Boy!

Don't you sass me!" Which meant not to talk back at or question him. "You will do as I tell you to do. Don't you ever question me about anything that I tell you! You will do as I say and not as I do!"

I think he meant whatever he does, even if I think that it is wrong, I mused, *I should not question him.*

"Now, get up on this porch and out of that water! Get yourself cleaned up." He reached down, offering his hand out toward me. I thought his hand was an effort to help me out of the water and up onto the porch. This I proudly accepted as a gesture of thank-you for what I had done and one of love from my grandpa. I felt so proud that maybe I had pleased him and thought everything would be better now that I showed him I was becoming a good grandson. Smiling up toward my grandpa and reaching up with both hands, I took ahold of his rough hand as he hoisted me up toward the porch. I felt so thrilled that I might have finally reached the compassionate part of my grandpa, that I might finally receive love from him and that he felt I could possibly turn out to be a good farm boy that my grandpa would be proud of. I did want so much to please him, and knowing that he was my daddy's father, I thought that he just had to be as good a person as my daddy.

When I reached the porch with my bare feet, I suddenly felt something hit me on the top of my head. Looking up in Grandpa's direction, I could see that he was striking me with his bare knuckles on the top of my head, saying, "I think maybe someday I will knock a little sense into that thick skull of yours!"

"Grandpa, I'm sorry, but what did I do?" I took a step backward to get away from his hard pounding and slipped off the porch, submerging back into the muddy water. When I regained a foothold of the ground, I bobbed to the surface through the swirling muddy mire to see that he was laughing at me.

"I thought I told you to get out of that water and get yourself cleaned up?" he exclaimed, chuckling. "Now go over there toward the end of the porch. I believe the steps are just under that water. And get yourself up and inside like I told you."

The expectations of compassion or any sort of kindness and/or love were again shattered.

Every morning, my grandma was busy in her kitchen, cooking breakfast on a wood-burning stove. The entire house would be filled with the aroma of sizzling bacon and hot buttermilk biscuits. As she cooked, my sister and I could hear the singing of old gospel songs, such as "Crying in the Chapel," "Amazing Grace," and "How Great Thou Art." My grandma was such a good, spiritual Christian woman, and I could feel and see always the love of God all around her. Whatever space she would occupy, there would be such an amazing spirit that manifested itself through her. Even to this day, I can't understand how two people like my grandparents, who were so much different from each other, could have possibly been married, and for as many years. She was a precious, loving person, and along with that Christian spirit, she held all of us together during the time that we spent living on that farm outside of Ripley, Tennessee. The opposite was my grandpa. I never heard him say a prayer at any time. Prayers by our grandma were always given during meals, and later before we went to bed. Each evening, after supper and chores were finished, she called for all to join her for Bible study on the front porch. My grandma could not read or write, while Grandpa had, I believe, a third-grade education, and she pleaded with him to read from the good book, which was what she called the Bible. Even though she could not read or write, she could quote scriptures from the Bible that she had apparently memorized from the many preachers and sermons she heard as a young child.

Earlier in their lives, she and Grandpa had run away to get married when she was about twelve and he was sixteen years of age. He did not want or permit her to attend church very often, if at all, during their marriage. Grandma once told us that Grandpa said that whatever she needed to learn from the Bible, he could read or teach her. She would be so overjoyed when the time came after supper to gather all of us on the porch for gospel singing and reading of the Bible. Grandpa always had his pipe, smoking and staring across the crops of cotton or cornfields. Grandma pleaded with Grandpa to read scripture from the good book. Grandpa, I thought, used his skills of being able to read the Bible to tease Grandma most of the time. Granny, his mother, would also be in her wheelchair, backed up against the wall. Though this was my grandpa's mother, I did not think she was properly cared for. She would, as they called it, dip snuff and have it dried on her face, where it would drip down her chin and soil her clothes. She had such a terrible odor because of not being cleaned or bathed. She had also lost both her legs due to diabetes, and we were told that both legs had to be removed to save her life. Eventually, later, she did die of complications relating to the diseases. I did not know exactly what diabetes was at this time in my life, nor did I know if it was something that would also cause me to suffer the same fate as my granny.

"Now, you young'uns just sit there on those steps, and your grandpa is going to read a few scriptures from the good book."

Grandpa grumbled a few words under his breath. I could not quite understand what they were but knew that he was not happy with reading the Bible to us. Instead of reading, Grandpa reached across toward Grandma, and I could see that he had her blouse twisted with his hand and was pinching her. She slapped at his hand with each pinch while he just laughed and continued to frustrate her.

"Now, Mama, you know what I get when I must read this nonsense, don't you?" he asked. With another loud laugh, he pinched her on her breast, causing her to scream out and wince in pain. He held on to her breast, twisting and pinching as he continued to laugh and puff on that smelly pipe.

"Okay, Daddy," she said, "you know you can do whatever you want with me and when you want it. Now stop that!" She was still trying to slap and push at his hands. "Those young'uns are watching you, so you stop that now! And read from God's Word, then we can sing a few hymns," Grandma said. "The Lord has really blessed us with this house, and Mr. Burns's farmland has really produced a good crop this year. We need to give thanks to the Lord God that we have this house over our heads and plenty of food on the table to eat."

I did not understand at that time why, during the night, I could hear Grandma crying from their bedroom, and sometimes into the early mornings. I could hear her rocking chair as she rocked back and forth, singing the old gospel songs she knew so well, along with the faint sound of her crying.

After all week in the cotton fields, late on Friday afternoons, we picked at least four bushels of purple-hull peas to have them ready the next day to take to Ripley and sell around the court square. This would be my grandpa's way of relaxing after working hard all week in the fields. The next day, my grandpa got up very early and woke me up, saying, "Come on, boy, we are going to town. We got to sell those peas so I'll have my tobacco money for the week!" This was also his way of buying what he called his sweetening, which was really jelly or honey. His sweetening was his special treat, and he would be the only one that could share it with us. He also woke Pat to help haul the four bushels of peas from the front porch to the edge of the road. After we got all the bushels of peas next to the roadside, Grandpa was heard opening the front door and walking toward where we were standing next to the bushels on the side of the road.

"Where are we going with all these peas, Grandpa?" Pat asked.

"You're not going anywhere, girl! You get in that house and help your grandma. I and your brother are going to catch a ride with one of our neighbors when they come by. Your place is in the house and not prissing around town in front of all those men and boys!"

Her eyes filled with tears, and she started briskly walking back toward the house. She was met by Grandma, who had come out onto the porch to wave goodbye. Grandma hugged Pat close to her stomach, and I could hear her say, "There, there, young'un, we have got plenty to do here in the house," and could see her turn with Pat pressed to her side, going into the house.

Eventually, an old truck stopped and the old man inside asked Grandpa, "Guess you're headed into town with all those peas? This should be a good day to sell. The weather is sure agreeing with us."

"Yes, I sure hope so," Grandpa answered and looked around at me. "Boy, put those peas in the back of this man's truck so we can be on our way. Then hop on up there, boy, and see to it that none of those bushels shift. I don't want those peas all over the bed on his truck."

After a brief and bumpy ride, we arrived in the town of Ripley, Tennessee. There were several people that had all sorts of vegetables and fruit baskets spread out in various locations around the courthouse square. Grandpa shook the old man's hand and said goodbye, and I could hear him say, "There is old man Virgil," pointing to a group of men. "It looks as though he has a few peas himself." We took the peas out of the truck and placed them on the grass next to the street that circled the courthouse. "Boy, we are going to sell these peas so I can have a little pipe tobacco and some sweetening next week. There might be a little left to get a sack of flour and a few other things."

We sat and watched while people strolled around, buying different things from the other farmers throughout the courtyard. Several hours had gone by when I noticed Grandpa talking to someone nearby. They walked over to where I was watching the peas, and after a few minutes, I noticed the man take a large amount of money out of his pants pocket and start to count off some of it, handing it to Grandpa.

"Boy, help me put these peas in this nice man's truck. He just bought every bushel we have left," Grandpa told me. We loaded all the bushels into the back of his truck, and Grandpa handed me a few dollar bills. "You see that building?" he asked, pointing to a door across the street.

"Yes, sir," I answered.

"You take that money and buy yourself a cold drink or something. I will be right over there."

"But, Grandpa, what will I do? Where will I go?"

"Well, boy, you can't go with me right now. I have things to do and some friends that I need to talk to about the crops. You just walk around town here and stay out of any trouble, and I'll meet you at this bench right here later when I get finished. I'll expect you to be sitting over there on that bench when I get finished, you hear me, boy? That bench right there!" Grandpa pointed at a bench across from the building he had just pointed toward. "Yes, boy, and if anything happens, I will be right inside there. But don't bother me unless you have to."

"Grandpa, can I come with you? I'm afraid to stay here all alone, and I don't know anyone!"

"No! Now, you take that money I just gave you and try to find a cold drink, or maybe some marbles to play with." He then turned and started walking across the street and entered the building he had pointed toward, without looking back. The front of the building had some sort of bright-colored neon signs that flashed different colors.

Doing as my grandpa had said, I started to walk around the court square, pressing my head up against the many windows, trying to see what they had inside. I thought about my sister and really wished they could have come with us. I felt so saddened for them because they also worked very hard all week, and so I felt that they, too, deserved to be able to enjoy coming to town.

In this one store, while peering through the window, I spotted two beautiful dolls that stood up and were dressed in what appeared to be fairy-tale dresses. My thoughts were, because my sisters did not get to come with us, these dolls would be a nice present for them. Also, feeling so guilty that I had gotten to come to town, I thought buying them these dolls would allow them to understand that I loved them and felt bad. I did not want my sisters to be sad or angry toward me, and I hoped that these dolls would make them both happy. I just could not wait to see the joy and excitement on their faces when I gave them these two beautiful dolls.

I excitedly walked inside, but then, at first, I felt a little strange and embarrassed, wondering also what people were going to think about a young boy buying two dolls. Slowly walking up to the counter, where the dolls were propped up, I was approached by this nice, pretty woman. "Hi, there, young man! And what can I do for you this fine day?" she said, smiling across the counter at me.

"Ma'am," I said, embarrassed. Then I attempted to explain, "My sisters could not come with me today, and I was just wondering how much those two dolls are." I pointed toward them. "They needed to stay home and help my grandma with the housework. I came into town with my grandpa to sell peas over there on the courthouse yard," I told her, turning and pointing.

"Young man, you are so thoughtful! And no need for you to be embarrassed about wanting to buy these dolls for your sisters. Let me put them both into this bag here with the handles so they can stay together and you won't have a hard time carrying them."

Reaching inside my pants pocket, I handed the lady all the money that Grandpa had given me, except for the nickel I had spent on a cold drink. I smiled the biggest smile I think I ever had as the pretty lady counted all the change and dollar bills on the counter.

"Oh no! Young man, you will need another ten cents to have enough money to buy your sisters these dolls. I'm so sorry, but do you have any more money?"

Looking up at her, I must have had a face that looked as though my dog just died. I tried to act as though everything would be all right and then remembered where my grandfather was and how much money that man had given him. I hoped and silently prayed to God that my grandpa was where he said he would be and I could get an extra ten cents so I could buy these dolls for my sisters. "Ma'am," I said, looking up at her, "please wait. I'll be right back. Just keep them in that bag and don't allow anyone to buy them! My grandpa is across from the courthouse, and he has ten cents. I'll be right back, okay?" I hurriedly ran out the door and across the yard of the courthouse and did not stop until I entered the door where Grandpa had entered earlier.

The room was filled with stale smoke, and I noticed that several men were seated on stools up against a long counter. Over in the far side of the room, I spotted my grandpa. He was stooped over a table and was hitting a small white ball with a long stick. I ran over to him as he looked up and glared at me, drinking from a large brown bottle of Busch beer.

"Grandpa!" I yelled, raising my hands to get his attention and running to where he stood.

"Boy," he said, "what are you doing in here? I told you not to bother me in here while I am talking business with these fine neighbors of mine! Did I not tell you to stay around the courthouse and I would meet you near that bench?"

"Grandpa, I found something, and I need just ten cents more to buy it. Please, can I have it?"

"Yeah, boy, anything to get rid of you!" Reaching inside his overalls, he handed me a bright, shiny silver dime. "Okay, now, young'un, get out of here and don't come back in here with any more nonsense!"

I could smell a bad odor on his breath and felt his spit hit my face when he spoke. The smell sickened me, and so I turned around and ran back through the door. Running as fast as my legs could carry me, I went back across the court square and did not stop until I entered the store where I left the dolls on the counter. Before I got to the counter, I could see the bright, pretty smile coming from the same lady I had spoken to earlier. My eyes must have been as large as saucers, because the lady said, "Boy, now you just calm down and let me see what you have!" She smiled. "Young man, you sure want these dolls for your two sisters, don't you?"

"Yes, ma'am." And I placed the dime on the counter next to the bag.

Gathering all the money, she opened the register and placed it inside. And as she smiled across the counter and down toward me, I felt embarrassed because she was so pretty. Then she said, "I can see by the smile on your face that you are almost as happy as your two sisters will be when they get this beautiful gift that their precious little brother got for them."

"Oh, thank you, ma'am. I know they will be too!" I then turned around and walked toward the door that I had entered. I turned around briefly and shyly smiled at her. She waved and smiled back, saying, "Now, you come back, young man, if you need anything else."

I continued walking around town, not knowing how long I would have to wait for my grandpa. I thought maybe I had better not bother him again and did not want to get him angry. The bag with the dolls was not going to leave my sight; I held on to the bag with a viselike grip, walking around from store to store. After all, I thought, this bag contained the only thing that was normal for the first time since we stayed with our grandparents. I felt so overjoyed and just knew that I was going to make them so happy. My sisters had dolls when we lived in Ohio, but our grandpa would not allow us to bring anything such as toys and told us just to bring clothes. He said that they did not have enough room in the car to haul unnecessary, foolish things like that.

When my grandpa had given me the money after we sold out the purple-hull peas, I felt that we were rich and believed he wanted to reward me and for me to have a good time. I felt that he would think as I did that I spent the money and had something to show for our hard work. I also thought the dolls were going to allow my sisters, his granddaughters, to be happy. I felt as though my grandpa was really starting to like us, and now today, he had spent time with me by taking me with him to town. I felt so special and thought that he did have a good spirit inside him. I was starting to feel bad that I had thought that his Christian spirit was not the same as Grandma's.

Dear God, I began to pray in my head, *please forgive me for thinking such bad thoughts about my grandpa. He is a good grandpa and Christian, just like Grandma. I promise to always obey him and be a good grandson. Amen!* I thought that he needed to spend some time at that smoky place with all those other men and drink beer and play games. He had worked so hard all week, and this, I knew, had to be the time that he relaxed, and he wanted me to have fun in town as well.

I started to get tired after walking around town most of the day and sat down on the bench across from the building. I waited and began to daydream about my mama and daddy and the family lifestyle that I had known in Ohio. We had been staying with our grandparents, it appeared, a long time due to the seasons that came and went. Each day I thought about my daddy and dreamed that someday he would drive into the front yard of my grandparents' home. The dream was that Mama would also be with him and they would be smiling and laughing. I could see Mama get out of the passenger seat and could hear her cry out, "There are my babies!" All our eyes would fill with tears of joy as we started running toward one another with open arms. Everybody would be hugging and crying. Daddy would encircle all of us as he came up from behind Mama. "Oh! Daddy! Mama!" the three of us children would cry out. "We missed you!" Then I would ask, "And, Mama, can we go home now?" in this dream, both of our grandparents were standing on the porch side by side, watching all the love that we were giving one another. Both of our grandparents smiled and gave each other a slight kiss and embraced with the realization that we now were going to be a family again.

Abruptly I was brought out of the daydream by the loud, rough voice of my grandpa. "Heh! Hershel, wake up there!" And I felt his rough hand slap across my face, forcing me off the bench and onto the ground. "This man is going our way home, and he has been nice to offer us a ride to the house, so get yourself up from there and get into the back of his truck over there."

"Yes, sir, Grandpa," I said, picking myself off the ground and quickly following behind him toward the truck.

Grandpa, I noticed, was not walking as he normally did. He was staggering and almost fell. He caught himself by stumbling against the man's truck. Because of the startling way that I had been awakened, I had forgotten the package containing the two dolls I bought for Pat and Cynthia. Looking around and across the street toward the park bench, in surprise, I noticed the bag was still under the bench. Quickly I yelled at Grandpa, telling him, "Please wait! I have got to go back and get the presents that I bought for my sisters!" And I started to run across the street.

"Boy, you get back here in the truck! This man was nice enough to give us a ride, so we can't keep him waiting for nonsense such as that!"

Hurriedly I ran as fast as I possibly could, picked up the bag, and ran back to the truck, climbing into the back. "Okay, I'm ready, Grandpa!" I said, almost out of breath and clutching the bag tightly to my chest as the truck started to slowly drive away. With the sack clutched against my chest, this finally allowed me to smile with happiness. Just thinking about the excitement that my two sisters were going to feel when I gave them these dolls caused me to feel a sense of deep fulfillment. I visualized their smiles as they looked at the dolls and then thanked me with hugs of affection.

"Boy!" I heard my grandpa start to yell out from inside the truck's cab. Riding in the back of the truck with the wind blowing around me, along with the passing of other vehicles, made it very hard to hear what he was saying to me.

"Yes, Grandpa?" I turned around and leaned over the edge of the truck to hear what he was saying.

"What was so important that you had to jump out of the truck and had us wait on you?"

"Grandpa," I excitedly began to explain, "you know the money you gave me along with that extra dime after we sold all those peas?"

"Yes," he replied.

"I took the money and bought Cynthia and Pat something!" I was excited and wanted Grandpa to also be happy for me that I had thought unselfishly about my sisters.

Grandpa turned slightly toward me and said, "You did what, boy?" I could detect a slight aggravation in his voice.

I again repeated what I had just told him and lifted the large bag off my chest and up toward him. "Their present is in this bag. I wanted to try to make them feel better because they did not get to go with us."

"Let me see what in the world you got in that bag for those sisters of yours!" I handed the large bag to his hand as he reached around the outside and grabbed the bag. Taking it inside the cab of the truck, he opened the flap and looked inside. I peered through the back window as my grandpa took the two dolls from the bag. Our neighbor looked over at my grandpa, and they exchanged glances. He started to laugh and hit his hand onto the steering wheel of the truck, looking back and forth toward me through the window then at Grandpa. "Boy, what in the [saying a bad word] is this?" And he took both dolls from their individual boxes. Suddenly, as if in defiance, Grandpa took the head of each doll and pulled them off, throwing both out the window and into the night.

I stared in horror and disbelief while he took both their arms and then their legs off, throwing them, too, out the window. Raising myself up and leaning over the side of the truck, I tried to see where they landed. He crumpled the bag and boxes that had contained the dolls and threw them forcefully also out the truck window and into the dark night.

"Boy! If I could get my hand on you, I'd beat you until I thought you had a little sense beat into you! Don't you waste my money on any such nonsense as that ever again!" Grandpa said. "Maybe I should think seriously about not ever taking you into town with me again, if that is the way you are going to act."

"No! Grandpa," I cried, "that was my sisters', and I wanted to get them something to make them happy because you would not allow them to go to town with us."

"Boy, if this is how you are going to act when I take you with me, then I sure can find something for you to do around the farm. The barn has a buildup of cow and mule manure that has needed some shoveling for some time. Yes," he said, "that will keep you busy tomorrow, and we don't usually do any work on Sunday, but I will make an exception this time in your case." He nodded to himself. "I give you my hard-earned money to buy you a drink, and you waste it on those heathen sisters of yours, buying dolls. Furthermore, those girls don't need to go into town. They already go to that school and waste enough time. Girls are for cooking and cleaning and have plenty to do at home without wasting their time prissing around town in front of all those men, anyway."

Turning around, I stared into the darkness of the road, to where I thought the dolls had been thrown. The white middle lines in the road were briefly illuminated by the truck's rear lights as each section of the road disappeared into the darkness of the night. Staring out toward the back of the truck, I could feel my eyes fill with tears, which dripped off my cheeks and onto my trousers. I drew my knees up into my chest and just sat there, emotionally traumatized. Why had it mattered to my grandpa that I spent money on my sisters? He had given it to me to buy what I wanted, I thought because he loved me and wanted to show that he appreciated the work I had done all week. I loved my sisters and felt awful that I got to go into town and they had to stay on the farm with Grandma and Granny.

The neighbor's truck began to stop, and I looked up to see that we had arrived at Grandpa's house. I pulled myself out over the truck bed just as Grandpa opened the door—we almost stumbled into each other. He attempted to stand up straight in his drunken condition.

He had to hold on to the truck door to keep from falling. Running by him, I could hear his slurred speech saying, "Get in that house, boy! I'll deal with you in the morning."

During the night, as I lay in bed, fearing about what my grandpa was going to do to me, especially in the condition he was in, I could hear him go from room to room, grumbling about something that I could not understand. Covering my head with my pillow, I feared that the door would swing open and I must endure that other evil personality that frequently came out of my grandpa when he drank beer. I prayed each night that the other person, or spirit personality, would stay out of my grandpa.

Please, God, I silently prayed, *help me and my sisters to be good and always obey our grandpa and grandma, to do all that they tell us. Forgive me for causing my grandpa to get angry. Help me, God, to understand why we can't be with our daddy or mommy. I promise, Jesus, to be good if you would please allow Grandpa to go to sleep and not to be angry anymore. Amen.* I then squeezed my eyes shut and continued to whisper repeatedly, "Thank you, Jesus! Thank you, God! Help us, please, God!"

Some of the time, Grandpa showed that he could have happiness and at times was even playful, but there were other times he hurt us by grabbing us with his strong hands. This occurred when we walked close to him, then with lightning speed he'd reach out and grab one of us by the leg or another part of the body. His hands clamping down hard felt as though we were being squeezed by a vise. He always laughed at us, especially when he finally saw tears streaming down our cheeks and heard us cry out in awful, excruciating pain.

There was another emotional scar that occurred one summer night that I will always remember. We had been singing with Grandma out on the front porch some of her favorite hymns. This was one of the times when Grandpa had gone into town alone on a Saturday and had been gone all day. I was afraid that he had been drinking all day and would return drunk. This was one of the constant fears that I had while living with my grandparents, and I am sure that my sister Pat also had the same concerns. Grandma always listened when a truck would suddenly stop by the road. That would be the sign Grandpa had caught a ride home with one of the local farmers. This time, Grandma stopped her singing and instructed all of us to go quickly and get into bed. "Now, don't any of you young'uns make a sound, and I'll get your grandpa to bed." I knew that the next day would be Sunday, and Grandpa did not do any farmwork that day, which meant that he would be staying up late.

Lying very still in my bedroom, alone, I tried to silence even the breath that I breathed. If I could have stopped momentarily the sound of my heartbeat, I would have. I felt and heard my heart trying to beat out of my chest. Suddenly, my fears were intensified with the sound of a loud bang that traveled through the walls from the kitchen. Grandpa could be heard stumbling through the kitchen and mumbling something that I could not understand. He eventually stumbled outside as I heard the kitchen's screen door creak open, then slam shut. I started to pray not only for myself but also because I knew that when he drank, he started to intensify his physical and verbal abuse toward my two sisters.

"Please, Jesus. Please, God," I began to pray, out loud this time, "give my grandpa a sleepy head so he will feel better." I squeezed my eyes tightly shut and continued to pray that my grandpa would eventually sit down in the rocking chair on the porch and fall asleep.

Sometime during the night, I could hear my two sisters crying and Grandpa yelling at Pat that she had not cleaned the kitchen like he had told her to. I slipped out of my bed and walked toward the kitchen and stood in the doorway. Grandpa was standing over Pat, who was on her knees on the kitchen floor. She was trying to mop up water that had been spilled but had not been there earlier. Cynthia was sitting on one of the stools in the corner, crying hysterically. He was standing over her and had a large leather strap in his hand. The strap was the one that hung in his bedroom above the mantel, which we were told was for stubborn, disobedient young'uns. Grandpa stood behind Pat, holding the strap above his head, then slung it down upon my sister's behind. My sissy yelled out in agony and apparent pain. Each time the strap waved above Grandpa's head and he brought it down forcefully, I could hear the slap of leather upon Pat's flesh, giving off a loud popping sound throughout the kitchen.

I screamed at my grandpa, "Please, Grandpa, stop hitting my sissy! Please stop! She cleaned the kitchen with Grandma earlier today. Please stop hitting my sissy!"

Grandpa reached down and slapped her behind with his hand, then looked up at me standing in the doorway. "Boy, what are you doing there?" With a startled look on his face, he looked down at Pat. I could see that this was the evil spirit or personality that entered my grandpa when he drank. "Girl, get up from there and you young'uns go into my and Mama's bedroom and stand at the foot of our bed until I tell you otherwise."

"Yes, Grandpa," we all three answered and quickly went into their room. We stood with our backs against the foot of the bed so we could watch Grandpa as he approached.

Grandma, hearing what sounded like a roar coming through the house from Grandpa, and feeling us against the bed, rose up. "What in the world are you young'uns doing out of bed?"

"Mama, you lay back down," Grandpa answered. "These young'uns were told to do some chores that were not done. They are going to stand there because, apparently, they don't need any sleep, or they would have done what they were told."

Grandma spoke up. "Now, Daddy, you have been drinking again. You let those young'uns go to bed."

"Shut up, woman!" he said, pointing his crooked finger in her face. "And you lay back down! I am the man of this house, and these young'uns are going to do as I say. If you don't mind what I'm telling you…" He raised his hand above his head, looking down toward Grandma. She quickly lay back down but looked up at Grandpa with a frightened, worried expression on her face. I could see Grandma mumbling something and knew that she was praying, as she usually did when Grandpa drank beer.

"Now, you three hold on to that bed railing and stay there until you hear me tell you to do something different. I told each of you young'uns what was going to happen if you gave me any more trouble!" Grandpa took that large leather belt and came around the foot of the bed and began to beat each of us. After each slap of the snap on either of us, I could hear a growling sound deep within him. I don't remember all that had happened that night, as in any of the other times, but I believe, due to the severity of the trauma of that night, it was apparently lost in my subconscious. Eventually, he sat down on the bed and started to take his clothes off, except for his long undershorts, then lay down next to Grandma. We stood there in the dark bedroom, whimpering, staying as quiet as possible, for what seemed like hours. Eventually, Cynthia and I could not stand on our feet any longer, and with total exhaustion, we slowly sank down to the floor and leaned against the foot of the bed. I was sure that if Grandpa woke up, I hoped I had had enough time to get Cynthia up again and be standing. Pat sat on an ottoman stool that leaned against another wall, but had fallen asleep.

I heard Grandpa snoring and felt it safe enough to relax my body but was afraid to leave the bedroom. The snoring was followed by the horrible odor that came with each breath that he took.

Sometime during the night, I was awakened by silence. The silence frightened me, and I knew that Grandpa was not asleep. I felt the movement of his body as he shifted his position, and looked to see him sit up on the edge of his bed and place his bare feet on the floor. Pat, I could see, was still asleep and curled up against the wall on the stool. Grandpa, in slow motion, stood up and began to walk toward my sister Pat. First, I thought he was angry that he had caught us not standing at the foot of the bed, as we were told.

Please, God and Jesus, I started to pray silently, *forgive us for not doing what Grandpa had told us to do. God, we must have gotten sleepy. Please, God, we did stay in Grandpa's room instead of going to our own rooms. Please, God, have our grandpa forgive us, and I promise to be a better grandson and to do whatever he tells me from now on. I also promise to work harder in the cotton field, and I'll always make sure that Grandma has enough wood to cook with.*

Oh, God, I continued praying silently, pleading to God for mercy and forgiveness that I had been so weak to have fallen asleep with Cynthia next to me. *I should have been a better brother. Now I fear that Cynthia is going to get more whipping, or worse, because of me!*

Peeking through my tight eyelids and still praying, I noticed Grandpa walking past me to where I cuddled with Cynthia against me and the bed. Slowly, as if trying not to wake anyone up, he crept toward Pat. Pat was asleep with her legs curled onto the stool, clothed in her cotton nightshirt and underclothes. Grandpa stopped next to Pat and just stood there looking down at her. I feared the beating she had received earlier was about to continue because of her also falling asleep. I started to pray again for God to please help my sissy and to soften my grandfather's evil heart so that he would not hurt my sissy. Watching him, I prayed.

Grandpa bent over Pat, and slowly reaching out with both hands, he began to reach toward her. God had answered my prayer and plea, I thought. Grandpa was going to wake her up and tell her to get up and take us to bed. But suddenly, and with horror, my thoughts were shattered beyond anything that I could ever imagine. Instead of Grandpa waking Sissy up, I was confused and horrified, trying to understand this strange behavior from my grandpa. His breath became louder and stronger. It was as though we were in a bad dream. My heart rapidly began to beat as though it was going to come out of my chest, and I thought I would lose all the air from my lungs, which made it impossible to say or do anything. I believe that I was in some sort of shock and/or trauma because of what I was witnessing. Suddenly, Pat opened her eyes and swung away from where she lay. I believe it was a natural, horrifying reflex, with her not being exactly aware of what Grandpa was doing. We looked to see our grandpa having what I now call a demonic stare and glow with the usual beet-red face.

Pat screamed out in horror, swinging her entire body toward the corner of the wall.

Grandpa abruptly stood up, yelling at Pat, "You shut up, young'un, before you wake Mama up!"

"Papa?" Grandma arose from her sleep and spoke. "What are you doing over there to that young'un?" She could see and hear Pat in the corner crying. "You young'uns now get up and go to bed!" she said as she looked at Pat sitting still in the corner, crying with both legs drawn up to her chest. "Do as I tell you, young'un! Get up from there!" She then pointed at me and Cynthia. "Take your brother and sister and go to bed, now. Do as you're told before anything else happens!"

Later, I lay in bed listening through the wall at the whimpering coming from my sister's room. Without making a sound, I slowly crept out of my bed and into my sister's room. "Sissy," I whispered. Pat rose up, and I could see her head's silhouette against the light of the full moon that shone through her bedroom window.

"Bubba," she whispered, "you had better get out of here before Grandpa sees that you are out of bed!"

"Sissy, I heard you crying and was worried about you. What was Grandpa doing?" I asked. "I am afraid of being in that room tonight. Please, sissy, let me stay in here with you and Cynthia tonight!" I started to slowly walk toward her bed.

"Okay, Bubba," she said, pulling back the covers. "You better get back to your bed before Grandpa and Grandma get up." I slid over to Pat, and we all three embraced, comforting one another under the covers.

"Bubba," Pat whispered, "when you hear Big Red, the rooster, crow in the morning, you had better get up and get back to your room."

We all fell asleep cuddling under the warm covers and the comfort of the feather mattress underneath.

I did not understand at that time what had taken place that night with my grandfather or what his intentions were with my sister Pat until later, as I grew older, then the realization of what he was capable of doing that night would haunt me to this day.

The following Monday morning, my sisters and I got up early, as was our custom. There were chores to be done. The water had to be drawn, and wood for cooking needed to be gathered before we caught the school bus. My sister acted especially nervous this morning and was preoccupied, seemingly trying to hurry with the chores. I was probably in the first grade, and Pat in the second, because of her only being a little over a year older than me. Cynthia was several years younger than me and was yet to be in school. This day, Pat seemed to be carrying Cynthia around the house as she did the chores more than what she normally did. Pat was continually hugging and kissing her on the cheek while looking in my direction to see that I was okay.

We waited on the front porch for the school bus, and I remember that we always enjoyed going to school. That was the only enjoyment or normal thing in life that we looked forward to. To be able to get away from the farm and our grandfather was, in my view, a blessing from God. If it had been our grandfather's decision, he would have kept us home, but because of legal issues, children were required to attend school. I felt that the time we spent attending school was a comfort to our emotional stability. During this particular school day, while going with my class to lunch, I noticed that my sister was going into the office with another lady. I wanted to leave my group and go to her because of being concerned, but I did not want to get into trouble. If the school sent home a letter saying that I had done something wrong, my grandpa would have beaten me with a switch from a tree limb. When he punished us, we would have to get our own switch from a tree in the front yard, and if he did not think it was strong enough or would break, we had to get another one.

Later that day, after school and back at the farm, I noticed that my grandpa was not at home, and asked Grandma, "Where is Grandpa?"

"Son, your grandpa and Mr. Burns had to go into town to get your grandma some medicine. I haven't been feeling too good lately and thought it best to see that doctor Mr. and Mrs. Burns go to. Sometimes these old country remedies that I try do not seem to work. Your grandpa, bless his poor soul, doesn't like to spend his tobacco money on those city remedies when we have God's medicine from this great earth he has provided. I have not gotten any better, so I asked him this one time if he would allow Mr. Burns to take him to talk to their family doctor about what might be wrong with me."

"Okay, Grandma, do you want something from the kitchen? Maybe a glass of tea or something else?"

"No, son. That's sweet, though," she said, smiling. "Now, just get outside and make sure that all your chores are finished before your grandpa gets home. You know how he is when the chores are not done."

Outside with Pat, I found out that when I noticed her earlier going into the office at school, she had informed one of the teachers what had occurred with Grandpa late Saturday night and/or Sunday morning. She had apparently accused Grandpa of something very wrong. Pat pleaded with the teachers in the office, crying hysterically that our mother's mom, our grandmother, lived in Memphis, Tennessee, and she wanted them to see if she could be contacted. They searched through their available contacts, and not only did they locate our grandmother but we also were told that our mother had moved to Memphis. Pat told me she had talked to Mama while in the office at school and told her what had happened the other night with Grandpa. I was filled with the excitement that after all this time, our mama was found and was not too far from where we lived with our grandparents.

I asked, "What did Mama say? Are she and Daddy together? And will they come to take us home? I thought they were still at the house in Ohio, where Uncle William and Grandpa picked us up. Maybe Mama went to Grandma's in Memphis when she could not find us at our house after we left!"

"Bubba, Mama was very mad at what I told her, what Grandpa tried to do to me the other night, and said she would come to pick us up today."

"I'm sure glad that Grandpa is not home, or there would be a lot of trouble!" With the terrible comments they spoke toward each other, we knew that mama did not need to be at the house when Grandpa arrived home.

"Does Grandma know that Mama is coming?" I asked.

"Yes, Bubba. When we got home from school, I went to her bedroom and told her. She looked very weak but smiled and said that it would be the best thing because we needed our mama."

We all three went into Grandma's bedroom and stood at the foot of the bed, looking at her weak and sweaty face. "Grandma," I asked, "are you okay?"

"Yes, Bubba," she said, reaching up in her weakness and patting my face. "Your grandma will be okay. Papa and Mr. Burns went into town to get some medicine, and your grandma will be just fine. The

Lord Jesus has always taken care of your old grandma through a lot worse thing than this. The good book tells us that when we pray and believe, we can move mountains. God will continue to answer prayer this time also. I have raised seven boys and one girl, your aunt Francis, with God's help. If my God had not been there to answer my many prayers, I could not have survived." She smiled. "Now, you young'uns, when your mother arrives with her people, you go with her. I'll be just fine."

"But, Grandma," I said, "I don't want to leave you here alone. We don't know when they will be back! Grandpa might stay in town, as he does sometimes, and drink that stuff that makes him mean to you."

"Now, you do as I tell you, or I'll have to give you a switching like your grandpa does!" She smiled, looking up at us. We knew that Grandma had never used a switch on us in all the time we spent with her and she was only trying to look serious. Your grandpa is with Mr. Burns, and he will not drink while they are together," she told us. "Both of you come here and give your grandma a hug. I don't know when your mama will bring you back to see me."

"Oh, Grandma!" We rushed around the bed and leaned over her, noticing that her body was hot and soaked with sweat.

"Grandma, we will be back, you'll see. We love you, Grandma!" I said as we all hugged her close.

"I love you young'uns, too. Now go, like I said. I think I heard a car pull up out by the fence."

At that very moment, we heard a car pull off the road and stop. Both Pat and I ran over to the bedroom window and looked outside and could see that our mama quickly got out of a large car on the passenger's side. I could also see two other men in the car, one in the back seat and another behind the steering wheel. Excited as we were to finally see our mama, I found it hard to express any sort of smile. I looked at my sisters, and we all turned and faced Grandma, noticing that in all her fever and sickness, she still managed a smile.

She asked, "Is that your mama?"

"Yes, Grandma," we all said, trying to be excited but still very concerned with Grandma and her condition.

"Now, do what I tell you, but first, come give me one more hug!" Grandma said. "I love all you young'uns and only want the best, so come here before your grandpa and Mr. Burns get home."

We all gave her a loving hug and started to cry because we did not want to leave her alone, sick as she was. Pat went into the other room and picked Cynthia off the floor, where she had been playing, and quickly ran through the front door without looking back toward me or Grandma. "Bubba, come on, Bubba!" Pat shouted. "Let's go, before Grandpa gets home!"

"What about our clothes?" I shouted.

"Come on, Mama is waiting, and the clothes here were what Grandma made for me and Cynthia. Don't you remember Grandpa would not allow us to bring too much stuff and we had to leave all our good clothes other than just a small sack when we left? Mama will get us some more clothes. Now, come on!" Pat screamed again.

I ran behind her and did not stop until we ran into our mama's arms as she rushed toward us. "You," she said, looking at Pat, "take your brother and sister and get into the car." She pointed toward it with a very stern look that I quickly remembered. "Is your grandpa in there?" she asked, still glaring at Pat.

"No, Mama. He went into town with Mr. Burns to get Grandma some medicine. She is in the house and very sick."

"Well, that [curse words], it is better for him that he is in town, or there would have been a lot of problems!" She gritted her teeth and slung her long black hair around her face and shoulder in disgust.

"Mama," I said and got out of the car, walking toward her, crying, "we just can't leave Grandma alone in bed. She is so sick."

"Your grandpa will be back soon, and he will have to watch after her. Now, get your little behind back in that car! We have got to go."

"Mama, when he goes into town, he drinks beer and comes back home hitting and pinching Grandma!"

"Son, I told you that we have got to go, and I don't want to be here when your grandpa gets home, because one of us will not live to see tomorrow!" Mama reached inside the car window and brought out what frightened me so much I began to cry.

I heard Pat from the back seat scream out, "Bubba! Please get in the car!"

Mama again gritted her teeth and slung her hair around. "I don't think your grandpa will try anything with me or his grandchildren again!" She held up a large silver gun and was waving it around, pointing it toward the air. I backed away and ducked behind the side of the car. I was frightened and saddened that after all this time, I missed my parents and had prayed constantly for them to come and take us home.

Mama spoke. "Son, either you get back in that car and go with me or go back inside with your grandmother. We have got to go right now!"

"Please, Bubba, come on, get into the car like Mama says!" Pat pleaded.

I wanted to leave with my mama but just couldn't leave Grandma alone. She was sick. And so I started to walk back toward the house. "I don't think he will try anything with his grandson."

Mama looked in my direction, saying, "I'll send someone to get you in a few days, your uncle Howard or uncle Ronnie. Now, let's go!" My mama got into the car and slammed the door shut.

My decision was made, and the finality of it was when I heard the car start and looked back across the white fence to see my sisters and mama drive away, eventually disappearing over the hill toward what I thought to be Memphis, Tennessee. Standing there watching the only life and family I knew disappear over that hill devastated me. I began crying hysterically and started running as fast as my bare feet could carry me out of the yard and up onto the pavement of the old county road. Running faster and faster, crying, "Please, Mama, come back soon and get me! I'll be waiting for you right here. Don't forget me, please, okay, Mama?" Tired of running, I got to the top of the hill and could see there was not a car anywhere in sight. Turning around, I walked slowly, crying and emotionally drained, toward the old farmhouse, where my grandma lay very sick.

Leaving the Farm with Daddy

Several weeks had gone by since our mother had come to take us away from our grandparents' farm. However, I had stayed or was left behind because of my concerns about leaving my grandma alone while she was extremely ill. Patricia and Cynthia left with our mother that day, leaving me alone on the farm with my grandparents. I was frightened and did not know at that early age in my life what exactly depression was or how to cope with it; I only knew that now I was somewhat alone and sad, without my sisters there with me for us to comfort one another. Our being together all this time after we had been separated from our parents was the only thing that had held us together with any sort of family-type environment or rational sanity. It seemed after they left as though the days turned into weeks, then into months. I spent a lot of time on the porch, looking out onto the fields and just thinking and praying that someday I would again see my paternal side of the family.

Grandma had gotten better, we knew, because of the medicine that Mr. Burns and Grandpa brought back from Ripley late that night after my mama left along with my sisters. Even to this day, I knew that Grandma's faith in prayer was the main belief that healed and saved her life at that early time in my life. Grandma tried to help solve the loneness that was deeply embedded inside my young emotions after my sisters left. Seeing my mother when she arrived that day had lifted my spirits briefly, then losing not only her but also my two sisters when I saw them driving farther and farther away had shaken me to the very core of my emotions. My grandmother loved me with all her heart and tried to soften the burden of loneliness and grief that she knew I felt. She scolded me for not doing as she requested and leaving that day with Mama, but she also understood why I stayed, which was because of my love for her and because I did not want to leave her in her sickness or while she was by herself.

Living in the rural county of Tennessee, one would find there was not much to do in the way of recreation, and I had to solve that dilemma with whatever fantasies my thoughts could dream up. There was a large barn out in the far field that I found was a place of comfort and solitude. It was filled with bales of hay that were stacked throughout the entire inner part of it. There was a large rope that hung from the middle rafter, and when Patricia was with me, we used it to swing from the far end of the barn. We stood on a stack of hay toward the back of the barn, then, holding on tight to the rope, would swing all the way through the barn until we would go out of the opening. When we looked down, we were at least fifty to sixty feet above the ground. It was really scary being so high. And it was not just in the barn; after we swung outside through the opening, we could look down at all the farm animals that were so far beneath us. This type of fun we tried not to do often because the only thing that kept us from certain death was the tight grip our hands and feet had on the rope.

I did not swing on the rope anymore after my sister left. It had been scary enough while they were here, and I did not want to take the chance of falling and getting hurt while I was alone. After supper in the evenings, I would enjoy going out away from the house and feeding the animals in the different areas surrounding the barn and several of the sheds. This was my chance to get away from the house and the uncomfortable feeling around Grandpa, who liked to smoke his pipe and/or visit with Grandma on the porch. I felt that this helped me with some sort of comfort and get my mind off the depressing thoughts that were so many times plaguing my mind. After feeding the pigs, I would walk out in the far pasture, where the two mules Old Dan and Blue would be grazing. They were an unfriendly couple, but they were all that I had on this night, and I insisted on trying as I had before to get close enough to possibly pet them. But I wanted to also make sure that I had enough running room to save myself if either of them got a little aggressive. I would always take a large switch with me but never wanted or intended to use it on either of them; it was just as a precaution. I always felt a sense of peace when walking around the farm and through the fields. I would pray as Grandma taught me, and thoughts about my family always ran through my mind, with the way that I missed them so much.

While I lived with my grandma, these were the first real realizations I had of the existence of a higher power that controls everything. Whatever anyone wishes to call this Creator will be entirely up to the reader of this writing. I understand that this Creator, as my grandma and the Bible instructs me, has many names. Whatever his many names at this time in my life did not matter; I only knew him as God and knew he was there to listen to and comfort me. God's presence would always be there beside me to listen as I spent a lot of time walking around the fields and inside the barn. I spent a lot of hours sitting high on top of the hay bales and just looking throughout the countryside. Most of the time was spent staring out and thinking; today I think they call it meditating. I prayed as my grandma had taught me and did find somewhat of a little comfort and knew that God would bless me someday and I would again see my family. I was also so thankful that Grandpa brought the right medicine that helped Grandma to get better from whatever sickness she had. I knew, through my prayers, that God took care of all the details that enabled Grandpa and the doctor to provide the right type of medicines for her sickness.

"Thank you, God," I prayed, "for Mr. Burns, that he had a good truck that drove them into town to get the medicine!" My thoughts at that time were that God had better things to do than listening to a small boy like me. "Dear God," I continued, "I know that Grandma has a lot of faith in you, and she talks about you, God, all the time, but I was so afraid that you might need her more up there in heaven than I do in here. I just wanted you, God, to know that I'm sure glad you didn't because I really need her here with me right now. I love her so much and wouldn't know what I'd do without my grandma." Tears began to fall from my freckled face and into my clasped hands while I prayed and thought about the possibility of being without her. "God, that tobacco juice, or snuff, I believe, was probably not going to heal Grandma this time as it did my cut hand. I'm glad that she knows and accepts that you do provide other types of medicine for us to use. I miss my mama, daddy, sissy, and Cynthia. Will you please tell them, wherever they are, that I really miss them a lot? And will you keep them safe? Tell them not to worry about me, that I am all right, and that I helped to take care of Grandma while she was sick. And oh yes, I almost forgot! Tell them that she is better now. Also, God, tell them, if they want to come see me, that I am still here at Grandma and Grandpa's. I hope that they remember how to get here, but if not, I know you will please show them the way back to me!" Both my hands went to my face as I began to sob even more to the point that I could just faintly hear the mules begin to stomp and snort around in the distance and then heard their dusty footsteps fill the air as they came closer to the barn.

Maybe, I thought and, I guess, secretly hoped, they were just curious of all the sobbing I must have been making and all the loud praying. I knew they kept to themselves and would just walk away if you started to get close to them, unless, of course, they knew of it or heard the grain being dropped in the trough.

I must have lost track of time because it was starting to get dusk, and as I looked up at the sky like I had always been, I was amazed at all the vastness of what I considered just a tiny part of God's heaven. I stared up through the millions of twinkling stars, glancing briefly down through the fields, and could see an occasional deer in the distance cautiously walking and grazing on the leftover corn that had fallen on the ground after the harvest. This beautiful sight somehow brought a sense of peace to me and of the time my grandma spent teaching me to sing the old religious hymns late into the night. She would say, "Son, just look up into all that beautiful sky that our God has blessed us with. He has allowed us to have eyes to see and has miraculously created lungs in our bodies with which to breathe that good, healthy air. Our God is sure something else, isn't he?" She always got so excited when she spoke about God, and this time she began to wave her arms and hands back and forth above her head toward the heavens, saying, "Thank you, God!" I watched her entire body seem to pulse and vibrate. Looking down at me, she continued to say, "Oh, my precious grandson, our God is so great and beyond any of our imaginations!" Then she looked back up toward the stars that covered the whole of God's heavens, talking with all the sincerity that was within her.

"God, the great Creator," she said, speaking with such a powerful spirit that I could not describe or explain even to this day, "he has created all that we can see and things that we can't see, but we must have the faith to know that he loves us enough to send his only Son, Jesus, to die and be persecuted for us to be saved and have eternal life in heaven."

I looked around at my precious grandma while she stood there looking up into the heavens, and I could see that she had tears rolling down her cheeks. I could feel the entirety of the porch shake and vibrate as though there was an earthquake, but there was nothing other than the porch seeming to shake or move. The trees were perfectly still, along with the leaves, and there was just a slight breeze that brushed across my cheeks.

"Are you okay, Grandma?" I asked. I knew that sometimes when praying, she would be overcome with the Holy Spirit and shed tears of joy.

"Yes, my little grandson, our God is so great that even though he has created all the heavens and the earth, he still has enough love to bless your old grandma." She looked down at me, placing her hand on my head, and said, "And of course, he loves you, my child, too." Thoughts of my grandma were always fond memories scattered throughout my life, and I know that God has a special place for grandmas like her.

I sat there in the barn, watching millions of stars twinkle, and prayed as only a young child knew. I could still hear the mules moving around and could tell that they had gotten close to the large opening at the front and below where I was sitting. It started to get a little dark, so I got up and began to move my body around the bales of hay and get closer to the opening so I could look down at them. I worked my way around some of the bales and sat back down directly in front of the opening. Looking down, I became frightened of the height and quickly but cautiously sat down on the closest bale. Old Dan and Blue were feeding on some straw that had fallen from the barn loft, and I asked them both, "Hey, boys, looks like you are really enjoying that straw. So how is it?" They both looked up toward me at first, then suddenly jerked their heads to stare straight ahead toward the middle of the barn. I noticed that the light on the pole at the road had suddenly brightened up the back side of the barn, and that was what must have caught their attention. But no, that couldn't be what it was, because there was no light in any other part of the barn or anywhere else.

I sat there with both my legs hanging off the bale of hay, with nothing between me and the ground below, which was a little frightening, because I had always been afraid of heights. The large opening at the front of the barn was the same that I and Pat swung out of hanging on that long rope when she was with me. I then noticed both the mules' ears suddenly perk up and their nostrils flare open, then both, as in a sequence, let out a loud snort. "What is the matter with you two?" I asked and shifted on the hay bale to be able to look down through the cracks on the floor planks at the ground below me. The road pole's bright utility light that I thought had briefly lit the stall down below was no longer there. The mules didn't seem to be frightened, just alert, as though something had suddenly caught their attention. Maybe Grandpa had come out to the barn to tell me that it was time to come to the house, I thought. But Grandpa usually just yelled from the house, and it was not that far. Sound really traveled a long way out in the country, or maybe people that lived in the country knew how to yell louder.

I sat there just looking around at all the fields and the beautiful blue sky. "Wow," I said to myself, then looked down at Old Dan and Blue, "God sure knows what he is doing. Sure is beautiful out here, isn't it, boys?" I found solitude and seclusion, which was why I came out to the barn every day and in the afternoon before dark. Though I missed my sisters and family, it did somewhat soothe my loneliness. I didn't want to cry anymore and thought that crying only made me feel worse, but the more I tried, the more I got mad at myself and the more I tried to shake my head to possibly force the sadness from me. This did not allow the tears to go away, and the more I tried, the more they kept flowing.

The barn was a secluded place that I could come to and pray after my sisters left. I asked God questions about why things happened the way they did. My grandma always told me that God would listen to me in my prayer. Looking up toward the heavens and the beautiful sky, I realized it was beginning to get dusk, as the sun was sitting in the far distant cornfield. I asked God to please protect my daddy, wherever he was. "And please tell him that I love him very much!" Feeling my face begin to dampen with the tears that rolled down my freckled cheeks then dripped off my lips and my chin, I got up from the bale of hay that I was sitting at and, as if I were a stubborn child who was mad that he had not gotten his way, knelt behind the hay. Folding my hands together, I looked up toward the heavens, angrily pleading, then quickly stopped and asked God to forgive me.

"Oh, please, I'm sorry, God!" I said, wiping my tears away from my cheeks, and again I blubbered out, "I'm so sorry, God. I did not mean to sound angry, and please don't be mad at me!" I took a deep breath and again folded both hands over my eyes and wept. "I just miss my daddy, mama, and sisters so very much! Do you hear me, God? Are you there?" I cried out. I stayed with my hands folded over both eyes, just crying and hearing the mules stomp around below me, which was somewhat of a comfort, that I wasn't completely alone. I heard both simultaneously give out a loud snort and stomp their hooves, causing me to open my eyes and again wipe my tear-soaked face with my sleeve.

Rising from kneeling behind the hay, I looked down and out from the opening. There standing between Old Dan and Blue was a white-bearded old man, petting both mules with partially gloved hands. I was startled by this sudden appearance and wondered who this old man was and if he had heard me crying. I felt a little frightened that while I was in deep prayer, a strange man had surprised me without my hearing him approach. His clothes seemed to be soiled and worn, his shoes caked with dried mud.

"Hey, mister!" I yelled down and warned him that he needed to be careful standing that close to Old Dan and Blue. "They can really get mean with everybody except my grandpa, and they don't like him that much either!" I let out a small chuckle, I think just to release the tension. "That one on your left, his name is Dan, and if he gets the chance, he will bite you. The other one's Blue. He will try to rear up with his front quarters and knock you down, but before he does, he will try to also get in a few bites!" The scruffy old man continued to pet both mules, and if I did not know better, they seemed to be trying to keep the old man between them with their bodies. He was mumbling something, looking at both, and kept turning his head back and forth between the mules and seemed to be whispering something in their ears. I had never seen these mules behave as gently as they did with this stranger, and I watched both mules circle him, rubbing their bodies against him gently as if they had known him all their lives.

"Hey, mister, my name is Hershel, but they all call me Bubba. Don't know why, though. Guess it was some name that my sister started calling me and everybody else started calling me that too. I live with my grandparents over there in that house," I said, pointing toward the house. "Do you live around here?"

Taking his hands off both mules, he turned toward me, saying, "Hello, child. My name's Gabe." He then smiled up at me.

"Mister, those mules have never allowed anyone to get close to them, and Grandpa even must corral them up in this barn to bridle them for the farmwork. They surely have not ever allowed anyone close enough to pet them, not even me, and believe me, I have tried a lot of times!"

He took a step toward the entrance of the barn, and I was again amazed beyond belief to see both Old Dan and Blue step quickly toward him as if they were newborn calves going after its mother. They both appeared to have a calmness that I had never witnessed before, and their eyes were fixed, looking directly at this strange old man. "Why don't you come down here, child, and humor an old man with a little conversation?" His voice, as my grandmother's, had a soothing, calming effect, and maybe that was what it was that the mules sensed too.

I hurried toward the back of the barn, where there was an opening to the loft and a wooden ladder that led down to the ground. This strange old man had some sort of curiosity about him, and I was more than happy to have someone else to talk with. And I felt safe.

"Now, you be careful climbing down those steps," he said, "and don't forget to count each one. You have climbed them so many times, haven't you? And you know exactly how many there are. Be careful to watch out for that long last step."

I thought of how he knew about the long way, where you had to drop after the last step. Quickly climbing down, and just after getting to that last step, I jumped, but landing, I stumbled with embarrassment backward on my backside in the dusty barn floor. Quickly I tried to get to my feet, to hide my embarrassment, walking out of the barn and wiping my pants to get the dust off. I then stood next to the old man. He was still standing between both mules, and to my amazement, neither of them attempted to leave. Standing back, looking, I could still see that he was continually whispering something in each of their ears and rubbing both their foreheads.

"Mister," I said, "those mules sure do like you."

"Well, hello, my child." He turned to look at me. "And they like you too."

"I don't think those mules like anyone," I replied.

"They told me that you help take care of them and that they are thankful to you," he said. "Come over here and see for yourself."

"Oh no, mister, they don't like anybody, not even Grandpa." I had mumbled those words to myself. "And I can understand why. He is mean to them and hits them with a large leather strap."

"They don't seem to be mean right now," he said as he continued to pet each of their foreheads and along the neck. "Old Dan here said that you were afraid of him but he can't understand why. They really do like you a lot."

I took each step closer cautiously until I got close enough that he reached out, taking my reluctant hands and placing them up toward each of their heads. "There, you see? They do like you! And you thought they were mean!"

"But, mister, these two mules have never allowed anyone to get close to them except Grandpa, and that was only when he hitched them up for plowing." Old Dan and Blue were large animals, and standing in front of them was frightening. My head only came to each of their nostrils. "Mister, where are you from? I didn't see you come from the road, and sitting up there in the barn loft, I can see everything for miles around."

"Child, you must have been busy with something else or was looking elsewhere. I saw you from behind that bale of hay and thought also that I heard you asking God the Father something."

Looking over at this white-haired and white-bearded old man, I noticed that his eyes were a glistening blue. They also had, surrounding the blue, a perfect white without any sort of strained tiredness that anyone would expect from an old man like my grandpa. His eyes seemed to pierce through me, and when I looked into his face, calmness came over my entire body.

"My child," he said, reaching toward me, taking my hand in his, "God the Father always hears prayer, especially from his little children and one as yourself who is truly precious to the Father. You see those two mules over there?" He waved his open hand toward them. "He provides for them and everything that your little eyes can see or will ever see. I have been here for a very long time and have seen the Father do miraculous things." He led me over to an old bench that leaned against the barn while continuing to hold my hand in his. The old man waved his other hand up toward the now star-filled sky. "Child," Gabe said as I looked over at him and again felt such an indescribable peace fill my very being.

"Yes, sir," I said, slowly uttering the words.

Waving his hands slowly back and forth, he looked up. "My child, the Father created all that your eyes can see up there and throughout the whole heaven that you can't see. He hears your cries and pleas late at night. And remember, didn't he help you with all those chickens when the creek was flooding? The Father is with you always and loves the spirit of a child when you speak to him."

"Yes, sir. My grandma told me that also," I said. "But I really miss my daddy, my mama, and my two sisters a whole lot. I want God to tell my daddy to come here and take me home with them. I want us to be together again. And show my mama how she can stop drinking that bad, smelly stuff that makes her be mean to everybody."

"My child," he responded, looking over at me, "the Father will always guide you through your life if you ask him. He will reveal to you what decisions to make, but the Father will not force anything upon you. It will be up to you when the Father answers, and you have free will to choose and make your own decisions. My child, if you ask the Father to show or reveal to you the right decisions to make, it will be entirely up to you to follow the Father's directions."

"Yes, sir," I said as this old man's presence kept me transfixed on his every word. "Where again did you say you were from? Do you farm around here? Do you know my grandma and grandpa?"

"Yes, child, I know them. I'm from here and from there. I'm from everywhere." While he spoke, he again looked out, waving both his arms around toward the sky and up and down at the fields. "I'm from where the Father needs or wants me to be." He smiled over at me and placed his hand upon my head, which somehow comforted me, but I did not know exactly why. "Child, let's pray. Turn around there and kneel behind this bench. Close your eyes and ask the Father what he wants you to have. If there is anything special, as you said earlier, ask and I know that you will receive." He smiled down at me and laid his hands on me, and still there felt a comforting calmness, and it was but the same comfort that came when my grandma prayed with me. I did as the old man asked and knelt behind the bench, folding my hands together and closing my eyes. There was a sense of peace that surrounded and enveloped me that I had not felt before. The emotions that had caused me so much sadness began to leave me.

At first, he began to pray and, leaning down, started to whisper softly in my ear. "Child, the Father of all creation loves you and hears your cries at night. You need not ever fear that he is not with you. The Father will always be close to you. All you will ever need is to just call upon him. As you mature and grow, you will learn all the spiritual names that the old prophets call the Father. You, child, are the Father's precious children. Now, with your eyes closc, talk to him. He is here with you to listen, as always." I felt his soft hands slide down my shoulder, then eventually felt it leave.

"God, thank you for everything. Please take care of my mama and daddy, wherever they are. Keep them safe and tell them that I miss and love them. Thank you for taking care of Grandpa and, especially, Grandma when she was very sick." I knelt there for what seemed like a long time and prayed for all the things I usually prayed about. Instead of feeling a sense of sadness, I felt overjoyed, beyond anything I had felt in a long time; and instead of tears dropping down my cheeks, I felt and somehow knew that God was there in the spirit beside me and did hear everything that I had prayed about. "God," I continued to pray, "thank you that my mama came and got my sisters, and I ask that you, God, keep them safe, please. Please, God, if it is okay with you, I ask that you bring my daddy here to take me home with him. I do love Grandpa and Grandma, but I really miss my real family. So, God, I ask, as Mr. Gabe here with me says for me to ask and you will provide, whatever that means. I think it means that you will give it to me. Isn't that right, Mr. Gabe?" I looked up to where he had been standing when we started to pray. "Mr. Gabe!" I shouted, startled, and began looking around in all directions to see where he was.

Quickly I stood up and was puzzled at not seeing Mr. Gabe anywhere around me. Turning around and scrambling throughout the barn for this gray-haired old man that called himself Mr. Gabe, I yelled, "Where are you? Thank you, Mr. Gabe, for teaching me that prayer!" I continued looking around in all directions and did not see him, but I did not understand why he did not say goodbye before he left. I also noticed that Old Dan and Blue had completely walked away from the barn and back out into the field, as they were before Mr. Gabe arrived. I searched the entire barn, inside each stall, because I thought that possibly Mr. Gabe was just a drifter passing through and had gone into one of the barn stalls to rest or perhaps sleep before continuing on his way. I yelled out to both the mules as if they would answer, "Hey, boys, where did Mr. Gabe go?" They both looked in my direction, then turned and walked away, grazing on the ground at the grass sprouts.

Then suddenly, Grandma could be heard from the direction of the house. "Woo-eel! Bubba, grandson, you had better get up to the house now! Come on now, boy!" I could see her waving in my direction from across the short distance. "Grandma's got a little sorghum and biscuit for you!" Then she put her one finger up to her lips as if to say, "Be quiet. We don't have to let your grandpa know."

"Okay, Grandma!" I said, waving back at her. "I'm coming! Be right there."

When I got to the house, I told Grandma that I had met an old man and described him, all his white hair and tattered beard. "Grandma, he told me his name was Gabe. Do you know any farmer around here with that name?" I asked. "Grandma, we also prayed together while Old Dan and Blue allowed him to pet them."

Grandma pulled me close to her and said, "Grandchild, there isn't anyone around these parts by that name, and no one lives within miles of here. I and your grandpa have been sitting right here, snapping peas, on the front porch all afternoon, and no one had passed by us."

"But, Grandma, he was so spiritual, just like you, and those mules Old Dan and Blue have never allowed anyone to come near them, and surely not allow a stranger to pet them!"

"Now, son, it is perfectly fine to have a good imagination, and your daddy also had the same. If you talked with an old man as you say, he would have had to pass by me and your grandpa, and there has been no one that passed by us."

"But, Grandma!"

She interrupted me. "Now, that will be enough of that. You get inside and wash up." She reached over and patted me on the cheek, smiling, and said, "The only similar name like Gabe that I have ever heard of is that of the angel Gabriel. He was the angel sent by God as a messenger. Now, you do as your grandma says, and I'll be in shortly to get some sorghum and that biscuit I promised."

That day, during our conversation, and with the information my grandmother tried to explain to me about the angel Gabriel, it did not make any sense in my young mind. That night, though, I did sleep better than I had in a very long time, and without any of those bad nightmares that so frequently interrupted my rest. Too many nights as a child, I would wake myself up screaming out and find myself drenched, soaking the bed with my sweat-drenched body. The nightmares instead were replaced with what I call heavenly thoughts, and perhaps visions of peace, with only good thoughts in the dream. Before I drifted off to sleep, I kept hearing what the old man Gabe had whispered in my ear: "The Father of creation is always with you and hears your every thought and prayer."

As I slept, I dreamed of my sisters, mama, and daddy. We were near a beautiful crystal-blue lake and having a picnic at the water's edge. It seemed as though there were several thousands of white swans swimming around. I did not want to leave this beautiful place; I just wanted to stay here and feel the slightly warm breeze that contained the sweet smell of honeysuckles gently flowing across the lake, brushing my face. I looked over at my mother and daddy and could see that they were embraced in each other's arms and laughing at the excitement of all the swans gracefully swimming around the mirrored blue water. My dad spread out a large blanket and began filling it with baskets of food and fruit. My sisters were wading around in the nearby water's edge, laughing and splashing each other and kicking up the water toward each other.

Suddenly, I came out of this beautiful dream and was awakened by my grandmother kissing me on the forehead. "Time to get up, son," she said. "I have a surprise for you! Now come on, get out of that bed." I always could smell the delicious aroma of Grandmother's country breakfast, but this time I just wanted to go back to sleep and re-enter the dream. The dream seemed so realistic, the colors so vivid, the lake so blue, the swans seeming as though they were made from silky white cotton. "Come on now, son!" I heard her yell again from the kitchen. "I have something very special to show you. Now, get in here, and don't make me come and get you again!"

"Okay, Grandma, I'm on my way!" I responded, not only wanting to see the surprise that she had promised but also feeling excited to tell her about my dream.

Walking through to the kitchen doorway, which was an archway without the door, I suddenly stopped and screamed out, "Daddy! Daddy!" He got up from across the table from Grandma when he heard me scream.

Daddy turned around, smiling, with his arms open, and said, "Come here, son. I sure have missed you! I burst into tears and ran into his arms, hugging him as tightly as I thought possible.

"Oh, Daddy, I sure have missed you so much!" I told him. "Where were you? Grandma, my daddy is here!" I turned around to show her my excitement. Turning toward her, I could see that she was also happy to see Daddy and the excitement that I was trying to share with her. She had large tears rolling down her high cheeks, and she had the biggest smile I think I had ever seen on her face. She wiped her tears away and tried to speak, but I could see she was overcome also with emotion to finally see her son and grandson reunited.

"Well," she said, getting up from the table, "I think I will go and stock the old woodstove and leave you two alone to catch up on things." Then she turned and walked into the other room.

"Daddy, I did not think you were ever coming to get us and did not know where we were. I and Grandma kept praying that you would come see us. I thought maybe you might have gotten hurt again!" I said. "Daddy, Sissy and Cynthia were here with me, but Mama came a few weeks ago and took them with her."

"Yes, I know, son. I heard from your mama. And what do you think about this? How would you like to go with me tomorrow and find your sisters and your mama?"

"Oh yes, Daddy, I would love to, but we need to make sure that Grandpa is home. I don't want to leave Grandma alone."

The rest of the day was spent with Grandma and Daddy visiting and talking about old times, particularly when he was a child. They laughed, talking about him and his six other brothers and one sister, my aunt Francis, and all the experiences they had had on the farm growing up.

"I know you must have had a very poor time with seven boys and one girl?" I asked.

"Yes, I guess you could say that, Bubba. But we did without a lot of things that people take for granted now. The good Lord was always there to provide, didn't he, son?" She looked over at my dad.

I sat on the steps at my dad's feet, looking up at the excitement on their faces as they talked about those early years, and I could see they both had the look of endearment on their faces.

"We made the best of what we had and were in God's good graces. We had to grow all we ate and raise our own livestock for plowing or to eat. We grew our own potatoes, corn, okra, tomatoes, squash, and everything we needed to survive in God's blessed world, didn't we, son?" She looked over at Daddy again with motherly love, which gleamed on her face. "We raised our own chickens, hogs, goats, chickens, and chickens, and what we didn't eat as meat fed us with eggs. People these days think that God's provisions just naturally wind up in the stores, but we didn't have the money to buy those things, and even today, Daddy wants us to raise our own food instead of buying that bad poison they call food in the store. He uses the spare money we have left from the crop harvest for his sweetening, which is what Grandpa calls his jams and jellies. There are only very few things we needed to buy from the stores in town, only the essentials, like tobacco, snuff, flour, and sometimes sugar. You know how Daddy's attitude would be if he had to do without those things, don't you, son?" She looked over again at Daddy.

Later that afternoon, Grandpa got back from one of his frequent trips into town and was surprised to see that Daddy had arrived.

"Son," Daddy said, "we are going to leave early in the morning, and I want you to go to bed now."

"But, Daddy, I want to stay here with you!" I had not seen my daddy in a very long time, and I really did not want to allow him out of my sight, for fear that he might leave without me.

"Now, son, you go ahead and try not to be worried. Daddy is not going to leave without you ever again," he told me, giving me a loving embrace, and patted my behind, sending me off to the bedroom.

During the night, I was startled and awakened by the loud voices of Daddy and Grandpa arguing. I could hear the anger in my daddy's voice, which I knew was very unusual because I had always known my daddy to speak in a soft, calm voice. He could be heard telling my grandpa how disappointed he was that he could ever hurt or treat his grandchildren the way that he had. They argued late into the night, and the last thing that I heard my dad say was, "If it weren't for my kids' Grandmother, I would probably never allow my children to come here again!"

The next morning, it was still dark outside my bedroom window. I felt my daddy's body stirring beside me, which was a comforting feeling because I now knew that he was still here and it had not been a good dream; it was real, and my daddy was here! I felt him nudge me, telling me, "Come on, son, time to get up. We got a long way to go and a lot to do today!"

We both went into the kitchen, where Grandma was standing beside the woodstove, and suddenly feeling our presence behind her, she turned and handed Daddy a steaming cup of coffee. "Good morning, Mama," he said. "Thought we would get an early start this morning." He leaned over her shoulder, kissing her on the cheek.

"I'm going to miss this young'un!" Grandma reached down and pulled me against her apron, hugging me tightly against her body. "He has really been a blessing to his old grandma and reminds me of you, Robert, when you were his age. Except he is a good young'un and you were always into something. If I had not hidden most of what you did from Daddy, you would have gotten your britches whipped clear off your behind!" They smiled at each other, and both then let out a small chuckle.

"Mama, we have got to go," Daddy said, reaching over, giving her another kiss on the cheek and a big bear hug. "Where is Daddy?" he asked.

"Well, son, you know Daddy. He must be out to the barn, feeding the pigs. He knew that this young'un was going with you and would not be able to do the feeding this morning. Also, he knew that this young'un was leaving, and he had gotten fond of him and thought maybe it would be better to leave things as they were without all the nonsense goodbyes, as he calls it. You know, son, your dad was never much for all those types of emotions, especially with you boys."

"Bye, Grandma!" I walked over and attempted to hug her.

She grabbed ahold of me and said, "Take good care of this boy, Robert. Neither he nor those precious girls are responsible for all the nonsense that you and Jeanette have brought upon your family." Grandmother held me tighter than she had ever held me, and I looked up to see tears streaming down her round cheeks. "You hear me, son?"

Daddy took a step closer and hugged Grandma again, telling her, "I will, Mama. Don't you worry. You have worried enough already taking care of yourself and Daddy."

"Now," Grandma said, "take this flour sack with you. I have put a few biscuits in there for you to eat on the way to wherever you're going. I just knew that you probably would not take the time to sit down and eat breakfast with me before you left this morning."

"Thank you, Grandma!" Then I hugged her flour-speckled, dusty apron at the waist and reached for the flour sack.

"Well, you know where your old mama lives, so come back when you can, son." She looked nervously over at Daddy as if he would reassure her that he would.

"Yes, Mama, we will," Daddy said, looking toward Grandma then back at me. "We'll come back soon to see your grandma, won't we, son?"

I looked up at Grandma and asked her to please tell Grandpa bye for me. "And tell him I love him. Please also tell him that I needed to go with my daddy and help him. Grandma, will you please do that for me? Where is Grandpa, anyway? Can I go tell him good-bye? I looked back and forth at both of them.

"No, Bubba," Daddy said. "We have got to get on the road. You will see your grandpa again real soon, and he is more than likely in the barn, feeding the hogs and the rest of the livestock. That's where your grandma told you he was earlier."

That day, I had very mixed emotions about leaving my grandma. I loved my grandma so much; she had been the virtual foundation of my spirituality then and for the rest of my life. My daddy never asked about how we were treated on the farm by our grandparents. I don't think it was anything he wanted to discuss with his children at that time. There were so many incidents that occurred on the farm, but that is perhaps another chapter in my life, and like my life, I prefer to move on. The holy book that my grandmother calls the Bible tells us that nothing can be gained by looking into your past occurrences; the future is what you have control over, and the future is what you can shape and mold into what you want it to be. This is not the exact quote from the Bible, but God knows what is in my heart. And really, isn't that all that matters?

"Daddy, where are we going?" I rose from the passenger seat so I could see out of the front windshield of this large car. I looked excitedly over at my daddy as he seemed to carefully steer the car down Tennessee's Highway 51 toward Memphis. This car was the same type that I remember in Ohio, a large four-door Buick.

"First, son, we're going to Memphis where your mom and sisters are supposed to be, and then to your uncle William. You remember him, don't you? He was your uncle that came and got you kids along with your grandpa and brought you to live with your grandparents. I think maybe he and his wife, your aunt, will allow us to stay with them until your daddy can find a house of our own," Daddy said.

"Do you know where Mama and my sisters are living?" I asked. I again mentioned that Mama came and I did not really know how much time had passed when she took Pat and Cynthia with her. "Daddy," I continued, "I stayed with Grandma because she was sick, and I was afraid to leave her alone." I looked over toward him for his answer, but I also noticed that he had that familiar worried look on his face.

As we drove toward Memphis, I felt thrilled that I was finally with my daddy and we were on our way to see Mama and my sisters. At this early age in my life, I still felt worried because of the things that had happened to us in the past, and I did not know what lay ahead once we reached Memphis. The only comfort to my worries was that I was finally with my daddy, and I knew that he would not let anything happen to us.

"I really missed you and Mama and was praying along with Grandma that you would come and get us. Why didn't you come, Daddy, with Mama when she came?"

"Son, please." He seemed to be getting aggravated at me. "I have been busy. I and your mama do not live together anymore. Try not to think about things like that. You are too young to understand grown-up problems, but always try to understand that I and your mother will always love you and your sisters. You children will always be the most important part of our lives. And promise me, son, that you will always remember that."

Looking over, I noticed he had a strained, sincere look on his face. He placed his hand on my head, giving it a small endearing nudge. "Okay, son?"

"Yes, Daddy, I promise," I said. "But when we find Mama and my sisters, can we then go home, please?"

"No, son." And I noticed his eyes begin to tear up.

"What's wrong, Daddy? Why are you crying?"

"I'm okay, son. I had just been driving for a long time. Guess I am getting a little tired too." He reached over and patted me or the head again, and I could see that he was attempting to force a smile. "Everything is going to be all right." I could tell that my daddy was worried, and even at my young age, I understood that Daddy was emotionally drained. He kept driving and looking out the windshield, then occasionally lovingly over toward me.

"Daddy, I just want to be with you and Mama and for us to be a family again. I and Grandma prayed that you and Mama wouldn't be mad at each other."

"Son, I know that you want all of us to be together again. That's also what your daddy wants more than anything else in this world, but now we have got to go to your uncle William's house in Memphis. And hopefully, they will allow us to stay with them for a while until I find a place." Daddy looked at me. "Son, you lie down over there now and get some sleep and I'll tell you when we get there."

Eventually, we arrived in Memphis and drove around for hours, it seemed. "This is where you were born, son." He pointed in the distance at the tall buildings that made up the Memphis skyline. I could see the Up sign high atop one of the largest buildings, and all the lights brought a sense of fascination and intrigue. This was a lot different from the quiet life of the country and my grandparents' farm. The buildings were clumped together in a maze of colored lights and concrete. Driving through the downtown area, we were surrounded by the tall buildings, and my eyes were fixated on all the lights and the way they seemed to align upward all the way up to the sky.

I fell asleep again after we left the area of downtown, and it must have been late in the evening when we arrived at Uncle William's house. "We're here, son. Time to wake up." I felt Daddy nudging me. I could see that we were directly across from what appeared to be a large warehouse that was at least two stories high and a large four-lane avenue that separated us. I had not seen my uncle William since he and Grandpa came to get me and my two sisters in Ohio, and I remember that he was a kind and gentle man, as was my daddy. He would later in life become a very devout Christian and a sincere, devoted preacher of God's Word. Most all my uncles, including my daddy, did later in life become Christians and preached to a lot of different church denominations and vast congregations. My uncles considered themselves to be evangelists, traveling wherever they thought God led them to go and preach. God used my uncles and my dad throughout all their lives so they could become vessels for Christ in helping bring many people to give their lives to God, accepting Jesus as their Savior.

Walking into the house, we were greeted by the large towering man that was my uncle William. His large frame towered above not only me but also my daddy. Through the years, I would always associate him with the TV show *Bonanza* and the character Hoss Cartwright because of their similar calm and caring personalities. "Hi, Bubba!" he said and clapped his large hand on top of my head, which felt like the weight of a small body. His large fingers were as large as Polish sausages, draping over my head and almost going all the way down to my neck on each side. I felt my neck wobble back and forth from the weight. He laughed and said, "What is wrong?" seeing that my head and neck were going from one side to the other, then chuckled and loosened his grip. "Robert," he then said, walking over to speak to my dad and putting his arm around his shoulder. "How are you and Jeanette getting along? Let's go into the kitchen, where we can have a cup of black coffee, and catch up on what has been going on and what we need to do to straighten things out." Uncle William looked at me and pointed at a door across the room, saying, "Bubba, you can go on into that room. The boys are supposed to be in there, asleep. I have laid a pallet of blankets in the corner so you can make yourself a place to sleep for tonight, and we will work out something different tomorrow."

I did not want to leave Daddy and looked over at him with concern.

"Now, you go on in there and I'll see you in the morning," Daddy said. "We have a long day ahead of us."

Reluctantly, I left him and Uncle William and found inside the room the pallet of blankets placed to one side. I was really exhausted, and as I looked at the pile of blankets, they must have looked so inviting that I just laid my head down just to rest a minute but, after my head felt the softness of the blankets, I could no longer remember anything until the next morning.

For several days, we stayed with Uncle William and found out that my other uncle lived in Memphis with his family and my other cousins. At first, initially, when my daddy went to look for work, I went with him, staying in the car when he went inside, applying for work. But I think he got worried about leaving me alone outside and thought it would probably be best that I stay at Uncle William's house. My aunt, William's wife, and he would be home to look after me.

One day, Daddy returned with my sisters, Pat and Cynthia, whom he said had been with our mother's mom, our other grandmother. I was so excited to see them and had so many questions to ask Pat, like, Where was Mama? And were she and Daddy getting along when they spoke to each other? She told me that she and Cynthia had been staying with our mother and Grandmother since she left me behind on the farm.

"Bubba," Pat said, "Mama is still the same as she was at home, and I don't think she and Daddy will be getting back together. One night, she was forced to take me and Cynthia with her because most of the time, when she left, she would leave us with Grandma and not return for a couple of days, and Grandmother would really get mad at her. She told Mama that if she was going to go out and do some running around—whatever that means—she would have to take us with her. I think Grandma got angry and argued with Mama about leaving us for days without calling her or asking if we were all right or needed anything. Just the other day, I could tell that Mama was mad and told me and Cynthia to come with her, that she had somewhere to go and wanted us to meet her friend. We arrived outside of this place that played very loud music and had all those beer signs on the windows. Mama pulled her car around the back of the place and told both of us to come with her. We followed her inside this black metal door and were met by the rolling waves of tobacco smoke, which made me think the place was on fire. There were both women and men all drinking beer, laughing, and smoking, and as we passed them sitting on barstools, I felt their eyes staring at us, which made me feel like I was a caged animal in the zoo. I felt frightened and really wanted to get out of there.

"'Mama,' I asked her, 'could we please go back to Grandma's house? I don't like it in here, and these people keep staring at us.'

"Instantly, she grabbed me and Cynthia by both our arms on either side of her and pulled us through this awful place and forcefully back out the door and to the car. 'Get in that car!' And just when I felt relieved that we were going to leave, she instead drove farther to the back of the building, pulling into the most desolate part of the lot. Getting out of the car, she slammed the door, yelling at me, 'Now you stay in this car and lock all the doors and I'll be back later.'

"I started to yell and cried, 'Please, Mama, don't leave us here by ourselves. What if a bad or drunk man comes out of there?' I pointed at the place. 'And he hurt us!'

"'Shut up!' she said. 'They don't want a whining little thing like you! Your grandmother should have let you stay with her. She probably would have if you had not kept on whining to come along with me!' She slung her black hair around her shoulder and made a crying-like gesture, with her lips puckered, to show her anger and disgust. 'Now, you wanted to come with me, so just shut up and do what you're told! Keep the doors locked.' Mama slammed all the doors shut and looked to make sure all the locks were down.

"I cried for her to come back, and she did, Bubba, but only briefly. She opened the door and grabbed me by the hair, pulling me out of the car and onto the broken-gravel parking lot. She slung her hair around her head and yelled at me, saying, 'You are not going to mess up the rest of my night, you little thorn in my behind! If you know what is good for you, you'll get back inside that car and do what I tell you! And don't you move from here until I come back!'

"'But, Mama, I must go pee!'

"'Get yourself behind this car on the other side and squat down! No one will see you, and even if they do, they won't want a little squirt like you, anyway.'

"'I don't want to do that, Mama. It is dirty everywhere, and someone might see me! Can't we go back to Grandma's house?'

"'You get over there like I told you! I got to get back inside. You've wasted enough of my night as it is.' Before Mama went inside, I also got Cynthia out of the car and helped her to squat down and relieve herself. We both squatted down while Mama angrily stood nearby, jerking her head and hair around, yelling at us to hurry up. 'Now, hurry up and get in that car,' she said, shoving us inside and slamming the car door shut with me and Cynthia inside.

"Bubba, we stayed in the car almost the entire night and eventually fell asleep. During the night, I was awakened by people coming and going from that place. I kept very still and quiet and told Cynthia not to move around too much and to certainly whisper if we talked to each other. Finally, I heard what I thought was Mama's voice and peeked up and out the window to see. She briefly talked to a strange man and then got into her car and drove us away. I felt relief that we were finally leaving that place and prayed like Grandma taught us that we were going back to Grandmother's home.

"First, I sat there with Cynthia in the back seat as she slept, then rose up and whispered toward Mama, asking, 'Are we going back to Grandmother now?'

"'I thought you were asleep? Just lie back down.'

"And a short while later, I felt the car slowly pull over to the curb and stop. Hoping we were finally at Grandmother's, I rose up just as Mama opened her door and slammed it shut behind her. Instead of us being where I had hoped, I looked out and saw Mama speaking to the same man she was with in the parking lot back at that beer joint. They both embraced and then briefly looked back at our car. I ducked down quickly in the seat so they would not see me. I did not want to get Mama angry at me again. I then slowly peered over the front seat toward them. My heart sank. I noticed that we were not at Grandmother's but instead were at a poorly lit building with numerous doors with numbers on them.

"The man took out a key and used it to open the door, then Mama and this man went inside. I cuddled up to Cynthia and tried to go back to sleep, and I must have because later I was awakened by the sunlight and Mama opening the car door. Mama finally drove us back to Grandma's, and the next day was when we heard a knock on the door and were glad to see Daddy when it was opened. I was relieved, as was Cynthia.

"Oh, Bubba, we were so happy and relieved to see him but were concerned and asked if he had seen you at Grandpa's. That was when he told us that he had taken you from Grandpa's and you were with Uncle William at his house here in Memphis. He asked if we wanted to go see you and stay with him for a while. Bubba, I was so worried about you! I did not want to leave you there at Grandpa's, but you know how Mama is, and I knew that you were worried about Grandma and didn't want to leave her while she was sick and alone. How is Grandma now?"

I responded, "She got better after she took the medicine that Grandpa and Mr. Burns brought back from the doctor."

"After we got here, I was so glad that you stayed with Grandma instead of coming with us and Mama. Since we have been here with Mama, she has left us alone or with Grandma, telling us to stay in the house and not to answer the door. When Grandma came back home, she would find out that Mama had already left with someone, leaving me and Cynthia alone for her to watch and take care of us.

When Mama did eventually come home was when she and Grandma argued."

We stayed several weeks with Uncle William, then with another uncle, just back and forth, as Daddy attempted to always take us with him when job hunting but found it a little difficult and stressful leaving us in the car while he talked with possible employers. During the time he left to look for work, he asked relatives sometimes to watch after us until she returned. He trusted that they could keep us safe. We tried to adjust the best we could to whatever situation that came our way and continually kept trying to comfort one another. I believe that we tried to reassure one another that everything was going to be all right and prayed this was just temporary and would soon be over. We continually moved around from one relative to another while in Tennessee and eventually moved to Oklahoma with another uncle, who was stationed in the military there, and I believe the reason for this move was that Daddy was concerned with what he heard either from our mama or other relatives. Apparently, the juvenile authorities were seen frequently driving through our Grandmother's neighborhood and had asked questions concerning apparent complaints that we were frequently left unsupervised. Apparently, after hearing this, he decided it was best that he take us away from Memphis and to his brother's home in Oklahoma. We enjoyed a brief period with this uncle, and he was a lot like Daddy, with similar personalities. We enrolled in school and felt as though life was finally starting to seem to have a real family atmosphere, whatever we thought that was.

Daddy started seeing a nice lady, and they seemed to try to spend time together and took us along with them on family-type outings—i.e., the zoo, fairgrounds, and sometimes we went to the ballpark to watch baseball games. We had a hard time accepting her with Daddy, but he did seem to be happy. They did get along better than what we remembered he had with our mother, and eventually, we tried to like her and did, after a while, adjust.

I have very fond memories of our stay in Oklahoma, and I, along with my sister Patricia, enrolled in extracurricular activities for school. We applied for gymnastics and high jump, and I remember that was the first time that each of us was awarded the first-place trophy for running and high jump. We were so proud that we had made so many new friends at school and in our uncle's neighborhood. I don't remember what occurred and can only speculate on the reason, but we left Oklahoma and this first-time-in-a-long-time normal existence. Maybe it was because of too many people being in one house, and I guess when you have so many different people and/or personalities in one house, there probably will be a disagreement sooner or later. Daddy decided that we would move back to Memphis. Our uncle and his wife, our aunt, I will always remember fondly as loving and kind, and I thought they did their best trying to help us adjust and make the best of a bad situation. I believe my sisters also regretted that Daddy decided to leave this only stable existence that we had known for quite some time and move back to Tennessee.

Our lives during the next months would again be tossed into turmoil and disarray as we moved from relative to relative for Daddy to have someone to watch over us while he looked for work. He told us that he was going to take us back to Ripley, Tennessee. When he told us this, the only thought I had about Ripley was when we stayed with our grandparents. He could see the worried look on our faces and tried to reassure us that we were going to visit our aunt Francis, who was his only sister. She, too, was a sharecropper on Mr. Burns's farm that was in another section of the county. Daddy talked with our aunt and made financial arrangements for us to stay with her while he worked in another city. Aunt Francis was single but had kids from a previous marriage—four sons and one daughter. They all worked hard cultivating various types of crops on the farm. We again adjusted with our aunt and cousins as we had previously with the other relatives we had stayed with. Aunt Francis was a good, loving, spiritual woman, as was her mother, our grandma, believing in hard work and, especially, providing a godly home for her children. As I grew up, it was apparent to me that she was the cornerstone of what a good mother could and should be. This was also evident in her children and her grandchildren in the years to follow.

Our aunt's children had reached their teenage years except for one son, Jerry, and all of us children were able to help one another and work together on her farm. The youngest two—a son, Jerry, and a daughter, Ruth—were children, like us, but showed more maturity for their age, and I thought it might have been due to growing up on a farm. We enjoyed working and playing together, sharing all the chores equally. Our aunt Francis taught and instilled in all her children and us how a true Christian family should live. As I looked back in my life, I thank God and did realize just how fortunate we all were that he was looking after us and loved us so much that he provided me and my sisters a safe, spirit-filled home with our aunt's family. She taught us and instilled in us that a good moral character in a person would gain them respect from others and bring a smile to the Lord's face. Our aunt, as did our grandma, would tell stories about the Bible and the prophets, assuring us that when we got to the pearly gates of heaven, God would welcome us and say, "Come in, thou good and faithful servant." She reminded me so much of the devout spirituality of her mother, our grandmother.

Her eldest son, James, was a good man, always helping his mother with all the various farm equipment and the overall management of the farm. During the time we spent with our aunt, her two eldest sons, James and Bobby, when they reached maturity, left home and joined the military, which was the customary decision for young men in the South. This period, as I think back, was in the late 1950s or very early 1960s. This was the custom not only with my aunt's sons but also with most young farm boys in the South. They anticipated the time when they reached enlistment age, or even at an earlier age, getting their parents to sign for them if below the required age. This allowed all the young men the opportunity to leave the drudgery of the hard farmwork and acquire a dependable monthly military check. The farm was what work you put into it, but even then, sometimes that did not make a difference. The weather was something only God had control of and was what made the difference between making a profit at the end of the year and ensuring your survival.

As was on our grandpa's farm, we grew all the food that we ate, not only for us but also for all the livestock. There were crops to sell for profit, then other crops that we ate. During certain hunting seasons of the year, the older cousins would go out into the fields and woods and bring back a wild kill of squirrel, rabbits, deer, or anything that was eatable. Only a very small percentage of food was bought from the markets in town, such things as flour and sugar. Living with our aunt on the farm was also stressful and consisted of a lot of hard work, but there were no threats of severe punishment or intimidations as with Grandpa. Aunt Francis and her son James allowed for plenty of rest when we worked, and I could hear her yell from across the field in our direction, saying, "Come on, that's enough for today! It is too hot out here, and I don't want you young'uns to get a heatstroke!" At the end of each row, there was always a gallon jug filled with ice water she had brought out earlier that morning, and there was where we could always rest awhile in the shade under the trees. I can still, to this day, see her with her bonnet, which covered her head and face and shielded her from the scorching rays of the blistering sun. She also made sure that we were all properly covered with light clothes so as not to smother our bodies. She was concerned for us and wanted to prevent a heatstroke, which was very prevalent during those years. She told a story that occurred during her childhood about the time cotton was to be harvested and, she said, there were numerous laborers that died in the fields due to the blistering heat of the sun and hard labor. Times were hard in those days, and people had to make money any way that was available and sometimes took unnecessary chances to survive.

Sometimes, on Sunday or when we were not in school or in the fields, working, she allowed James to bridle up the mules for all of us to ride. We had more kids than we had mules, so many times we would have to double up to ride. James or his brother Bobby led the way, and we would follow one another through the fields and back into the far pastures. Jerry, the youngest brother and cousin, was much more adventurous and liked to get the wildest-spirited mule, and if I was riding behind him, he would do his best to frighten me. He would whistle, yell, and start kicking the mule on the side, causing her to trot, which caused us both to jostle up and down on her spiny back. And oh, goodness, how that hurt my bottom! I'd yell for him to stop or slow down because it hurt getting jarred repeatedly on her spiny backbone until she finally went into a full gallop, and there were many times that I thought I would fall off. We always enjoyed ourselves, though, and to this day, I don't know how we never received any serious injury. However, there was one situation that occurred after the ride that was somewhat frightening and a little comical.

After each ride, we needed to lead the mule that we were riding to the pond for them to drink before we put them up either in the barn or out to pasture. I asked Jerry and James if I could take the mule I was riding to the pond for watering. "Okay, Bubba," they both said. This allowed me to feel so mature, that I was in control of this large mule beneath me and that I was able to control and guide her to the pond. I had seen my cousins do this numerous times, and now I was to be trusted to do the same as they had. As I was approaching the pond, I wanted to make a lot of noise to frighten any of the water moccasins (snakes), which were always seen swimming around on the surface. We had been riding for some time, and the closer we got to the pond, the faster this mule began to trot, jarring me up and down. I tried to pull back on the bridle to slow her down and not fall and to let her know that I was the one that was in charge, but she just was too powerful and pulled against me. Finally, trotting up to the pond, and before I had time to adjust, she came to a screeching stop. She bent her front legs and leaned her head over toward the water to drink. Suddenly, I was slung over her head, flipping and tumbling into what I knew to be snake-infested water and feeling my body jolt and hit hard beneath the surface and to the muddy bottom. My cousins could be heard laughing hysterically as I attempted to catch my breath, which was knocked out of me by the sudden jolt of striking the water. I was drenched in water and mud all over my head and body. The mule was startled by my body being hurled into the pond, and when I regained my footing, I tried to come out of the water by jerking back against the reins, which I had refused to let go of. I held on to the reins as if my life depended on it, not only to make sure that she did not get away but also to help pull me out away from the snakes that I just knew were coming for me. The reins around her neck were my only security, and there was no way I was going to release them.

Cousin Jerry was laughing so hard he had gotten down on the ground rolling around back and forth, pointing at me. James, his brother, who mostly had a serious type of personality, was also laughing. After I had time to gather myself and think about what had just happened and the total muddy mess I must have looked at, I, too, started to laugh but managed to stumble out and collapse close to where cousin Jerry was lying, looking over at me and laughing hysterically.

"Bubba," James said, laughing but trying to put on a serious face, "get yourself up from there and go up to the house and get cleaned up before Mama sees you. Jerry, get that strap from Bubba and take that mule to the barn. Feed and put her away. I think she deserves and an extra helping of oats for what she has been through." And again he laughed real hard. "Come on now, get up from there and get to the house and draw yourself some water from the well and wash up. That dirty pond water has mosquito eggs in it, and you need to get it off before you get infected. And take that snake out from around your neck and throw it back in the pond."

I suddenly jerked around, standing up quickly, and saw that James and Jerry were laughing at me as I looked all over my body for the snake that he was apparently only joking about. "That was not funny," I said but was not laughing and began to walk up the hill toward the house, which was about a quarter of a mile from where we were. I was wet, and my entire body was covered with muddy pond water. I finally walked up the steep hill that separated the old farmhouse from the rest of the property.

My aunt also had the same agreement that my grandparents had with Mr. Burns, that she and her family would live in the house free of charge and cultivate the fields with hopefully lucrative crops and share in a percentage of the profits at the end of the harvest.

Aunt Francis apparently saw me coming up the hill, and as I started climbing up the stairs located at one end behind the farmhouse, I noticed she had a smile on her face. She said, "Boy, what in the world have you gotten yourself into?" After I told her what had happened, she said with a small chuckle, placing her hand on my shoulder and leading me down the porch to the large well that extended out, with a wooden porch encircling it. The well was attached to the middle of the porch toward the back of the house and about fifteen feet off the ground. "There," she said, pointing toward the well bucket. "Now draw yourself a couple of buckets and put it in that bathtub over there but leave a little room. I have a bucket inside and will heat up some on the stove to add to that. Now fill that tub. We will have supper shortly." She smiled. "I think maybe next time you might remember to slide yourself toward his rear when those thirsty mules get close to the pond. Those other boys should have told you."

I interrupted her and said, "No, ma'am, it was my fault. I just wasn't thinking and should have known better." My thought was, I did not want them to take the blame for a mistake I had made. I stripped out of all the muddy clothes, all but my underwear, and quickly got cleaned up in the long steel tub that was always turned upside down on the back porch. I usually left the water for at least another person to use, but because of the severity of the pond water's infestation with mosquito larvae, my aunt told me to empty it.

My cousins were like my big brothers, especially Jerry and his brother Robert. They were always making me laugh with all the jokes, and Robert had the ability to talk and sound like Donald Duck. The well water was very cold and delicious to drink; the cold temperature was because of it coming from deep in the ground, which led to the water needing to be heated to take a bath.

This stay with my cousins and Aunt Francis was the most memorable and pleasant experience of our lives. The old farmhouse was built on a hill overlooking a country road and other fields where a group of hogs was kept. We used to take cardboard boxes, tear them apart, and use them to slide down the hill on the surface of the tall green grass all the way to the bottom. There were ways that we found to entertain ourselves because there was no money that could be used to buy toys. Sometimes at dark we would gather lightning bugs and put them into glass jars, using the jars to light our way around sheds and barns and then later to illuminate the rooms when we went to bed. I always thought this was in a way of going back into the pioneer days of old.

There was an incident one summer night. I was on the very top of the hill and about to slide down while I sat in one of the cardboard boxes. My cousin Jerry was unaware that I was inside and shot through the box with his new Daisy BB gun, striking me in the back of the head. I think he was as stunned and afraid as I was, especially when he heard me cry out from inside the box. We were both afraid to tell his mother, my aunt, and I just checked with the help of Jerry to see if there was any damage to my head or scalp, and when there wasn't, we just put some ice wrapped inside a rag on the hit areas, and to this day no one was the wiser. At the time of this writing, my cousin Jerry has passed on from this life at the early age of sixty-one and, without a doubt in my mind, has found a place in heaven.

My dad visited several times while we lived with our aunt Francis, and we also attended school and were, as usual, very excited to see him. He would always stay for a few days or over the weekend, then tell us that he had to go back to work and would leave. One morning, I could hear my aunt's and daddy's voice coming from the kitchen, and I hurried to see him. I ran over to where he was seated and grabbed him around the waist, hugging him tightly. He reached down and kissed me on the forehead, saying, "I love you, son. I and your aunt are talking, so I want you to go in the other room until we finish, okay?" I reluctantly left the room but could still overhear them talking. "I think I'll take the kids back with me to Memphis. I have a good job opportunity there, and Bill [Uncle William] said that they could stay with him and his wife until I get settled."

"I don't know, Robert," she said. "Do you know for sure if William has spoken to his wife about it? You better make sure it will be all right with her. You also know how it can be with two families living together in one house, and you know, Robert, that it is okay here with me. This house is large enough for all of us, while they have a houseful of their own kids to look after."

"I'm sure that Bill has discussed it with her. I know what he told me, that is, to bring the kids there so they will be close to me, their father. I'm sure, Francis, everything will be fine, and you know that I can't keep asking you to look after them. You also have enough to do with the farm and your own family."

"Oh, Robert, you know that I love these young'uns just like I do my own, and they are a real help to me, and all of us get along just fine," Aunt Francis responded. "But I also understand that you miss your young'uns. But you know that if things don't work out at Bill's, you can always bring them back here. Will you promise me that?"

Dad said, "Yes, okay, I will, but I'm sure that William and his wife will help, and if things get a little tense, I can always take them over to their uncle Connie's house. I just want to have them with me. I'm their father and miss them so much, and with me is where they should be. Their mother is in Memphis too, and if there is any possibility that she will come back and be their mother and my wife again, I just must pray that God will bless us as he always has."

"I know, Robert," she said, "but you and I know how Jeanette is right now, and I really don't see her changing her attitude anytime soon, if ever."

I looked through the slightly open door and could see the extreme frustration on my daddy's face. He looked over at her and said, "I know, but it's hard for me to just give up on the mother of my kids, and while there is still a breath in me, I must always have some sort of hope." My daddy began to cry and bow his head toward the tabletop as Aunt Francis got up and came around to him, saying, "I know, Robert," placing her hand on his shoulder. "You know I'll do whatever I can to help."

Leaving Our beloved Aunt Francis

I felt saddened and lacked the ability to make any kind of rational understanding concerning the decision that our dad made in moving me and my sisters again, especially taking us away from our beloved aunt Francis. I thought at that time that living with her had to be the beginning of some type of normal family existence that we had not felt in such a very long time. Though I wonder, Did we ever know the real existence of a normal family beyond that which we had lived previously with our parents? Or was the happiness we felt with our aunt Francis the real lifestyle of a family? At first, we all missed our daddy and mother, but then we felt the warmth and love that Aunt Francis and our cousins showed. I know we learned to appreciate being in a farming lifestyle, along with the loving Christian spirit our aunt surrounded all her children with. She loved us and accepted us into her family, and this allowed us to feel the warmth and love that our hearts must have been without in such a very long time. As I said before, in my opinion, she was a loving example of what our great Creator, God, would consider being the ideal mother and Christian.

I did want, more than anything I could ever imagine, to be united with our mama and daddy, and I constantly prayed that this would be the blessing from God and that soon it would come to reality. Don't misunderstand me; we all were so happy to be back with Daddy and at the reality of being with him, but I just thought our mother would have love and compassion and understand that we loved and missed her, and especially Daddy. He wanted her to realize that he was trying to do whatever he thought possible to bring the family back together. I think my thought was that maybe, somehow, she would see that he alone would not be able to care for us and have the compassion that he would have to seek the help of friends or relatives. This was in my constant thought and prayer. And I could also see that Daddy's behavior had changed in that his usual happy attitude was not the same. I prayed that God would possibly help Mother to see that even though they had chosen to help us out of their kindness, still, she might offer to help Daddy—not, of course, out of being forced but especially since we all knew how stubborn Mama could be if anyone tried to force her to do something she did not want to do because she was our mother and she loved us.

We were extremely unhappy when we said our goodbyes to all our cousins and our precious aunt Francis, whom we loved and appreciated so much. Our stay with her in the latter part of the 1950s had left a great impression on me with how I created the moral foundation of my overall personality. I don't think that it truly registered at that time in my impressionable young mind what a great example of a true spiritual Christian person she was and how valuable she had become in our lives. Our aunt Francis, along with her mother, our grandma, taught us many moral Christian qualities that stayed embedded in my mind throughout my life. Even though they have both passed on to be with our heavenly Father, their spirits still linger in the deepest part of my heart and soul to this day.

After our arrival again in Memphis, we went to the home Uncle William shared with our aunt and attempted to settle in with their family. I can remember somewhat of a challenge with both families crammed into such a small house. This was the same home that we had stayed at the last visit, and I was worried about the length of time it would take our daddy to find a place for us to live. Even at a young age, I could feel the tension that was caused by our being in a cramped space, especially from Uncle William's wife. Looking back now, I ask myself, How could anyone blame her? She had her own children, and now three more children that had invaded her home and lifestyle. We tried to stay out of the way and were thankful when the time came to go to school. Yes, those were the thoughts I had at that time, and I know it sounds strange coming from a child, but I knew our aunt would have time alone without the three of us possibly interfering with their family.

Daddy got a job driving trucks and seemed to be pleased with promising us that finally, he was going to have enough money to move us into a home of our own. I knew, or rather thought, that he still had intentions of renewing his marriage with our mama but first wanted a nice home and more money for her to come home to. I felt compassion for my daddy, knowing that he always talked about making enough money to make Mama happy. Daddy could be heard talking to others, saying that he was the reason for their failed relationship and he needed to make enough money to fulfill all her demands and/or expectations.

Each day after Daddy left for work, my sister Pat took on the "big sister" role and the responsibility for the three of us. She always made sure that we had something to eat and dressed adequately for school. Our aunt, I thought, was a very good woman, but after thinking about the situation later in my life with all of us invading her and their lives, I knew she must have had a little animosity toward us, but because Daddy and her husband were brothers, I thought that was the reason she probably tolerated the intrusion. I tried not to think about or be saddened by the lifestyle or home that we had just left and we so much missed, as well as our beloved aunt Francis and the loving environment that she provided. I was in constant fear that this constant moving around might be the way we were going to continue to live our lives, and I wondered what tragedy would be next in our future. Yes, even though I was a small child, I had faith enough to believe there would be a future for us, because of the Christian homes that I lived in and the many prayers we were taught by both my grandmother and aunt Francis. I believed that God was with me always and that God would provide all things to those who ask and believe! I, too, was so fortunate and thankful to be with my two sisters and remembered how much I had missed them after Mama rescued them from our grandfather's farm.

Living with Uncle William, we always made sure that when we got up in the morning, we made our beds and even did some of the housework for the family and our aunt. The many household chores, we were familiar with because of our being taught by our grand-mother and aunt Francis when we stayed with them. I thought this would help make her like us, and maybe they would allow us to stay with them. Daddy also thought it would be a very thoughtful thing for us to do. He said, because we were staying with them, it was only the right thing for us to do most of the chores or whatever else we were told. We wanted and needed everybody to be content and to make our stay as less stressful for them as possible. I felt as though we needed to keep to ourselves to not get in their way. Daddy did not tell us this in so many words, but we did not want to do anything to disrupt their family's initial way of life.

I did not necessarily know why I felt this way; it must have been just a feeling. I felt it was possibly because of the many times that we had moved around and into the homes of relatives. If they wanted to include the three of us in their many family activities, they needed to first invite us to join them. I and my sister Pat knew the difference between our initial family and the families of the relatives that we stayed with and how to act accordingly. There was always the feel-ing of a divide between the families, and if we made the mistake of stepping into their family's love or lifestyle, then there would be the feeling of resentment. I did notice when it was time for family to eat, we did not feel a part of the family, unless, however, our daddy had gotten off work was with us, and then there was somewhat a feeling of acceptance.

I remember that Uncle William's wife had been in a very serious car accident that had left her partially disfigured. We all loved her and paid no attention to what she obviously considered a serious problem, but I felt this had left her bitter with the world in general. I remember that I and my sisters were so glad to be together again that we certainly did not want to do anything that would upset Daddy or anyone else for fear that they might ask Daddy to leave. And then where would we go? Sometimes, when traveling between relatives, we would live out of the car for days. Daddy would stop alongside the road in some of the many service stations, and all of us would take turns washing up in the bathrooms while Daddy protected us from the outside until we finished. We had been shuffled around so many places and relatives I thought soon we would run out of people to stay with or have nowhere else to go. My current thoughts relative to that time in my life included staying out of everybody's way and being quiet and as good as possible. I was constantly praying to God that eventually we would find our mother and could be a real loving family once again.

I don't exactly remember how much time we spent with Uncle William and our aunt on this visit but remember how fortunate we were to be allowed to stay with them if we had. I constantly smiled at Uncle William and our aunt, telling them how lucky they were to have a nice home and family, thanking them often. Uncle William one day motioned for me to come over to him, and as I got close to him, he reached out toward me with those enormous hands and pulled me against him, giving me a big hug, and smiled, telling me to stop thanking him. "Bubba," he said, "you young'uns are going to be all right, and you and your sisters can stay if your dad needs you to, but please, Bubba, you don't need to keep thanking me all the time!" What my uncle had told me somehow brought a little relief from the constant state of fear I was in. During these early years, my young mind must have been in a constant state of confusion, fear, and disillusionment.

Early each morning, we would always do our chores before going off to school. It had gotten to be the normal way of life for me and my sisters to attend a different school every year because of having to move constantly to live with different relatives. One day after school, my sisters and I were picked up and left at Uncle William's house by our aunt and told to stay there until our daddy got home from work. This was very unusual because usually someone was always there at their house, but this day we were left at the house alone. We went inside to check if there was any cleaning we should do before our aunt got back home. Both Pat and I laid Cynthia down in a small room that was closed off from the rest of the house and where we could hear and check on her periodically. Pat and I found some dishes to clean up, and we pushed some chairs against the kitchen sink and counter so we could reach them while we cleaned. She washed while I dried until all of them were finished, then getting down, we started cleaning the rest of the kitchen until even that, we thought, was spotless. We both smiled at each other with pride at the thought that we might make our aunt and uncle happy when they got home now that they would not have to clean up anything. I also thought that if we only knew how to cook, I was sure we would have surprised them with a good dinner too.

The rest of the children, our cousins, had not gotten home from school, which we thought was very unusual. After all the hard work from cleaning the kitchen and some of the other rooms, I thought it would be okay to go outside and play. Their house was set off from the main street, with a small yard in front and an alley along one side that led to another street. We had played here often, and so I thought it would be safe to play while we waited for everybody.

"Come on, Pat," I asked, "let's go outside and play. They should all be home soon."

"I don't know, Bubba. Maybe we should stay here. If something happens or either one of us gets hurt, there will be no one here to help."

"But, sissy," I said, "we'll be careful. Come on, please! And I want to be able to see Daddy when he gets home."

My cousin had that new bike that he said I could ride if I wanted.

"Well…" Pat appeared to be thinking, and with that oh-so-familiar worried look on her face, she continued, "But then…oh, I guess it will be okay. I can ride our other cousin's bike. I don't think she will mind, do you?"

I then exclaimed, "And then we can have a race!"

"I bet I can ride faster than you!" Pat said.

"No, you can't!"

She giggled.

"Let's go!" we yelled at each other excitedly and hurried out the front door, stumbling down each step, rushing toward the bikes, which leaned against the back of the house.

I had difficulty trying to keep the bike from falling over at first but was not going fast enough to cause any real damage to me and especially my cousin's bike. Pat had the same problems trying to keep the other bike up and rolling forward. During a fast ride, she fell and skinned her knee, then quickly got up and wiped it off with the hem of her dress—even that did not seem to slow her down, and we both kept riding.

"Pat!" I yelled back behind me to where I thought she was and noticed that she was riding up toward me as we both approached the front of the house. I was pedaling close to the street, looking back at her, which made it very hard to keep the bike up and rolling without it falling over. She started riding toward me as I stopped and put both feet on the broken blacktop alleyway. I looked around to see her riding up to meet me.

"I'm coming, Bubba!" she exclaimed, pedaling up and down in my direction as fast as her long legs could go.

My attention was suddenly averted toward the street, where a large dark car pulled off the main street and into the alleyway, stopping only inches from where I was straddling the bike. Hurriedly, I got off the bike and pushed and dragged it to the side to get out of the way and allow the car to go past if they wanted to go down the alley.

Pat also yelled at me, "Bubba! Watch out for that car! Get out of the way and let it go by you!"

"It's okay, sissy," I responded, trying to calm her, and tried to catch my breath. "I'm not in the way. The car has already stopped!"

She hurriedly pushed the bike she was straddling with her long bony legs against a fence that lined the alleyway close to the house and started walking briskly to where I stood. Grabbing me, she said, "Come on, Bubba," and started to tug at me and the bike, which I was still rolling across the alley in the direction of the front porch. She looked worried and told me, "Put the bike down over there, Bubba," pointing toward the side of the house. After I dropped the bike, she quickly grabbed my arm and began tugging at me toward the front steps of the porch, where we began stumbling up one step at a time.

Looking around, we both heard the car doors opening and slamming shut. "Hello, there, little lady and young man. Is your mama or daddy home?"

I looked at Pat and felt her pulling me closer to her side as we both looked in the direction of the strangers, a man and a woman, that stood on opposite sides of the large car. Both were dressed very nicely. The woman stood stiffly erect, with a large dark ankle-length winter coat. Later, as I thought, she could be described as the neighbor that stole the dog in the movie *The Wizard of Oz*. Adorning her head was a straw-type hat that had a flower arrangement around the top. The man did not seem as intimidating as she did, but he did remind me of a preacher type because of the tie that was so neatly pulled tautly around his neck. He also wore a long black ankle-length coat and a dress-type Sonora hat that had a small feather on the side.

Pat seemed to again pull me even closer, and I could feel her trembling body against mine, then she answered the man, "No, sir, but they will all be home in a few minutes. I and my little brother, Bubba, just got home from school, and our daddy is on his way home from work."

"Is this where you and your little brother live?" the man asked as he approached and put his hand on the top of my head, smiling down, looking back and forth at the both of us.

"Yes, sir," I answered. "We live here with our daddy and Uncle William and aunt—"

"Bubba!" Pat stopped me and looked over at me, squeezing my shoulder, which felt as though she had a death grip on me, sternly telling me that we were not supposed to talk to strangers.

"Oh, that's okay, young lady," he said, looking over at Pat. "We are here to help you. I and this nice lady are your friends. If no one is here with you, it is our duty as child protection officers to ask questions so we can determine that you are all safe. Isn't that right, Mrs. Raines?" He looked over again at the scary-looking lady.

The lady he called Mrs. Raines looked angrily over at the man and sternly told him, "We have wasted enough time here, and it is obvious that there is no adult around to care for these children. You take the boy and I'll take the girl, and let's get them into the car. Their parents will have to come up to juvenile court and explain why they are out here alone, without any adult supervision."

The man took me by the arm and proceeded to walk me toward the car as I nervously glared around to see where my sister Pat was.

"Bubba!" Pat yelled out. "Ma'am," she said, looking up at the lady, who was now pulling her toward the car, "our daddy will be here soon, and our uncle and aunt should also be home any minute now. I'm sure they are on the way. Where are you taking us? They will be worried if we are not here when they get home and won't know where to find us."

"No," the lady said, "that is not something you need to worry your little head about. They will be notified where you are, you can be assured of that. Now, get in that car!"

I was on one side, while Pat was on the other. We both were hurriedly shoved inside and could hear both the car doors slam shut behind us. The door that shut behind me had caught me, slamming into my hip before I could get out of the way. I felt terrified, not knowing what was really happening to us and why these strange people were making us go with them. Where were they taking us?

Pat, looking horrified toward the mean lady and then back over at me, with tears starting to fall from her eyes, asked, "Why are they taking us? And where are we going?"

"I don't know!" I cried back and could see the tears continue to fall from her face as she shouted over toward me. I wished we could hug each other. We almost forgot that Cynthia was asleep inside and thought that we could go out and be able to hear her as she woke up while we played outside the house.

"Mister!" both Pat and I cried out.

Then Pat continued, "Our little baby sister is asleep inside the house, and we can't leave her alone. If she wakes up and no one is home, she will be afraid."

"Okay, you two, just calm down," he said. "Mrs. Raines, you watch them, and I will check the house for the other sister." He looked over at the lady and said, "We were told there would only be two of them. It is a good thing that these two kids spoke up and told us about the other child, or she would have been left." As the man started to walk up the porch toward the front door, I could hear Cynthia crying, and we both looked up toward the house as the man went inside. Later, I heard Cynthia scream even louder. We both looked, worried, but could see the man come out with Cynthia in his arms as she kept screaming and thrashing around, attempting to get away from this strange man and loosen his grip on her. He finally opened the back door of the car and handed Cynthia to both me and Pat. We had been embracing each other, so it was easy for her to be placed on both our laps.

She looked up with her frightened tear-soaked red face first at Pat and then over at me. We hugged her tight and tried to calm her down, but she had been so frightened by the stranger it was hard for us to calm her down. She kept sniffling and tried to catch her breath as we both told her that everything was all right, that she was with her sissy and brother, Bubba.

The lady was writing something on a large folder and told the man, who sat behind the steering wheel, "Come on, let's go. They will be expecting us at the juvenile court. I'll finish with the rest of this report while you try to get us there without any more problems."

As we drove down the street, I kept looking around out of all the car windows, hoping that I would see Daddy arriving home, or maybe even Uncle William and our aunt. Cynthia was still sniffling and was visually still very upset and kept looking back and forth at me and Pat. I hugged her tight and said, "That's okay, sissy. Everything is going to be all right. Don't be afraid. Daddy will find us and take us back home again, you'll see!"

I heard what sounded like radio and noticed the man reach up toward the dash and take a small round object up to his mouth and begin to speak into it. "Yes, base, this is unit 531 and we have the children and are now about five minutes away. Have the bay door ready to open." The voice on the other end replied, saying that they would be ready when they got the signal from the buzzer when we approached.

It had gotten dark, and the lights were lit up all along the streets during the last minutes of our frightening drive. Looking over at both Pat and Cynthia, I whispered, "Pat, I'm scared. Where are we going? And who are these people?"

"I think they are with the police, because of the man speaking on the radio a few minutes ago."

"But, sissy, we did not do anything wrong, did we?" I asked with pleading eyes.

Just as I got those words out, we arrived at a large brick building, and the man drove the car around toward the back of the structure and down what appeared to be an enclosed underground tunnel. It got even darker when we reached the bottom, and a large steel door began to go up from the ground, revealing an open area that was dimly lit. The car pulled forward and eventually stopped close to a wall, and I could hear the steel door, as before, begin to move. I looked back to see it slowly lower until I could hear it rattle against the concrete floor.

"Sissy," I said, looking over at Pat, "we are closed in here with these strange people, I'm afraid. What are we going to do? They are not going to put us in jail, are they? I tried to be good to Uncle William and Aunt Dolly. What did I do, sissy?"

"Let's just do what they tell us, and I'm sure that everything will be okay."

Both the man and the lady got out of the car, and I could hear the lady tell the man, "I've got to take these girls to the dormitory on the second floor, and you see if that attendant is awake enough to admit that little man up on the third. I've got to get this paperwork to the office, then get myself home before the mister locks me out." The lady took ahold of Pat by one hand and told her, "Carry your little sister, or if she can walk, let her down. We have got to go."

I yelled out, "Sissy, no! Don't leave me! I want to go with you and Cynthia!"

"Now, that will be enough of that, young man. You have got to go with Officer Smith. You can't go with your sisters. They have got to go where the girls are kept, and you will be all right with the other juvenile boys on their assigned floor. Now, go along with this man and do as you're told. I'm sure that you will see your sisters later." Then she angrily spoke to the man towering by my side. "Take him," she said, pointing her index finger out to me, then him. "I won't have any of this nonsense and certainly don't have time for it." He sternly grabbed my arm and led me to another elevator adjacent to the one that the lady and my sisters were seen entering.

I yelled out and could hear Pat quietly start to ask the lady, "Where is he taking my Bubba? When will we see each other? Ma'am, please!" I could hear her cry out, "He will be afraid without us together!" Then I saw and heard the elevator door slam tightly shut.

"You'll be all right, young man," the man said, looking down at me. "What is your name, anyway?"

"Sir, my name is Hershel." I fought back to contain my sniffles. "But all my family call me Bubba," I continued. "When will I see my sisters? Are they going to be okay?" I pleaded, looking up at him with tears streaming down my face.

"Yes, son," he said. "Now, don't you worry any about your sisters. They will be taken care of and probably a lot better than anything you have been used to."

It felt as though the elevator had traveled upward then came to a sudden stop.

"Here we go, young man. This is where you will be staying for a while until one of your parents comes to get you." Taking me by the hand, he led me out of the elevator and down a long hallway toward a large door that had a wired, web-type window halfway up. Knocking on the door, he yelled out, "Hey! You in there! I have another little resident for you tonight."

I noticed a very heavy, burly-type man approach the window and look through at the man beside me and then down at me. "I guess you know what time it is," he said, looking at the man with a sleepy, angry expression. "I just took all the other boys to their beds, but I guess these parents will never take care of their own children, will they?" I heard the heavy rattling of a key being inserted into the lock and the clank of metal against metal as the door opened. "I guess one more won't hurt, and I'm glad we still have a bed left for him."

"Okay, here. I'm turning him over to you. I've got to finish with all the forms along with the other female officer downstairs before we can call it a night."

"All right, Officer. I'll take it from here," the burly man said. "Come on with me." He reached out, grabbing me strongly by the arm. "You look okay. Don't think you will need a shower, especially this time of night. You are clean, aren't you, son?" he asked, looking down at me. "Well…" He jerked at my arm as if I did not answer fast enough. "Did you bathe today?"

"Yes, sir," I quickly answered. "I took a bath today before we went to school."

"Well, that's better than some that they bring in here. Some smell to the point that I don't think they have had a bath in a week!" He walked me into another room, pushing and shoving me down onto a wooden bench that sat against the wall, angrily talking with a very scary voice. "You sit there for a minute while I get you a sheet to lie on." He rumbled through a steel-type cabinet, then said, "Come on with me. This will do for tonight." His grip on my arm was so tight I grimaced with pain as he led me across a large room containing windows all around the walls, and I noticed the bright streetlights below and the occasional sound of city traffic.

As he led me through another door, we entered a room that I noticed was lined with steel spring beds, and I could also see that most appeared to have a small person asleep on them.

"You sleep over here, young man, and I don't want to hear a peep out of you until the morning, do you understand?"

"Yes, sir." Then I thought but was a little afraid to ask that I really had to go to the bathroom badly. I had not gone since we left Uncle William's. "Sir," I asked, "can I please use the bathroom? I really must go!"

"Well, I guess." And he gave me a shove sharply toward the other end of the room, to a lit room. "There, that's the bathroom," he told me. "Hurry up. And don't you linger! And when you get through, this is your bed right here." He threw the sheet down onto the mattress.

"Yes, sir, I promise." I hurried toward the lit room at the other end.

Looking around, I could see him begin to walk toward the room we had previously left and could hear the door slam, and again the turning of the steel key. I quickly did what I had to do and went back into the room and spread the sheet over the bed, lying down. There was nothing else to cover with, so I adjusted the sheet and did the best I could to cover myself. As I lay there, I could see the dim lights in the other room as it was illuminated by the streetlights that shone through the windows. I was frightened beyond anything I had ever felt in my life. I lay there with my head partially covered with the single sheet he had given me and began to pray as I had with my grandmother and our aunt.

Juvenile Court, Memphis, Tennessee

There are times in a person's life when traumatic circumstances arise, and the mind has its own way of protecting itself. This self-protective response, I believe, is the mind's way of protecting the rest of the body. I don't know how it works, but I do know that it must undoubtedly work, or I would surely have been dead many times and years ago.

Whenever I was at the juvenile court, I would be with a lot of other boys. Some were very bad and I felt deserved to be at a place that they called juvenile court. It was a place for boys and girls that had done something very wrong in the eyes of the law.

I remember one night, I was awakened by the sounds of loud screaming and crying. I was in a long room lined with beds, and I looked to where the screaming was coming. The large man I had first met when I arrived several months earlier had a small naked boy and was holding him by one ankle upside down, swinging a large belt, hitting him throughout the boy's buttocks, legs, and back. The man was telling the boy as he violently struck his naked body that he should have gone to the bathroom as he suggested earlier, then he would not have soiled the bed.

I began to tremble as I witnessed this beating, covering my head with the small sheet that was given only for cover. This room was separated by a glass partition halfway up the wall from the adjoining room, which was used during daytime hours. I peered out from the sheet to see this large man change hands and grab the boy on the other leg and continue to beat him. I could hear the man tell the boy as he hoisted him up, swinging the belt with such fierceness that I could feel the air part from where I lay. The sound of the belt coming down with a loud slap across his nude body sent horror throughout every part of my body.

I heard the man yell out, "Now these bruises and welts have got to come from your fighting in the game room earlier today, don't they, boy?" Then I could hear another slap of the large belt as it hit the boy's body again. The boy was trying to get away from the man, but I could see that it must have been close to impossible. I could also see that the boy had what appeared to be a white rag crammed into his mouth. He was screaming during this brutal beating, but now as he thrashed around, I could see why his screaming was muffled and garbled. The man had stuffed the boy's soiled underwear into his mouth, causing the boy to gag. He was trying desperately to breathe and catch whatever air he could during the vicious beating.

Eventually, the man loosened his grip on the boy, and I could hear his body fall to the hard linoleum floor with a loud thump. As I cautiously peered out from under the sheet, I could see the boy pull the underwear from his mouth and throat, gasping for air. Gasping and crying, he, as much as I could tell, was trying to silence any loud noise that might be heard coming from him. I also felt tears streaming down my cheeks, feeling very horrified and sorry for him and the vicious beating that he just endured.

"Now, get up from there and take that dirty sheet and those panties you call underwear and go into the bathroom and shower yourself and clean everything that you have ruined!"

The boy scrambled and stumbled to his feet, attempting to suck back what had dropped from his nose. Gathering the sheet from the bed and his underwear, he began to walk around the large man. As he attempted to walk between him and the bed, the man gave the boy a shove with his foot, knocking the boy's body down to the floor, and he slid to the end of my bed. I covered my head and lay very still in fear, I thought, for my life. I could hear the boy get to his feet and stumble quickly past my bed and into the bathroom.

This is one of several instances that my mind will protect itself from to keep its sanity.

I was moved from there later by Mrs. Rains, the social worker, but have never forgotten that early-morning beating the boy had gotten, and I still wonder what had ever happened to him.

I remember when I was taken out the front door of juvenile court on Adams Street in Memphis, Tennessee. I looked back when I heard the voice of my sister Pat, who was coincidentally looking out the window from the second floor. I was being led by a lady social worker down the walkway toward a car that was parked next to the curb. Pat asked where I was going. Excitement could be detected in her voice at seeing her brother again after we had been separated from each other and our family for such a long time. The social worker, who we later knew as Mrs. Rains, opened the car door and asked me to get inside, then pulled a seat belt tightly around me. I looked over her shoulder, trying to see my sister Pat, whom I was hoping still peered out the window. I was also straining to fight back the tears that were beginning to form in my eyes. I always tried to be a big boy and not show that I was fearful of anything.

"Ma'am, could I ask you where we are going?"

"Son, that doesn't need to concern you right this moment, but if it will keep you quiet for a while, the court system of Shelby County has reassigned you and others that are not in the category of violent delinquents to other locations."

"What about my two sisters?" I asked. "They are not bad sisters. Can't they also come with us too?"

"Now, you just sit back and stop talking. Don't you worry about your sisters. They will go wherever the courts reassign them to also."

"Yes, ma'am, but do you think they will send them where you are taking me?"

"I don't know, but that is a possibility because they have told me to take you to St. Peter's Orphanage and they do have facilities for girls also."

When I heard these words, I felt a sense of relief that I might see my sisters soon.

When the lady spoke the words St. Peter's Orphanage, however, a fear came over me and I started to remember certain occurrences when I had been there before earlier in my life.

Her face was old and looked like a dried riverbed with lines deeply embedded in them as she looked down at me. She asked others in the room if I was the boy brought in last night by child welfare. "Yes, Mother Superior, this is the young lad," she said as she strolled over to where I was lying. As these strange women gathered around where I lay, an extremely sad, empty feeling came over me, and I felt tears well up in my eyes. I suddenly felt alone and began to wonder where my mother was and remembered her saying, "You're a mama's boy, aren't you?"

This was the last time I remember seeing my mother as she was walking and pushing me among some tall buildings.

There was a lot of noise—the honking of horns, people yelling—and a bad smell in the air made my eyes water. I felt sick to my stomach and thought I would vomit and lose what I had had to eat or drink previously. I was looking up at my mother and saw black mascara running down her face. The black mascara dripped from her eyes and ran down her cheeks, and I was aware that it wasn't because of the weather. It must have been in the wintertime because I had plenty of clothes on and a large scarf that I was wrapped up in that made it hard to move. I felt the cool air on my face as I attempted to look up and smile, sending out a chuckle now and then. I also felt a dribble of moisture running out the corners of my mouth, making it even that much colder.

She paused briefly, looking down at me, but then continued walking fast, managing a smile toward me. "You are Mama's precious baby boy. I love you so very much! Please forgive me, and always remember, no matter what anyone might say about your mother or what I'm about to do, your mother loves you very much!" I saw her chest rise as she took in a deep breath of air and wiped her face, smearing the mascara on her cheeks. She continued walking, passing through an alley lined with garbage cans filled to overflowing. The exhaust from heating ducts was sending a torrent of steam and a musty smell high into the air.

After walking for a while, we arrived in a parking lot lined with numerous large buses emitting diesel fumes, which made my eyes hurt. We entered a large terminal room, and I jumped when a large voice came over the intercom. "Buses for Nashville, Chicago, and New York are now boarding at gates 79 and 11. Proceed to the appropriate gate with your tickets. Thank you for riding with us, and have a good trip."

My mother set me down quickly next to a row of seats that contained small television sets and walked toward the ticket counters. Suddenly, the view of my mother was blocked by a large figure towering over me. "Hi, little man. What brings you here?" His clothes were soiled and torn, and his breath had the strong odor of what I now know to be Tennessee whiskey as he reached down to pet my head. There was some sort of crusty brown stuff smeared about his bearded mouth and chin. As he reached down and stumbled forward, a large amount of his brown spit began to drip out of his mouth, falling toward me. He stumbled and staggered over a row of seats, landing against another man's legs, which were stretched in the aisle as he slept. This other man woke up, pushed him off, and began to cuss. "You old [calling him a bad name]! Get out of here and off me before I kick your behind!" The smelly old man tried to regain his balance but was not fast enough and was shoved backward into where my mama had sat me down. His body hit the checkerboard floor with a loud thump. The stench from his soiled clothes rushed up to my cold nostrils. As he staggered to get up, his legs forced me out of my seat and backward under a row of seats. As I was forced backward, I looked up to see that a bottle was wobbling on top of one of the portable television sets, and that was the last thing I could remember. I felt my head being struck by the glass bottle falling from above me. Suddenly, I was covered with wetness that spilled from the bottle, drenching my face and chest, and my vision was blurred. I desperately tried to fight the dizziness and attempted to rise, looking for my mother, but instead, suddenly everything went black.

"Mother Superior, the boy was brought in early this morning, about 3:00 a.m.," Sister Anne replied. "He's such a precious little boy, don't you think?"

"Why is there a bandage around his head, Sister?"

"All child welfare said was that they were contacted by the police department. They told them that they had a small child at the bus station downtown that was found under some seats. My grace, Mother Superior, they told them the child had been there apparently over twelve hours, with no one seeing to him. It was told to the police by a bus attendant that a young lady was seen bringing a small child and setting him down around the time an argument between two men took place. One of the men involved in the argument that the police questioned was so consumed with alcohol they could not give anything that he said any type of relevance. He apparently was one of the homeless that frequents that place, panhandling. The police didn't take too much value in what he said and later just escorted him from the building."

"Goodness gracious!" Mother Superior gasped. "Okay, Sister Catherine, let's get this child all cleaned up. And he's obviously very hungry." Mother Superior looked at the other sisters standing nearby. "After you've given him something to eat, take him to the infirmary. Sister Martha will have to check his head to see the extent of the injury."

"Yes, Mother Superior. At once, ma'am."

I was taken down a dark hallway that seemed to go on forever. The walls were lined with paintings of religious events and stained glass windows. That made it impossible to tell if it was daylight or dark outside. I felt so alone and frightened. I had hoped I was having a bad dream and I would wake up with my mother smiling and tick-ling my belly. I longed to go back to sleep, but my head felt so badly. There was some sort of dried, crusty stuff on my face. I had found out later that it was my own blood. There were large rooms that lined the hallway as we walked along. I could hear other children laughing and talking, but I couldn't see them because of the darker rooms and hallway. Along the hallway where the walls met the ceilings, there was what appeared to be a faint glimmer of light coming from oil lamps running along the upper part of the walls. As we passed one of the rooms, I could see another lady dressed like the others, all in black, except for a white cloth around her face. She was standing in the doorway of one of the rooms, hitting her hand with a large flat stick. She yelled out suddenly, which made me jump in fear, "You children stop that whispering and get to sleep! Now, be quiet and go to sleep!"

As we continued down the hall, I noticed I was being pushed in a square glass container on wheels. Sister Catherine greeted the other sister that was pushing me, saying, "Good morning, Sister," as the other sister returned the greeting. Suddenly, I saw the sister in the doorway turn quickly and enter the room where the children's voices had been coming. "I asked you children to go to sleep!" Suddenly, I heard screaming and crying, along with a loud slapping noise. The screaming was joined by other loud screaming and a thumping sound, like bodies hitting a hard linoleum floor.

I felt my face go flush as sweat began to appear throughout my body. My breath came in short gasps as I attempted to hold back the knot in my throat. I felt so alone and frightened. I was in a strange place and didn't know how I had gotten there.

The hallway seemed to go on forever. We made right turns and then left turns, passing steel doors along the halls with small glass windows that contained wire embedded in the glass. I glanced up and noticed in several of the small windows there were faces peering through. As I looked at so many faces, I could see their eyes and the tears streaming down their faces. Their mouths were moving, but nothing could be heard through the thick steel doors and the glass. Eventually, I was pushed through a double door that opened in the middle. The room was dimly lit and had an alcohol and medicine smell. There were stretchers lined up against a wall and a large aluminum cylinder filled with hot water in the middle of the room. I could tell it was hot water because of the steam coming off the water.

"Good morning, Sister."

"Good morning," she replied. "This youngster was brought in early this morning, and Mother Superior wants you to clean him up and check his head where this bandage is."

"How old is this young fellow, Sister?"

"We really don't know. They haven't found out who he is yet and where he comes from, but just looking at him, I'd guess about four, five years."

"Gracious!" the sister gasped. "He has got something stained all over the side of his head and down to his shoulder. It has gotten all dried up. I'll take him now, Sister. I know you must see that he has a place to bed down. I will bring him up when I'm finished here."

When the other sister left the room, the sister turned and walked over to a large metal cabinet. She reached inside one of the drawers and got a pair of large rubber gloves, putting them on, which reached above her elbows. Then she put on a large black leather apron that also reached up under her neck and wrapped around her middle and tied in the back. She came over to me and began to take my clothes off, all the while singing something. Eventually, she stripped all my clothes off as I lay there naked. I was lying on this black leather stretcher, and it was cold to my naked skin. I attempted to get up, but as I did, she slapped me across the face, which made my ears ring and my vision of her begin to get blurred. She shouted at me, saying, "I didn't tell you to move or get up, now, did I? I need to take this bandage off your head. Just lie there and don't move until you're told you can move. Understand that, boy?" She squeezed me hard, with her pointing fingernails on both my cheeks.

As she shouted at me, her hand and fingers covered my mouth, making it very hard to breathe. And I couldn't breathe as her fingers were embedded in my cheeks, squeezing hard enough to make my lips pucker out. My cheeks where she slapped me hurt and stung. She began to unwind the bandage that was wrapped around my head, all the while humming something that I could not recognize until later. It was the battle hymn of the South Dixieland. Eventually, the bandage came off, and she let go of my head, which she had been cradling on her chest. My head fell back and hit the table as she let go. A flush of heat ran up through my chest and ended with what felt like an explosion all over the top of my head. "Well, boy, I don't know what all the fuss is about. This doesn't look so bad." She reached over on the counter behind her and got a bottle of liquid and some cotton. She opened the bottle and began to pour the liquid all over the top of my head. The liquid began to burn, causing me to burst out into a loud cry and bringing a flood of tears to my eyes. I attempted to rise in defiance of her holding my head down and her telling me not to move. She had poured alcohol all over my wound, and it began to drip into my eyes.

I was held down, with her fingernails embedded into the sides of my cheeks. Looking up, I attempted to shake the burning liquid from my eyes. Everything in the room began to spin around, causing my vision to be blurred. Though my vision was blurred, I could, however, make out the light overhead that glowed around her head, which made her look like the sun during a solar eclipse.

"Okay, young man, it will be okay now. I just need to clean some more around the small gash you got in your forehead." She patted more cotton balls soaked with alcohol. Afterward, she poured some other type of liquid that made a bubbling sound but didn't burn as before. He put a bandage on the cut, and I was picked up from under my arm and brought over to a large tub. As I looked down, I could see and feel the hot steam covering my nude body. She lowered me into this large tub with her hands holding me from under each arm. As my feet were lowered into the steam and water, I felt the scalding heat, which caused me to scream with pain. I attempted to kick my feet, raising them above the water to get away from the heat. The hot water was burning my feet and legs. I attempted to brace my legs on the side of the tub, and where my legs had submerged into the water were beet red, up to my thighs.

"All right, young man," she said. "We'll have to do this the hard way, then." After she spoke, I was held out from the edge of the tub and she let me go, causing me to fall backward, submerging me under the scalding-hot water. I regained my balance, and screaming from the top of my lungs, I attempted to climb out again. But before I could get my other leg over the edge of the tub, she grabbed me and forced me back into the middle of the water. I looked up at her and screamed while my entire body was covered with welts of red, tears streaming out of my eyes. I was screaming that the water was burning.

"Please let me out!" I pleaded. "I want my mama."

"If your mama wanted you, you wouldn't be here. So shut up! The sooner we get this over with, the sooner you can get out and go to bed." She picked up a brush and a bar of soap, dipping both into the hot water with her long gloves. With the foamy, hot water, she reached out and grabbed me behind the head, forcing me toward her. I was scrubbed from head to toe with the soapy brush, which felt like hard straw from a house broom. She had her left forearm wrapped around my chest, holding me tightly by the neck and head. The hot water was burning my skin, and I was kicking and thrashing around. She was taking the brush in her right hand and was reaching over, scrubbing me with it up and down my body. She would reach down, scrubbing me on my legs, coming up my body and in between my legs, and then she would scrub sideways. "You will not need this for a while," she said, scrubbing me up and down and then sideways between my legs.

I again attempted to get away from her, going to the other side of the tub. She reached out and grabbed me by the hair, pulled me back close to her, and picked me up high into the air, letting me go again. I fell back into the scalding water, submerging my entire body, and then came up and grabbed the side of the tub, again regaining my balance, attempting to get out of the tub again. She grabbed me by the top of my head, a handful of my hair in her hand, and slapped me across the face, making my ears ring.

I cried out, "Please, I'm sorry. I'll be good!"

As she held my head in her tight grasp, I looked up into her face and saw such evil piercing through those eyes, and those tight lips were pushed out in a defiant manner. It added to my horror. She then forced my head under the water. I stiffened my legs, pushing myself back up, gasping for air. She then forced me back under the water, holding me there for what seemed like an eternity. I stiffened my legs again, forcing my head above the water, screaming out, "Please, I'll be good! I just want to see my mama and go home. Where is my mama?"

"What did I tell you?" she said. "Your mother doesn't want you, or you would be with her now. So shut up, and let's finish this!"

I stood there with tears streaming down my face and mucus coming from my nose. I tried to be still in the scalding water. My entire body was streaked with red lines because of her scrubbing me with the brush. She had forced my head under the scalding-hot water, causing the soap and hot water to add a stinging to the welts on my skin that she was inflicting from the harsh brush. She then took a large bucket from the floor, filled it with water, and poured it over the top of my head.

"Okay, young man, let's get you out of there and put another bandage on you." The bandage she had put on me before had been washed away during the harsh scrubbing. I was bandaged again and was dressed in white shorts and a long white T-shirt. "Now, young man, let's get you a bed. You're big enough to walk." And she took my hand, pulled me through the double doors. She walked so fast I could hardly keep up and fell. My body twisted around while the sister kept a tight grip on my wrist and continued down the long hallway. "Well, boy, get up. Stop that foolishness!" She jerked me back to my feet. I felt a pop in my left shoulder while regaining my footing and had to run to keep up without falling again. I was running, trying to keep up with her down this long hallway. It seemed like it would never end until we finally came to a room where I heard what sounded like other children's voices.

"Sister, I have cleaned this boy up," she said to another lady standing in the room.

The other sister she was speaking to looked down at me and slapped her palm with a large ruler. "Well, I guess he looks tired enough to not give me any trouble, but if he does…" She paused. "I'll handle him." And she took the ruler, lifting my T-shirt, slapping my thigh with the ruler, which made me cry out in pain. I felt some large welts swell up on my thigh where she had hit me. Tears streamed down my face as she glared down at me. "Boy, that wasn't anything to cry about! There is a lot more where that came from that would make you cry."

I looked up at her, sniffling, tears streaming down my face. "Please, I'm sorry. I'll be good. I haven't done anything wrong," I said. "Where's my mom? Where am I? What is this place?"

"Shut your mouth, boy, and do what you're told! Speak when you're spoken to and not before. Do you understand? Do I make myself clear?" She raised the ruler again like she was about to strike me again.

I quickly raised my hands above my head, saying, "Yes, ma'am, I will," to shield myself from any further blows. I was trying to hold back the tears, looking up at her, and asked, "What do you want me to do?"

"Follow me, boy, and don't let me tell you again." She started back through the double doors again, where I hurriedly followed her.

I stumbled on my long T-shirt and fell on the checkered floor. I quickly got up, holding the long T-shirt in my right hand so as not to stumble again. I looked around the large room we had gone into and could see beds lined up in a row on both sides of the room. There were windows that lined the walls and streetlamps that gave a dim view of what seemed like hundreds of beds. As I followed her toward the end of the large room, I could see figures on most of the beds moving around. I could see other kids partially peering out from under the covers. She eventually stopped at one of the beds that were empty except for a blanket folded at the end.

I was standing there, waiting for her to say anything else, when suddenly she said, "Boy, what are you waiting for? Do I have to give you some persuasion?" She raised her ruler above her head.

I suddenly jumped up on the bed, sheltering my body with my hands and arms.

"Now, get to sleep!" she said, looking down at me with a slight chuckle, then turned and walked away. I watched her walk through the double doors at the far end of the room, where she turned on the other side and briefly looked through the small glass opening.

Once Again at St. Peter's Orphanage

When we arrived at the place the social worker, Mrs. Raines, called St. Peter's Orphanage, the horror of my previous experience suddenly flashed back through my mind, particularly the many terrible things that happened behind those steel gates. We arrived late in the day, and I could tell that Mrs. Raines was somewhat upset when she pulled her car around the large circular drive with hedges that contained a statue of what appeared to be a man with a flowing robe and hood draped around his neck.

"Come on, boy, get out of that seat." She quickly opened the passenger's door and proceeded to jerk me from the car. I was taken up the long rock stairs, and we walked through a large wooden door that made a loud creaking when opened. "Come on here now, boy!" She jerked my arm into a large room, turning around a corner and toward a long hallway. "Sister, are you there? I have another child for you. Where is the sister?" she said, jerking me down the hallway and looking into each of the rooms.

Suddenly, there was a voice behind us.

"Mrs. Raines, here I am."

Mrs. Raines suddenly swirled around with me in tow, causing me to stumble and fall toward the floor. "Oh! There you are, Sister! Get up, boy." She jerked me back to my feet. "I have another young man here that the court has sent over. Apparently, he was declassified and they sent him over here."

"Okay, Mrs. Raines, I'll take all the files and sort all the details out in the morning." She turned to me. "Come on with me, young man. We'll need to find you a bed for tonight, and all the other children will be happy to see a new face."

I turned to ask Mrs. Raines again about my sisters as I noticed she was going back through the door that we had previously entered. "Ma'am, please don't forget about my sisters as you promised!" I noticed the door slam behind her.

"Well, young man, you have two sisters, don't you?"

"Yes, ma'am. They are at the place that I just left. I think it was called the court."

She smiled down at me as I spoke. "Yes, young man. I'm sure that they will probably join you in a few days. Girls go for adoption quicker than boys, and we sure could use a few more little girls. I'll promise that I will see to it that your sisters get a nice place to stay."

I was taken to a large room that seemed familiar, as though I had been here before. It was lined with beds from one end to the other. The sister told me, "Take that bed there and I'll see you in the morning."

I lay there shivering, not knowing if it was from the chill of the night or from fright. I grabbed the blanket that was on the bed, pulling it up over my head, and lay back down. I heard voices coming from the room, which were very faint, but I couldn't understand them. I lay there very still, with tears beginning to well up in my eyes. I didn't know what was happening to me. It felt like a bad nightmare that I wished I could wake up from and this would all be a dream. In the darkness, with the blanket over my head, I began to cry; large tears started running down my cheeks. I found it hard to catch my breath and tried to stop any noise that might be coming out of my mouth from the crying. I didn't want anybody to hear me, because of what had happened before with these ladies; I wanted to just lie there underneath the blanket, feeling protected. I lay there thinking about my mother. I thought, *She must be very worried, not knowing where I might be. Everything will be okay. I just need some rest.* And eventually, I fell asleep with the cover tucked tightly over my head.

The next morning, I was awakened by a loud clanging noise and sat up quickly in the bed and looked toward the direction the sound was coming. I looked through the roll beds at the other end of the room and saw other kids. There was a mixture of ages, and I noticed they were sitting up in their beds, looking in my direction. The clanging continued and kept getting closer and closer. I finally saw a large woman dressed in black down to her feet. A white cloth covered her head except for her face. She began to walk up and down the rows of beds, looking from side to side, her arm waving up and down, making a loud noise with the bell.

"Okay, children, it's time to get up and get dressed before you all go to breakfast." She suddenly stopped near my bed and motioned for me to come out. "Well, come here, young man. You were brought to us early this morning, but we don't know what your name is." She again motioned for me to come toward her, her hand stretched toward me. I walked toward the end of the bed, and she asked me, "What's your name, young man? I'm Sister Mary Ann, but from this time forward, you will address me as Sister."

I answered her quickly, telling her, "My name is Hershel."

"Well, that's fine, young man." She then turned toward the other kids in the room. "Children," she said, "this young man's name is Hershel. Say hi, children."

All the other children responded by saying, "Hi, Hershel," in unison.

She turned toward another boy that was standing near the foot of the bed next to mine. "Billy, this is Hershel, and I want you to help Hershel today. Stay with him and show him how we do things around here."

"Yes, ma'am—I mean yes, Sister," he responded and turned to look at me. "Do you have any clothes?" he whispered.

"No, just this," I said, holding my T-shirt out from my chest toward him. "This is what they had given me last night."

"Okay, that's all right. Come on, follow me. I'll get some clothes for you from the sister that gives out our clothes." He grabbed my arm and hurried toward the door where Sister Mary Ann was walking, then called out to her. "Sister, this boy doesn't have any clothes with him."

"Well, all right, come with me, Billy, and we'll see what we can find for him," the sister responded. "You had better hurry because breakfast will be over soon."

I just stood there at my bed and watched them as they left. The other kids in the room were talking to one another and putting on clothes from a small trunk located at the foot of each bed. I saw some of them coming in and out of a passageway that was near the door through which the sister and Billy had left. I had to go to the bathroom and thought maybe that was where the passageway led.

I began slowly walking toward the other end of the room, crossing the room toward the passageway where some of the kids had been coming, and I had been right—it was a bathroom. When I finished, I returned quickly back to the room. I noticed one boy my size and age looking out of a window, his back to me. I could see that he was crying and had both his hands and his face pressed to the window. Tears were streaming down his face. The glass was all fogged up with his hot breath from crying. Moisture was running down the inside of the glass.

I walked over to him and asked, "Are you okay?" Even though I felt sadness within me and was frightened, not knowing where I was or what I was doing here, I desperately wanted to talk to him and, hopefully, to find a friend. My thought, I believe, was to reassure myself that everything was going to be all right.

He turned toward me with tears streaming down his face and managed to blubber out, "I'm looking for my daddy and mama." He sucked in another breath, still looking out the window. "I want them to come and get me and take me home!" He briefly looked at me then turned back to the window, pressing his face up against it, crying, "Mama, Daddy, where are you? I want to go home! Come and get me!"

I felt a knot in my throat, and tears began to fill my eyes and run down my cheeks. I attempted to stop the tears from flowing while walking back to the bed I had been assigned. I didn't know what else to do, so I sat there, waiting for that boy named Billy to get back. The room suddenly was empty except for me and the boy at the window. I could still hear him crying at the other end of the room.

Suddenly, the door at the entrance opened, and I could see it was Billy, followed by the sister he left with. They started walking in my direction, and I noticed Billy was carrying clothes in his arms. He continued walking toward me, but then the sister suddenly stopped in her tracks, noticing the small boy at the window crying. I heard her yell out, "Jimmy! Why aren't you with the other children in the cafeteria? I'm getting awfully tired of this behavior! Every time I see you, you're crying!" She reached down, grabbing his arm and force- fully jerking him toward her and away from the window. She started hitting him on his buttocks and lower back with a big flat stick that she carried around with her wherever she went. "If I've told you once, I've told you a dozen times. Your mom and dad aren't coming!" She continued to strike him with the stick.

He was running around, trying to break her grip on his arm, yelling while she was striking him. "I want my mother and daddy! I know they will come to get me! I want to go home! Please, Mama, Daddy, I want to go home!" he kept screaming out.

I was standing there, watching, and started to shake all over, frightened to death. Not knowing what to do or where to go, I just wanted to hide.

Suddenly, Billy came up to me and said, "Hey, boy, get these clothes on. Hurry! We got to get out of here and go." He handed me a pair of black shorts and a white T-shirt that had some sort of emblem on it with some writing.

I hurriedly pulled the shorts on and pulled off the shirt I had slept in and put the other T-shirt on.

Billy told me, "Pick up your clothes and come on." He started walking hurriedly toward the exit door, with me right behind him. When we got near the exit and close to the saint sister and the small boy, he sadly jerked free and began to run toward the other end of the room. He was yelling, crying, "No, no, stop, don't hit me anymore! I'm going to tell my daddy what you did!"

The sister was walking toward him, saying, "Little man, you're not going to tell anyone. You live here now. You're a ward of the state!"

Billy took my arm and said, "Come on, let's get out of here. You don't want to see any more." We hurried through the double doors, and Billy said, "Put those clothes in here," pointing toward a clothes hamper that was up against the wall.

We started walking down a long hallway that I remembered from the night before. It was lined with pictures of holy men and women, with small plaques that told who they were.

I asked Billy, "What is this place? And who are these ladies dressed all in black with just their faces showing?"

Billy answered by saying, "This place is for orphans that don't have families to take care of them. This place is called St. Peter's Orphanage for Children. The boy that the sister was whipping, his name is Jimmy. He's been here for about a week or so. He does that all the time, standing at a window, crying, looking out, thinking his mother and father are coming to get him."

"Well, aren't they coming to get him?"

"No, because Jimmy, his mom, and his dad, I overheard from the sisters talking, all were driving back from Nashville. His mother had to go see a doctor because of some stupid lump in her breast." I could see the frustration Billy had on his face as he continued to explain. "They were traveling back from Nashville to Memphis and were just a few miles from home." Billy paused again, and I could see his eyes begin to water with tears and could also see him fight all attempts to show his emotions. Then he continued, "His father apparently fell asleep while driving and ran off the road and hit a large tree. His mother, father, and three-year-old sister were all killed. Jimmy was asleep in the back seat and doesn't remember the accident. When they brought him here, I remember that he was asleep. When he woke up, I could hear him whining and asking for his mother and father."

As Billy was telling this terrible story about Jimmy, I felt overwhelmed with sadness and tears began to fill my eyes, all while we continued walking down the hallway.

We got to the end of the hallway and approached two large double doors. "This is the cafeteria where we eat," Billy said. "And I hope we are not too late because at certain times, they put everything away, and you can't get anything to eat until lunchtime at twelve o'clock." We both went in, and I noticed a large room filled with tables and several hundred kids seated around them. I followed close behind Billy to the right side of the cafeteria, where I could see the food was behind a glass container and in metal trays. As we hurried up to the counter, all at once one of the sisters stood up from one of the tables and blew a loud whistle.

"All right, children, line up over here. We don't want to be late for class."

Billy turned back to me with a frown on his face and said, "We're too late now," shrugging his shoulders at me. "We'll have to wait now for lunch, and I'm so hungry," Billy said.

The sister who had blown the whistle looked at both of us and asked, "Where have you two been? I guess you didn't want any breakfast, did you? Now, get back in line. And be quick about it!" She clapped her hands as she looked down at us with a slight grin on her lips.

"Yes, Sister," Billy said, turning to look at me, saying, "Come on and follow me. We got to go to class now."

I followed him to the end of one of the lines with the other kids. One of the other sisters began to walk toward the double doors, followed by a row of kids from one of the tables. We all walked through the double doors, one row of kids at a time, followed by another sister. We marched out line after line until eventually the entire row of kids was outside the building. I looked around and saw a large black wrought iron fence that encircled the entire courtyard and complex. As we all stood there, I looked around behind me at the building we had come out of. It was a large dark castle-like place, something from the Dark Ages or Knights of the Round Table, which I had been reading stories about.

On the other side of the fence leading from the cobblestone driveway through the iron gate, there was a large street sign that read, "Poplar Avenue." This large street was joined by another large street, adjoining other traffic going in all directions surrounding this large complex. I could see a large playground containing monkey bars, a seesaw, and a large sandbox. In the middle of the yard, on the driveway coming from the street, there was a large statue and a fountain with water flowing out of the top and running down to a pool at the bottom. The statue was made to look like the sisters, with a long robe-like dress, with only their faces showing. The other statue in the fountain looked like a man with a robe wrapped around him and a scarf over his head. The statue of the man had a smile on his face, looking down at the sisters. They were kneeling at his feet, looking up at him with their hands clutched in a praying-like manner.

I asked, "Billy, who is that in the statue?" pointing at the statue of the sister.

"Oh, that's St. Mary, Jesus's mother," Billy said.

Suddenly, I was startled as we heard a loud screech that had come from the whistle one of the sisters was blowing. Everyone in their individual lines stopped walking, and one of the sisters started walking toward the end of our line. While she walked briskly toward where we were standing, her black dress, swirled out in front of her with each step she took. "Children," she started, "we all know that when we are filing to and from class, there is to be no talking. Now we just stand here and wait until we find out who it was that had been so disobedient." She walked back to the head of the group briskly, and I could see the very stern look on her face, her black dress almost dragging on the ground.

She walked back and forth all the way down to the end of the row and then all the way back up again. She had this long stick in her hand as she walked. Suddenly, she looked around at all the children in our row and focused her attention on me and Billy. Then she started walking briskly toward us until she got to where we were and then stopped. She tapped her stick on her leg, looking down at us.

"Now, Billy, you have been here long enough to know our rules."

"Yes, ma'am—I mean, Sister. It wasn't me. It was this new boy, Hershel." He pointed directly at me. She looked from Billy's frightened face to mine.

"Billy," she said with a sharp voice, "step out here. Aren't you supposed to be assigned to Hershel, showing him the way we do things here at St. Peter's?"

Billy started to say, "Yes, Sister—"

But before he could get another word out, she briskly brought the ruler down in front of her robe-like black dress and looked sternly at Billy, stopping him from saying another word, pointing her hand and ruler at him. "Step farther out here, Billy." She pointed the ruler down in front of her at the pavement. The sister stepped around him, walking toward me. "Hershel, you're new here, and I'm sure you're not going to try our patience." She reached out and grabbed my cheeks, pulling my face up to where I was looking directly into her face. "I can assure you, you will follow our rules here one way or another. Step out here. Fall in line behind Billy." She reached for and forced Billy's head with her left hand down and between her legs and held him there. The sister ordered all the other sisters to have their lines turn around so they could view what was about to occur. She raised the stick above her head and brought it down several times on his back and backside.

I stood there watching this round stick come up and down, striking Billy about his back. I could see large red welts swelling up in those places. Billy was jerking around, trying to get away, but she held him tight between her knees. When she did lose her grip, Billy fell onto the hard pavement, barely catching himself with his hands.

"Get up from there, boy, and get back in line before I give you some serious discipline!"

Billy had tears streaming down his cheeks and was reaching up with both hands, attempting to reach behind toward his back to rub the soreness and soothe the pain.

Billy was crying, and I could see mucus coming out of each of his nostrils. I could also sense that he was attempting to quiet the loud noise he was making. His shoulders were bending back in another attempt to soothe the stinging of the welts on his back. All the other kids pretended to not pay any attention and just stood there like statues, staring straight toward Billy, as though they dare not lose their place in line or their erect stance. They just kept staring straight ahead toward the other sister, who had positioned herself toward the rear of the line, between them and us.

Then the sister that had just let go of Billy looked down at me with a bright smile on her face. She had a twinkle and glazed look in her eyes, as though she had just opened the most beautiful Christmas gift anyone could have ever given her. With this big smile across her face, she walked toward me, carrying this big stick and tapping her thigh with it. "Young man," she said, "your hand, give me your hand." She then reached out toward me.

I raised my right hand toward her, and she took it, grabbing my wrist, and I could feel the point of her sharp fingernails as they dug into my wrist. She turned it over with my palm facing up, looking at me, and stated firmly, "Young man, we don't speak while we are in line! We must be silent. We do not speak unless we are told to. If there is a question, we will raise our hand and wait until we are acknowledged to speak. Is that clear, young man?"

She raised the ruler and brought it down with such force onto my hand that I felt it all the way through my body, down to my feet. The sister struck my palm so fast and so many times I lost count.

"Now, you two get back in line, and I don't want to hear another sound from anyone, especially you two." She then looked around and marched defiantly back to the head of the line. She was viciously glaring at all the children as she stomped back to the front. It was as though there was some other person or thing that had taken possession of her body. Her face had somehow taken on a different appearance. Her face was visible from the robe and cloth on her head that she wore, which showed an evilness that I could not describe, and that frightened me. Her face was red, and the wrinkles that were there before seemed to be filled with a chalky dark-blue color. Her eyes were red, and their veins seemed to be bleeding. They were also glazed over and seemed to protrude from their sockets. When she eventually arrived in front of all the children, she blew her whistle, turning around with her back to us. We all began to march, following her. We kept marching across this huge compound that eventually led to another building.

When a different sister blew her whistle, all the lines came to an abrupt stop. Two of the children at the front of their lines quickly left their places and went to two big heavy wooden doors at the front of the building. The doors were held open as we march through them in single file. One line went to the right down the long hallway, while the other line went down the opposite hallway to the left. As each line went down their respective hallways, we each broke off and went into different rooms. Billy grabbed my arm and pulled me into a room one of the sisters had entered. Billy led me toward the back of the room, where we sat at one of the small wooden desks behind the other children. At the front of the room was a large black wooden table that a sister walked over and stood behind. Behind her was a black chalkboard that covered the entire wall. Above that were the alphabets, which I would find out later would help me learn to read.

The sister began to write things on the big black chalkboard while she spoke. Billy quickly handed me a piece of paper and a pencil, putting them down in front of me, then, just as quickly looked back to the front of the room. I didn't know what to do, so I just sat there like Billy, looking toward the front, where the sister stood. Periodically, I would look out of the large window next to me. I could see another large brick building that joined this building. On the top of the building, on the corners, there was some sort of scary-looking animal. This beast-type animal had long hooked teeth sticking out of its furry-looking mouth, which curled down toward his clawlike feet. There were individual beasts on each of the buildings, and their big claws were perched on each corner.

The sister spoke to a little girl in the front of the room and asked her to lead us in the Pledge of Allegiance. When the little girl stood up, the rest of the class also stood up, and we each put our right hand on our chest as we all spoke together, reciting the pledge. When we had finished, the sister instructed us, "Okay, children, take your seats." She looked at the little girl and smiled, then turned and walked toward the blackboard.

While staying at St. Peter's Catholic Orphanage for Children, we did everything as a group. When we went to the cafeteria to eat, we all did it together. There were certain times during the day that were allowed as bathroom time; then again, we all went together as a group. We didn't go to the bathroom when our bodies needed, only when the sisters allowed us to. Whenever the time came for us to go to class, go out to play, or go to the bathroom, it was all done as a group and in single file. I don't remember exactly how much time I spent at St. Peter's Orphanage, but it did seem like an eternity. I was a quiet, shy child and tried not to attract attention to myself for fear of some sort of punishment.

The children in the orphanage with me were of different ages and sizes. The larger children, some in their early or middle teens, were kept in another building, and periodically we would see them come and go in the compound's front yard.

Most of the activities at St. Peter's were led by sisters of the Catholic faith, but sometimes we would see a priest, who would be dressed in black pants, black shirt, black suit coat, and white collar.

After dinner and bath at night, on some occasions, one of the sisters, Sister Alice (who, as I can remember, was a very sweet lady), would take individual groups at certain times on pretend excursions throughout the orphanage. On a certain night, our group section was led by Sister Alice off the main corridor to a large room where there was a TV and where we sometimes took our nap. She was kind and very sweet; it was refreshing after being frightened all day by the other sisters at St. Peter's Orphanage. When she spoke, her voice was so soft and gentle.

"My name is Sister Alice, and you can call me Sister Alice, okay? But don't tell anyone!" She then put her index finger up to her lips, smiling and looking around the room at each child. We were not allowed to address the sisters at that time by their individual first names. Her face, which protruded from the headcloth she had on, I can remember to this day had an angelic glow about it. Her eyes were so blue I could almost see the ocean in them. She made us all feel so relaxed. Her smile was so bright and cheerful, and her eyes were a deep blue, almost like mine. I felt so close to her, sort of like having a mother again. All the children felt the same way I did about Sister Alice. This excited all of us because of the way that she had in expressing herself as she read a story.

As she read to us, we gathered around her feet on the floor. She looked at each of us with her bright smile; her eyes would sparkle, accentuating the story as she read. Some of the children would try to scoot closer to her, smiling up at her with affection. When she read, she also used her bright eyes to excite each one of us and to explain certain topics. In her expressive gestures, she would reach down and embrace some of us. I think she was aware that all of us kids were starved for affection. Some of us knew how grateful we were to be able to have such a sweet person soothe some of the emotional hurt we all felt. She could see and sense it every time she'd embrace us or just give us a pat on the head or shoulder, which would always bring a bright smile to our faces. Sister Alice always showed happiness with her bright smile and pearly white teeth, and I could tell she enjoyed giving all of us a little normality to our lives. She would somehow soothe all our hurts. The time I spent with her, even to this day when I think about it, brought a calm peace within my spirit. Sister Alice had us all believe that amid all the frightening days and nights we spent at St. Peter's Orphanage, there was a God. She told us that our heavenly Father was watching over all of us, keeping us safe.

After reading and watching TV, Sister Alice instructed us, "All right, now, children, we got to get you all to bed. Mother Superior will expect all of you to have your proper sleep." All of us children scrambled to our feet and tried to get around her, hugging her, trying to get all the affection we could, getting as close as we could. She reached down from her chair, putting her arms as far around all of us as she possibly could. We all enjoyed having a big group hug. Then she would usher us down the hall through the double doors and into the sleeping auditorium.

Each of us got to our beds, and Sister Alice led us in a bedtime prayer, as she did each night. "Our Father, who art in heaven..." When we finished our nighttime prayer, we all got up from a kneeling position and lay down in our separate beds.

One day, while I was in the playground, I was standing at the big wrought iron fence that surrounded the compound. I remember just standing there and looking out, holding on to the bars, as I often did from time to time, daydreaming and looking at the traffic travel up and down the streets. Thoughts crossed my mind, as they often did, and I wondered if one of the cars had my mother or father inside; I was just hoping to possibly get a glimpse of either of them so I could yell out through the fence to tell them where I was.

As I stood between the fence and a large hedge, I was hidden from the other children and the sister/nun that had been watching over us. I was so depressed emotionally, as I often was, and had been crying but did not want anyone to see me, for fear of the punishment I might receive. I remembered little Jimmy crying for his mama and daddy and the violent beating he received, and I did not want the same. I was daydreaming and had not heard the nun blow the whistle for us to come inside.

When I wiped the tears from my face and gathered my thoughts, looking around, I realized I was the only one left on the playground. I still didn't want to leave the fence, however. I kept staring at the cars and people, hoping and praying as I always had. I was also wondering if I could get outside the fence and begin a search for my parents. I looked around the compound and knew that the only way out was through the heavy steel gate that was kept closed and was only opened when a car or other vehicle entered. As I looked out and across the fence at all the traffic traveling up and down the intervening streets, the realization of what Mother Superior might do to me when she found out that I was not with our group hit me. I stood for a while, daydreaming. I realized how much trouble I must be getting myself into and began to run toward the main building. Just as I was about to reach the walkway and around some large hedges that led to the main building, I ran into a large man that I had seen supervising a group of older children.

"Well, young man, who are you?" he asked. "Aren't you supposed to be with the sisters in building 1?" I didn't think he was a priest, because he didn't have on the traditional clothing of a priest. He looked down at me with a large grin on his face. I was relieved to see a smile because it took away the frightened, worried feeling I had for not being where I was supposed to be.

"Yes, sir, I am. I was playing alone, and the next thing I knew, everyone was gone."

"How long, boy, have you been here at St. Peter's Orphanage?" he asked.

"I'm not sure, sir, but it seems like a long time. I should be going home any day now because my mother will be coming to get me."

"Well, son, I think I've seen you before, and I know you've been here long enough to know the rules. Better get inside before the sisters know that you're missing."

"Yes, sir," I said, and I began to rapidly rush past him.

As I did, I felt a hard blow to the back of my head that sent me facedown into the concrete walkway. I started to get up and noticed there on the concrete walkway was a stain from my injury. I felt my face with my hand and noticed that there was wetness coming from my lip, and it was dripping down my chin onto the front of my white shirt.

"Stand right there, boy!" I noticed him start to break off a limb from one of the hedges and pull off the leaves. "Boy!" he shouted while towering over me. "The Bible says, 'Spare the rod and spoil the child.' We don't want to do that, do we?" he said with a slight grin on his face. "I first knocked you down just to get your attention, because some of you kids are as stubborn as a mule, and we all know how stubborn mules can be, don't we? Now, get up from there and receive your required punishment, boy!"

I tried to get to my feet when all at once he reached down and jerked me by the left arm and wrist, hurling me off my feet. He still had a smirk on his face as he said, "Son, I told you to get up! You must move faster than that. No wonder you're out here all by yourself—you are too slow! I guess we will have to send you to that special, slow mental class with all those others." He said this with that same smirk on his face. He raised his hand and brought the stick down across my back and continued striking me from my back down to the entire length of my legs. Every time the switch struck me, it sent horrendous stings that felt like bolts of lightning coursing through my body. My entire back, buttocks, and legs were covered with large red welts.

I attempted to jump away from him every time he struck me with the switch, and I could hear the air whistle and snap as it parted. This seemed to make him angry, and each time he struck me, it felt harder and harder, faster and faster. It was stinging all over my back and everywhere else I was being struck. The wet red liquid began to trickle down from most of the welts and stripes that lined up and down my body wherever the switch struck. I was screaming at the top of my lungs, begging and pleading for him to stop.

"Please, sir, I'm sorry. I won't do it again. Please stop. I'm sorry!"

He finally let my hand go, and I fell quickly away from him, hitting the concrete sidewalk very hard. "Get up from there, boy, or do you need some more discipline?"

I jumped up, running to the door of the main building. As I ran, I was screaming out in pain, rubbing my legs with both hands, trying to soothe the hurt. My entire body, my back, my legs, every-where was stinging.

My whole body felt like it had been attacked by a swarm of hor-nets. I looked down at my hands and my legs, and both were streaked with warm bright-red liquid and smeared where I had been rubbing, trying to soothe the hurt. My hands were also coated with a warm liquid when I rubbed, trying to soothe the pain. I had gotten to the main building, basically falling through the door onto the floor. I sat there crying, rubbing my legs, still trying to soothe the stinging.

When I got up, I proceeded to walk toward the bathroom in the main hallway. I was wiping my face with my hand, smearing tears and mucus that had drained out of my eyes and nose. Every step I took sent excruciating pain throughout my body.

I went up to one of the deep sinks and climbed up on the stool that was positioned there to look at myself in the mirror. My face was flushed, and my eyes were red from the beating. As I stared into the mirror at my reflection, I could not seem to stop crying because of the horror of what had just taken place outside. I was shocked to the point that at that time I thought my entire body, both physical and emotional, was traumatized beyond repair. After what seemed like an eternity, I attempted to gather myself emotionally and filled my hands with cool water, splashing it onto my face. I took one of the white cotton facecloths, soaked it with cool water, and began to clean all the injuries that had been cut by the switch. The water stung each place I wiped, so I tried to fill the cloth with water and just wring it out over the welts. Each time I squeezed the cloth out over the welts on my legs, the sink washed the injuries and stained water down the drain.

Still, I was crying. I could not understand why I had been beaten so severely. I kept thinking to myself, Why? What had I done so badly that caused this strange man to hate and beat me this way? He seemed to enjoy taking pleasure in his brutality and verbal assault on me.

Germantown Foster Home

There had been so many orphanages that I and my sisters stayed at during these critical times in our early childhood that they would be too many to mention or write about. However, I will choose to mention their names first: juvenile court on Adams Street, St. Peter's Orphanage, Porter-Leith Orphanage, and then the last home that I stayed in, which was the most influential, leaving a morally sound structure within my mind and body. This foster home was located off Hacks Cross Road outside of Germantown, Tennessee, which was a suburb of Memphis, Tennessee.

I was again taken from St. Peter's Orphanage by the same woman who had brought me there. One day, one of the Catholic sisters came out to the playground, where all the children had gathered to play. I watched her in the distance as she stopped to talk with the sister who had been watching over us while we played, who was sitting on one of the concrete benches surrounding the compound. As they spoke, I saw the seated sister tell the other sister something while pointing in my direction. The standing sister then shouted out to me, "Young man! Come here, please!" She turned back to the seated sister to ask her my name, then turned back to me and shouted again, "Young man! Hershel! Come here, please!" I was still standing, looking at her as if I weren't sure if she was talking to me, when she called out again, "Yes, *you*, young man. Hershel, you, come here immediately!"

I replied, "Yes, Sister," and began walking toward the two women.

"Hurry up, young man! There is someone waiting for us with Mother Superior in the main office," she said impatiently.

I started to run the short distance between us because she had already turned away from me and started walking. We were headed toward the children's living quarters. I began to pray with every ounce of my inner being and caught up with the sister. "Did my mama or dad come to take me home?" I asked excitedly.

She paused a moment, then reached down for my arm, and then my hand, holding it tightly. "I'm not sure, young man. I was just asked by Mother Superior to bring you and your belongings to the main building," she said, and we continued to the living quarters.

My thoughts and prayers had finally been answered! I thought. I was going home! I was excited, gathering my things from my locker in the living quarters. The sister stood closely, tapping her foot and watching me as I packed. "Boy," she said, "make sure that you take everything and put it in that cloth bag because if you forget anything, it will be donated to the church."

I answered quickly, "Yes, ma'am," but I really didn't care; I was just in a hurry to see my mama and daddy. I wondered if they had already gotten my sisters.

The sister looked around the room and asked, "Is that everything?"

"Yes, ma'am, Sister!" I answered excitedly. "That's all. I have everything. I'm ready to go!" I said, taking the cotton sack from my hand and swinging it around so she could grab my other hand. She began pulling me alongside her.

The exit we walked toward led to a long hallway that connected the main building and the children's quarters. I did not mind that she was walking so fast and dragging me along, because I also wanted to get to where we were going quickly.

As we entered the room that Mother Superior used as her study and holy prayer space, the sister spoke. "Mother Superior, here is the young man that you sent for."

I had expected to see my mama and daddy waiting for me in the room with Mother Superior, but I saw immediately that there in the room were two women with her, neither of whom was my mother. The excitement began to fade from my face as I realized one of the women in the room was the very social worker who had brought me here. She was sitting across the desk from Mother Superior and beckoned to me. "Come here, young man." She tapped her long fingers on a place at the right front side of Mother Superior's desk, where she expected me to stand. I stood quietly in a daze, completely confused by what was going on. It was then that I looked over toward the other woman in the room and recognized her as Mrs. Raines. I remembered her name so easily because it sounded like rain falling from the sky, and I associated it with that.

"Oh, hi, ma'am," I said when I recognized her. "I remember you."

She did not answer and instead just looked from me to Mother Superior, who snapped, "Young man, you have been here long enough to know that you don't speak unless you are addressed to do so!"

"Yes, ma'am—I mean Mother Superior," I answered politely.

She stood quickly and angrily slammed the ruler that she carried with her always down onto the desk, making a loud slapping sound. "We do *not* speak unless we are *addressed* to do so!" she repeated, glaring at me icily over the desk. Then she slowly sank back into her seat. "Mrs. Raines," Mother Superior said without turning from me, "I see that all the necessary documents are to transfer this young man to another facility." She finally looked away from me to face the other woman, but when I heard this, my heart sank.

Any hope that I was going home was shattered. My eyes began to tear up. All that I wanted was to beg and plead to be reunited with my family, but I dared not say or ask anything; instead, I focused on trying to stop the trickle of tears that ran down both of my cheeks and dropped onto the tile floor. I did not want the wrath of Mother Superior, and I knew that she would not appreciate anyone crying without a "real" reason. While the two women continued talking, I attempted to slowly raise one hand at a time to my face to wipe the tears away, before they were noticed.

Mother Superior stood and walked around the desk to stand between Mrs. Raines and me. "Let us pray for a good *future* for this young man and for you also, Mrs. Raines," said Mother Superior, reaching out to hold on to each of our hands. She then began saying her Hail Marys with the string of black rosary beads that always hung around her neck, touching each one in turn.

Again, I found myself going to some unknown place with this woman that I only knew as Mrs. Raines. "Ma'am," I asked, hoping she wouldn't get mad at me for speaking to her, "where are you taking me now?" I looked over at her as she drove. "I was sure hoping," I told her, looking over and up at her as she drove, "that when I got to Mother Superior's office, my mother and daddy would be there to take me home."

"I'm sorry, young man, but I'm taking you to another place. I'm sure you will enjoy it much more than the orphanage, though. Now, you just sit back. We will be there shortly."

"Yes, ma'am," I said, settling back into the seat.

During the drive, I began to wonder again about where my family was. I also worried that if they kept moving me around, I might never see my sisters again. I began thinking back on a time when I had stayed at juvenile court, the last time that I had been able to speak with my sister. I had been leaning against the window one day when I heard voices coming up from the second floor, below me. I also remembered a woman telling me once that the second floor was where my sisters would be taken. I started to say something out of the window, in hopes that one of the voices below might belong to my sister Pat, or that whoever was down below might possibly know her.

The voice answered back, "Hello? Where are you?"

Excited that they had heard me, I answered, "I'm up here! Do you know my sister Patricia?"

"Bubba! Is that you?" a voice yelled back from the window below.

"Yes, sissy, it's me!" I answered with relief as I pressed my face against the screen.

Each day we had talked with each other this way, from one floor to another. It had brought comfort to both of us. But thinking of those times now did not bring me the same comfort. It seemed like remembering times with my family only allowed the sadness and the tears to worsen; however, those memories were all that I had left to hold on to.

After driving for a while, Mrs. Raines pulled off the blacktop road onto a smaller gravel drive. "Here we are, young man. This will be your new home for a while."

I looked around and realized that this place was much different from the bustling city of Memphis. We were out in the country, facing a stately brick home surrounded by large trees in all directions. When the car came to a stop behind the house, I also noticed a beautiful lake peeking through the trees down the hill from where we were parked.

"Let's get you settled in, young man," she said as she opened the door for me.

I saw a small group of boys about my age playing in the yard, and I recognized one to be a boy named Donald, whom I had known from St. Peter's Orphanage and the juvenile court. As Mrs. Raines led me by the hand to the door at the back of the house, I yelled out loud enough for him to hear, "Hey, Donald! Are you staying here now? I thought your mama had come to take you home when you left the other place?"

When Donald heard me, he ran toward me, leaving the other boys looking on. He smiled like he'd found his long-lost best friend. "Hershel! Wow, are they bringing you here to live too?"

Mrs. Raines jerked my arm and said, "Hush up now. I don't have all day. You two will have plenty of time to get acquainted later. Now, come on!"

Entering the house, we were met by a nice lady that greeted us with a smile. She said to Mrs. Raines, "I've been expecting you." Then she turned to look at me, saying, "This must be the boy they spoke about."

Mrs. Raines answered, "Yes, Mrs. Hildebrand. This lad's name is Hershel. He's been moved about from place to place for some time now, and the court system felt he would be a good candidate for this new project and home that the Optimist board has financed."

The lady spoke with a cheerful smile. "Hello, there, Hershel. It's so good to have you here! We have three other boys your age that I am sure you will enjoy getting to know, but for now, let me show you where you will be staying." She led me past a large brick fireplace, down a short hall that had two doors next to each other. "This will be your bedroom," she said, indicating the door on the left. "Make yourself comfortable, and go ahead and unpack your things on that bed over there. We will sort it all out after I speak with Mrs. Raines. The bathroom is through that door," she said, pointing toward the other end of the room.

"Yes, ma'am," I answered.

"What a polite little boy, Mrs. Raines!" she said, turning to face her, and walked back into the hallway, where the two of them began speaking quietly.

Looking around the bedroom, I noticed a long window that ran along the wall near the ceiling, bringing in the bright sunshine from outside. There were two single beds in the room, and when I was walking into the bathroom, I noticed that the adjoining bedroom was identically decorated. The bathroom had two showers on one wall and two bathroom stalls on the other, along with a long mirror over a counter with two sinks.

For some reason, a deep sadness came over me, I think, because it reminded me so much of a "real" home, and there was a sense of permanence to it. I was overwhelmed by it all, so I ducked into one of the bathroom stalls and began to cry. The large tears flowed down my face and into the toilet, making small ripples with each drop. I began to pray, as I had so many times before. "God, please, why can't I go home with my mama and daddy?" I offered the prayer, whispered under my breath, and stayed there crying until I thought nothing was left, feeling exhausted.

Then I heard a man's voice. "Hello, are you in there, young man?"

I attempted to wipe my face with the tissue that was in the stall with me. "Oh, yes, sir," I said, attempting to sound as though I had not been crying. "I'm here."

"Okay, young man, I'll wait for you outside with the other boys. When you get finished, come on out and join us."

Cleaning my face hurriedly, I splashed some water on my cheeks to look more normal. I regained my composure and found my way to the back door, which I had come into earlier with Mrs. Raines. Once I walked outside, I saw an older man surrounded by the many boys that I had seen playing outside earlier. "Hey, Hershel, Come over here!" It was Donald, calling out to me from the group.

As I got closer, the older man reached out his hand toward me. "Hershel, I'm Mr. Hildebrand. We are all so glad to have you here, and I understand you already have met Mrs. Hildebrand when you arrived," he said, smiling kindly. "The boys and I were just discussing how we can improve the landscape around here. As you can see, the driveway hasn't been finished, so our first group project will be to lay some concrete, and later we will sow some grass seed."

Mrs. Hildebrand preferred that we address her as Mom and Mr. Hildebrand as Papa. They, however, never tried to take the place of our biological parents; they simply wanted the household to be as closely bonded and as loving as possible. The years that I spent with them were structured like a normal family environment. Mr. Hildebrand would teach us many things, always with love, but rules were expected to be followed.

The Hildebrand home was in Germantown, Tennessee, just south of Memphis, adjacent to Hacks Cross Road, in a beautiful country setting. Just down the hill were two lakes, one of which I had seen through the trees when I first arrived. The lakes were separated by a levee and canal that attached the two together. Across the larger of the lakes was a park with a building that accommodated meeting for the Optimist Club and other organizations. Mr. Hildebrand, "Papa," instructed us to never go to the lake's edge. He lectured us on the dangers of poisonous snakes and the possibility of drowning. Though you could see the lakes from the house on the top of the hill, there were so many trees scattered over the property that there was no clear view of the lakes' edges.

Mrs. Hildebrand, if my memory serves me correctly, was a retired schoolteacher, and she did her best to teach us proper etiquette, correct grammar, table manners, and the proper way to place silverware at a table setting, and how to act like a gentleman. My life at the Germantown foster home would take on a dramatic change in the lifestyle with which I had become accustomed in the other state and federal government institutions. This home, I would discover as I looked back, was a blessing from the heavenly Father. In the months and years to come, the Hildebrands and others associated with the Optimist Club would provide the true building blocks that molded me into what I consider to be the good, moral person that I am today.

At the time of my arrival, there were only four boys that lived in the home, including myself, two in each room. That changed later, and before I left, there were either six or eight boys altogether. We had a system for keeping our belongings separated; we would use color-coded strips of cloth to label all our clothing and toiletries. My color was blue, so every pair of underwear, every towel, and the toothbrush that belonged to me were labeled in blue.

We went to school at Germantown Elementary, and the first year that I lived there, I was in the third grade. The atmosphere of the public school was so different from the one I experienced at St. Peter's Orphanage. Life surrounding our education felt so normal. We caught the bus to and from the school each day, and our homelife was separate from our school life.

On November 22, 1963, I went to school in a great mood, excited because it was my birthday, and I knew that Mom Hildebrand would be having a birthday party for me, as was her custom for all the boys in our house. However, at some point during the day, classes were stopped and there was a buzz of commotion among the teachers. The students were all told that we would be leaving school early because something terrible had happened to the president.

I didn't exactly understand the significance at that time, and I excitedly spoke to my teacher, telling her that today was my birthday. "Yes, Hershel," she answered. "Now, go back to your seat. We are going to turn on the speakers to explain what happened to our president before we dismiss class." She seemed very depressed, and I thought I detected tearstained red eyes.

Just then, the speakers that hung in the corners of the room screeched loudly, then a sound like a television broadcast came through them. Walter Cronkite's voice filled the room.

"From Dallas, Texas, the flash apparently official. President Kennedy died at 1:00 p.m., central standard time, 2:00 p.m. eastern standard time, some thirty-eight minutes ago. Vice President Johnson has left the hospital in Dallas, but we do not know where he has proceeded. Presumably, he will be taking the oath of office shortly and become the thirty-sixth president of the United States."

Looking up from behind my desk, I watched as my teacher's hand was lifted to her open mouth as she gave a gasp in disbelief. She then tried to regain her composure over the shock of what she had heard. She looked around the room, trying to comfort us. "I don't want any of you to try to understand the magnitude of what just happened at this time, students. When you get home, I'm very positive that each of your parents will explain it all to you."

Again, the speakers screeched. "Attention, all students. This is your principal. Due to the tragic events of today, all further classes have been canceled. Your teachers have been instructed to assemble all the students in the appropriate areas, where either the buses will be waiting or parents will pick up their children. Today is Friday. We pray that class will reconvene Monday, November 25. Have a good weekend, and may God bless all of you."

During the bus ride home, there was a sense of solemn quiet unlike any other day. The radio was heard talking about events that occurred in Dallas, Texas. As we traveled on the bus to our separate locations, all that could be heard in the distance was the bus driver changing from channel to channel, apparently trying to keep updated on the events in Dallas, Texas. As the school bus came up to a screeching halt at our location, Donald, Jimmy, Michael, and I stepped off the bus and began to walk up the short gravel driveway to the back of the house. The excitement I had felt earlier in the celebration of my birthday was gone to some degree due to the events of the day. However, through the years of trauma in past events, I had learned not to expect good thoughts to take precedence over other events, but I still, in the back of my head, had hopes and dreams that my birthday would turn out to be a good one.

As we entered the house, however, I was surprised to see a huge cake on the dining room table adorned with candles that had not yet been lit. Mama Hildebrand asked that we change out of our clothes in the laundry room, which was where we always changed our school clothes, and into play clothes. As we all stood there in our underwear and tossed our clothes into separate hampers, I looked up at Mama Hildebrand and could see she had a big smile on her face. I asked, "Mama, did you hear what happened?"

"Yes, Hershel, but today is your birthday, and we're going to celebrate with some cake and ice cream. You boys go into your rooms and put on your change of clothes and come back because we're going to gather around this table and light these candles for Hershel's birthday," she said with a big smile.

Each of us took turns lighting all the candles, then we joined hands and all of us began to sing "Happy Birthday" to me.

In the days that followed, it seemed the whole world was in shock concerning the news of the assassination of President John F. Kennedy. I could tell that most people were solemn and somewhat in disbelief that this could happen to such a well-loved president. I believe that if I had not been in such a loving foster home with Mama and Papa Hildebrand, this public display of evil would have made a different impact on my life.

The very next day, Papa Hildebrand sat all four of us boys down and explained in a loving way what had occurred. Papa Hildebrand, I remember to be a loving and thoughtful man, and I knew that he wanted us to know the difference between right and wrong. Today, in retrospect, as I've stated before, Mama and Papa loved us and cared about us and tried to give us the building blocks of good, moral Christian ethics.

During the holidays of Thanksgiving, Christmas, and others, I don't think any of us—speaking about us boys—had any idea or thought of being depressed, except for the vague thought of our parents and other siblings, but even that thought was soon lost in the excitement of all the love that Mama and Papa showed us during these holidays.

However, there was also a very serious side to Papa. His rules were to be obeyed, and understandably so. The lake, for example, was off-limits unless an adult accompanied us. All of Papa's rules were explained. He said, "I'll first tell you what a rule is, and then I'll explain to you why that rule needs to be enforced." The lake was off-limits due to numerous poisonous snakes and the fear of drowning. Papa did possess a large thick flat paddle, which he showed to each of us. This paddle, he explained, was also used on his own children while they were growing up. Mr. and Mrs. Hildebrand, due to their age, had already raised children of their own and had grandchildren. I felt somewhat relieved and honored to know in an unusual sort of way that same paddle that he had disciplined his own children would also be used to discipline us if need be!

Papa, early each Saturday morning, would wake us about 4:00 a.m. He could be heard coming into each room and raising his voice. "Come on now, boys! Let's wake up now. We've got a bowling appointment at 5:00 a.m.!" Papa was an excellent bowler and had arranged with the Whitehaven bowling center to reserve lanes for our boys' home with special rates. I, Donald, Jimmy, and Michael enjoyed each Saturday morning bowling.

On special holidays like Christmas, Mrs. Raines, the social worker, would come to each of our homes and take all of us to Memphis to shop. This was so exciting for each of us because, coming from the type of family environment and homes that we did, we did not know what it felt like to really enjoy a normal Christmas. Of course, sometimes Mrs. Raines was occupied by another juvenile officer to help. We were taken to certain stores and tried on numerous clothes. Being told to take these pants or shirts in the dressing room and see how they fit was one of the most exciting feelings ever felt. I can't remember ever having new clothes at home. I can still remember to this day the smell and stiffness as I went into the dressing room, trying on different clothes, and then smoothing my hands up and down brought such enjoyment.

These were the outings that I knew regular parents must have with their children. Wow! Was this what normal families did to spend the holidays? I wondered. Just before school would start, we were also taken out to shop for school clothes. The Christmas holidays were especially exciting. There was a section in part of the living room where we placed a real tree, which we had gone out and cut down and decorated with Christmas ornaments.

I and Donald previously met while we both had been placed in juvenile court on Adams Street in Memphis, Tennessee. We both felt comfortable somewhat, having a past, even though that past had no significant enjoyable history. We—meaning I, Donald, Michael, and Jimmy—kept busy with Papa Hildebrand, who taught us how to landscape the new property. The house had just been built for boys like ourselves who had no other place to go, presumably by the Optimist Club of Shelby County, along with other funding. The house was the most beautiful house that I had ever seen and consisted of red brick surrounding the entire structure and an open-ended carport at the rear of the house, with a small shop on the right side of the garage. This shop was where all the landscaping tools and most of Papa Hildebrand's prized tools were kept. My thoughts at that time were that we were some sort of experiment, but of course in a good way. We were not bad boys in the sense of the word—i.e., juvenile delinquents. We were just boys that were abandoned by our biological parents, for whom the Shelby County court system was looking to provide a good, stable environment in hopes that they would take responsibility for the young and unfortunate boys and girls as ourselves. I also believe now, looking back, experiment or not, they wanted to show that the less unfortunate could be taught morally, physically, and spiritually to become individuals of good human qualities.

In my opinion, now thinking back, the accumulation of certain organizations and the joining of Mr. and Mrs. Hildebrand was a great blessing to the overall foundation of our future qualities. We deftly were given the guidelines and blueprint of becoming well-rounded and morally sound, both physically and spiritually, by Mr. and Mrs. Hildebrand and the organizations through God, who provided this home. It would be up to me and each of us boys to use this opportunity and the guidelines that we were taught in this most impressionable time of our lives to achieve success in any endeavor or career that we chose in the future.

There were so many enjoyable times riding our bikes in a home-made trail that we had constructed through the woods adjacent to the house. As I've stated previously, we lived in a very rural area south of Hacks Cross Road and Germantown Tennessee. It was exciting riding our bikes in the trail, winding around large oak trees, then circling back toward the house after about several thousand yards. We made a game out of racing one another like racecar drivers or playing a type of Robin Hood, fighting to rid the forest of the bad sheriff of Nottingham.

During all this loving supervision from our foster parents, through the years we helped with the construction of the driveway and the sowing of yard grass. We also had between the house and what I called the forest of Nottingham an aboveground pool that we enjoyed during those hot summer days.

I remember on one particularly hot summer day, the anticipation of finally getting home and off that school bus and all of us boys racing one another up the driveway and around the carport toward the back door. Mr. Hildebrand met all of us panting boys at the back door, stating, "Hold on there, boys. How would you like to take a dip in the pool?"

We all hollered approvingly, "Yes, sir!"

"All of you wait right there and let me get all your swimming suits." Papa returned shortly with a handful of swimming shorts and threw them all up in the air for us to catch. As they came flying down, each of us scrambled to retrieve our swim shorts; all the other boys retrieved theirs, but mine was missing somehow. I could see the boys going into the garage to change, and I was still staring around on the ground in bewilderment, looking for my swimsuit. Mysteriously, my shorts were nowhere to be found. I looked all around the yard steps and tried to figure out if maybe the others had gotten them mixed up by mistake, or perhaps they were just playing a joke on me. Yes, that was what it was.

Walking toward the pool, I noticed Jimmy, Donald, and Michael had changed and were playing and splashing around in the pool. "Hey," I asked, "I can't find my swimming shorts. Have either one of you seen them?"

They all stopped their splashing and looked up and came over to the edge, looking concerned.

"No, Hershel, we haven't seen them. I'm sure Papa threw them out with all the others like he usually does. Did you look really good?" Donald asked.

"Yes. Maybe I'll just go look again." I turned and rushed back toward the back door.

I continued inside and noticed Mama Hildebrand standing in the kitchen, just off the laundry room. "Mom?" I asked. "I can't find my swimming trunks, and I've looked all through the yard. I know Papa threw them out with all the others." I stood there with a concerned look upon my face.

"Papa!" Mom yelled to be heard throughout the house. "Hershel is missing his swimming shorts. Did you forget to throw his out with all the other boys'?"

"No, Mama!" he hollered back. "They were all together when I pitched them up, and I know that I threw them all out together!"

I could hear Papa walking in our direction through the house. He took me by the hand and knew he could see the sorrowful look I had on my face. "Come on, son, you're going to be okay. I just know that those shorts got to be out there somewhere." He stood at the top of the stairs outside the back door while I walked down and stood about the same area as before when he threw them high into the air.

Standing there in the yard, I turned around and faced Papa, and stepping back into the yard farther and looking up toward Papa, I suddenly saw what had occurred. Lying above Papa on the edge of the roof, I could see, was my swimming shorts. "Papa!" I hollered. "There they are!" Papa walked down the steps to join me in the yard, looking in the same direction I was pointing. We both then started to laugh, and Papa grabbed me around the shoulders embracing me.

"Well, Hershel, I guess we have solved this mystery, haven't we?" he said, giving out another laugh. "Mama!" Papa yelled toward the back door. "Come out here!"

"Yes," Mama said as she stuck her head out the door.

"Come here and look!" Papa laughed again. "We have just solved the mystery of the missing swimming trunks." He was still laughing as he spoke.

Mama walked down the stairs and proceeded to stand on the other side of Papa and turned to look where he was pointing toward the roof. "Well, well," she said, chuckling, seeing the swimming trunks perched on the very edge of the roof. "How in the world did you do that, Papa?" she asked.

He laughed and said, "Instead of tossing them straight out, I must have thrown them up, and apparently, Hershel's was the only one that flew back toward the roof." He then told me, "Come with me, Hershel. Let's get a ladder and a stick and we'll get it down."

Mama reached over and gave me a big hug and embraced me, saying, "I'm so sorry, Hershel, but at least we know what happened. It will be too late to swim by the time we get them down from there, Hershel. But I'll make it up to you, I promise, in another way, okay?" She looked down at me with her big loving smile. Her loving hand on my shoulder, her smile, and the concern that she showed in her eyes seemed to make it all better. "Now," Mama explained, "we got to get them down and get the other boys inside and cleaned up for dinner, then we got homework to do. Please come inside, Hershel. I need your help."

This house was exactly what a home should be in all sense of the word, in my opinion.

When we came into the house by way of the carport, we routinely took off all our clothes after school and especially playing in the yard, inside the laundry room, except for our underwear. We then scurried through the house to our rooms and our bath. After our bath, we changed into our pajamas, then went into the dining room for dinner, after which homework would be done.

Mama Hildebrand was very fluent in the art of grammar and fine etiquette. It was understood that she was from a fine, influential

Southern family. It was also believed that she had been an English teacher. She constantly corrected our grammar when we made mistakes. She tried to teach the proper way to set a dinner place setting. She was a very eloquent woman, with all the charm and beauty of an exceptional Southern lady.

I explained earlier that we were surrounded by woods, and just down the hill there were two large lakes that could be seen from the back of the house. All of us boys were told that the lakes were off-limits unless some adult accompanied us. Papa, on numerous occasions, would surprise all of us boys and take us on a fishing excursion. He would look at all four of us back and forth excitedly and begin to teach us and explain his method of catching a monster catfish or largemouth bass. He took pride in explaining his fine art and/or scientific method of fishing. He, Papa, took patience with each of us to make sure that whatever he said or things he showed us in his fine art of fishing, we understood. Papa enjoyed the fact that when we moved here, most of the landscaping and outside carpentry work was left unfinished, and it was his pleasure to teach us these skills. We spent many hours learning how to spread concrete sidewalks and smoothen out the concrete driveway that led to the garage. The unfinished garage and the adjacent workshop, we also helped to build. This atmosphere of family and working together was one of a real home, and Papa and Mama Hildebrand were truly sent by God to give comfort and love to all of us boys.

However, life was not without discipline, and this discipline was explained to each boy. Briefly, I'll attempt to explain. Mr. Hildebrand had still in his possession the same round paddle he had used to discipline his own two children, who were by then already grown. He first explained, looking directly into our eyes, what we had done wrong, then asked if you understood why it was wrong. He had a chair where he sat next to a stool as we were asked to lie across it, and the severity of the offense that we committed would determine the number of times the panel struck our bottom, but I recall it was no more than five times.

One afternoon, I believe it was in the spring of that year, because the large trees had green foliage prevalent throughout the wooded areas, in our backyard, where we had a large tree, Papa taught us how to put a large steel bolt on a small twine and, with all our strength, heave that over the largest limb to make a tire swing.

One morning, while playing in the yard by myself, I looked down through the trees and high foliage and saw what I thought was movement. This wasn't anything, in my opinion, unusual, because living in the country, we saw all types of wildlife, from deer to raccoons, squirrels, rabbits, and coyotes—just about any type of wild animal prevalent in this part of Southwest Tennessee and Mississippi. As I sat on the large makeshift seat that hung from the large oak tree, swinging myself around and around, my curiosity got my eyes fixated down the hill through all the trees and high growth. Living in the country, you become accustomed to recognizing the movements of certain types of animals, but something was different about this movement; it didn't seem like one of an animal. But what was it? I stopped swinging and just sat, holding on to the ropes, gazing out toward the lake with my eyes squinted and my head leaned back and forth in an attempt to get a better view through the numerous trees that dotted the hill down toward the lakes. Getting my body through the ropes and off the swing, I decided to walk down and get a better view.

I cautiously began to walk down the hill toward the lakes but also knew there was only a certain distance to the lakes that I was allowed to go. Each step I took was cautiously planted onto the ground so as not to frighten off what it was, but also so I did not stumble on the loose sweet gum balls that were all over the hillside. The hillside was also scattered with a small lava-type black rock that was pitted with poor-type air pockets that would cut your skin if you fell upon them. As I got closer to make them out, where I could see the edge of the small lake, I was shocked at what I thought I saw.

"Hey, mister!" I yelled out.

I was amazed to see standing at the edge of the lake, with a cane fishing pole, was a white-bearded old man that looked very familiar.

"Oh!" he said, turning toward the sound of my voice. "Hello, child, how have you been? I just thought I would get a little fishing in."

"Mister, do I know you?" with curiosity I asked.

"Child, I travel around quite a bit, you know. That might be very possible," he said.

"I'm Hershel. I live up there in that house on top of the hill." I tried keeping my distance due to his tattered clothes and unshaven appearance.

"Yes, I know that, child. And I do believe we've met before. I'm Gabe," he said. "And please tell me how those beautiful mules Old Dan and Blue are doing."

"Oh, yes! Mr. Gabe, I remember now. We had visited before. It was on my grandfather's farm, while you were passing through. Yes, Mr. Gabe, those two mules you're talking about, Old Dan and Blue, it's been a while since I've been around them, but I guess they're still okay."

"Well, my child, I'm sure they are. Our heavenly Father has a way of taking care of all his creatures."

Even though my curiosity at seeing this old friend seemed to thrill a deep, innermost peace, I wanted to get closer, but I knew the rule of getting any closer to the water's edge and the danger that is involved. To my excitement, I asked, "How have you been, Mr. Gabe? I'm so glad to see you again and want to thank you for praying with me the last time we were together."

He looked around again toward where I was standing and placed his cane pole across what appeared to be a forked branch he had apparently pushed into the muddy ground.

"I'm not allowed to get any closer to the lake, Mr. Gabe," I said.

"Yes, child, I understand," he said before I could finish explaining, "and that is a good rule to follow, my child. I know that your mama and papa here at this nice home give you these rules to protect you."

"They are not my real mom and papa. They are my foster parents."

"Yes, my child, but you do call them Mama and Papa, don't you? They are serving the role to all you boys as guardians."

"Yes, sir, Mr. Gabe." I looked at him as he walked slightly up the hill toward me.

As he got directly in front of me, he dropped to both knees, and taking his hands, he began to wave them around my cheeks and head without touching me. "My goodness, child, you've grown, haven't you?" he asked with a big bright smile that I now remembered. "And into such a healthy, handsome child too. Our heavenly Father's protection is still upon you and will for the rest of your days."

I looked toward his face and was mesmerized by a sense of calmness and love the likes of which I had not felt in such a long time. Though Mr. Gabe had torn, tattered clothes, long white beard, and long hair, this did not take away the feeling of spirit that surrounded him, which was something that I had not felt since our last encounter. This strange, beautiful feeling that he possessed was by far beyond my explanation or comprehension. My entire body and being was filled with a sort of love and peace that enveloped me from the top of my head down to my small body and seemed to roll like some sort of wave down to my toes. I continued to gaze at him and somehow wanted to take in everything he was saying. My eyes were fixated on his eyes, which seemed to cause me to have an unexplainable feeling of being able to comprehend all the beauty that was around me. I could see and hear immediately a flock of bluebirds that had suddenly swooped down out of the deep blue sky and fluttered around Mr. Gabe's head, then as quickly as they came, they flew away.

"Mr. Gabe," I excitedly screamed out, "did you see those beautiful bluebirds? They almost landed on your head! And oh, the beautiful sound that they were making!"

"Yes, my child. They could see God the Father's spirit upon you and wanted to get close, and the chirping they were making was the singing of adoration of the Father's spirit upon you. So always remember and know that your heavenly Father is just a breath away, as in the chirping of those bluebirds," Gabe said. "The heavenly Father wants you to know this world will have many trials of life that you will encounter. Your life will be long upon this earth, and you only must remember that the Creator of all things is only just a whisper of your breath away. You can call upon him, my child. And never give up. Have faith and believe the heavenly Father is with you to guide you through any trial that you might encounter throughout your life on this earth." As he spoke, his eyes seemed to pierce right through me, the hair on the top of my head seemed to have a life of its own, and a breeze of air blew around me. Then suddenly, a small whirlwind enveloped me, traveling from the top of my head down to the ground, then could be seen traveling across the lake, vanishing into nothingness. I felt cleansed and/or refreshed. I just did not know but thought suddenly that Mr. Gabe possessed something very special as if he was somehow connected to the very presence of God.

The description was beyond my comprehension, and I had never seen such amazing eyes or complexion before or since, even to this day. He possessed deep blue eyes I can only describe as, if God took the color of all the blue oceans and all the stars in the universe and blended it together, that would be the color of Mr. Gabe's eyes, which had a sparkle that I can only describe as a large twinkling diamond sphere or star that could be gazed upon the heavens on a beautiful spring night.

As I gazed into his eyes, the center seemed to burst out toward the edges. "Mr. Gabe," I said, looking up at him as he stood before me, "I'm so glad to see you again and remember all the things you spoke about before concerning the heavenly Father. Wow!" I looked into his face and told him how strange it was for us to meet again after all this time, and in a different place, too, both of which were quite a distance apart. "Have you been traveling, Mr. Gabe?" I asked.

"Hershel!" I heard someone yelling my name from the house. "Where are you? Time to come in now! And dinner is almost ready!"

I recognized the voice to be Mama Hildebrand and quickly responded, "Yes, ma'am, I'm on the way up. I found an old friend of mine fishing down here in the lake, but don't worry, I'm not that close to the water's edge!" I focused my vision through the trees and tilted my head around and noticed that she had walked out into the backyard and was bobbing her head around to see where I was. I hollered up the hill toward her and was waving so she could feel at ease that I had not gone too close to the lake.

"Who is this friend?" she questioned.

"Ma'am, it's an old friend of mine, and you'll never guess it, but I met him earlier on my grandfather's farm."

"Okay, I guess."

But even at this distance, I could see a puzzled look on her face as she stared down toward me, bobbing her head back and forth to get a better view around the obstruction of trees and shrubs. She was continually looking down in my direction through the trees as if frustratingly trying to focus and get a view of my friend Mr. Gabe. I could see her hand go up and down in the air toward me, as if in a confused manner, then she turned to walk back toward the house, shrugging her shoulders and turning her head from side to side. Before going inside, she yelled out, "Young man, you tell your imaginary friend that you must leave now! Now, come on up to the house, and don't forget to undress inside the laundry room before getting in the shower." Then she added, "Now, come get yourself up here and into the shower before dinner."

"Yes, ma'am." I knew I must have sounded frustrated. "I'm coming now!"

I turned around to tell Gabe goodbye and to also say how good it was to see him again, but as I turned, I was saddened to see that he had left, and looking across the larger lake in the distance, I could see Mr. Gabe walking down an embankment and beginning to enter a large wooded area. Sadly, I yelled out, hoping he could hear me at that great distance, "Mr. Gabe, hope to see you again soon! And take care of yourself! Thank you!" As I waved at him, I desperately felt emptiness within myself. "Mr. Gabe, hope to see you soon!" The sound of my yelling must have traveled across the vast still waters of the lake, because I could see Mr. Gabe suddenly stop then turn, raising his hand into the air, waving in my direction. A smile came across my face. I was glad that he had heard me and was waving back in acknowledgment.

Even through the great distance, from across the lake, I could hear his voice say in a whisper, "My child, always know that God, our great Creator, is just a breath away. Pray to him daily. He will always be there to listen and provide for you as one of his precious children." Then I noticed, as he turned, a sudden great gust of wind blew through his shoulder-length white hair and beard, just as he faded out of sight down and behind the embankment of the distant pond.

There must have been a scattered shower on that side of the farther lake because suddenly I noticed a bright, colorful light envelop a small portion of the woods he had entered.

I briefly stood, looking across both adjoining lakes, and thought about all the words Mr. Gabe had softly spoken. These words and thoughts filled me with great calmness and peace. Looking toward the colorful rainbow in his direction, I began to pray. I don't remember exactly what prompted me, except that I felt it would be a way to thank my heavenly Father for bringing this special spiritual feeling that I sensed within me. I clasped both hands together in front and fell softly onto my knees, looking toward the dusky dark-blue sky, and began to pray. I looked up, praying softly, and continued to feel a great, soothing peace within me. The twinkling of stars and the passing of an occasional comet that streaked across the lit sky caused it to change colors from blue to light purple, and suddenly it brought tears down my cheeks. But these tears were different, not tears of sadness or of the deep, traumatic depression I had felt before; instead, I felt a great feeling of love, calmness, and serenity. I felt an inner peace and *heard* a quiet voice inside me say, "Your life sometimes might be difficult, child, but always remember, I will be with you always. When you stumble, I will help you get up and help to carry you through those troubled times. Whoever or whatever will come against you, I will be there to hear you and comfort your cries. You will conquer this life and accomplish great things throughout your time. There was a beginning, and then there was me. All your questions will be answered and revealed throughout different periods of your life when you call upon the Lord. And this never-ending creation that you see in the heavens above you is just a small example of the greatness of your Creator. Your Creator, my child, is forever, even after the end of the world."

Slowly, I felt a whispering of wind breathe on my face and engulf my whole body.

Suddenly, I was awakened out of my prayer and meditation by a voice coming from up the hill and the house. "Hershel! You better come on. Mama Hildebrand has dinner almost ready!" I recognized the voice of Donald, one of the boys that I knew from earlier at the facility of the juvenile court on Adams Strcct in Memphis, Tennessee.

"Okay!" I yelled back. "I'm on the way!" I hurriedly began to run up the hill, going around the small brushes and trees until I reached the back steps.

Donald asked, "What have you been doing down there? And you know you're not supposed to get close to the pond."

"I know, Donald." I looked at him angrily as I answered. "But I saw an old friend that had visited me while I stayed with my grand-parents on their farm near Ripley, Tennessee."

"Hershel," Donald said, "I asked Mama where you were earlier, and she said she spotted you down the hill and told me that none of the other boys were with you, saying that you were alone as far as she could tell."

My thoughts were that Mr. Gabe's presence must have been blocked from her view by all the other trees and bushes.

"Come on," Donald said, looking at me, frustrated. "We have got to get cleaned up before dinner."

I began to strip down to my underclothes, as was the custom each day before dinner, and headed quickly through the house toward our bedrooms and bath. I paused briefly as I went around the kitchen pantry, noticing Mama Hildebrand bending over and peering through the oven door, apparently checking on whatever she was preparing for dinner. "Hi, Mama!" I said as I rushed around the corner. "You'll never guess what happened down close to the lake!" I said. "I saw an old friend, but I'll tell you about him later!" Then I continued to rush through the house because I was shy to be seen in my underwear.

"Okay," she replied, and I could tell by the slight smile on her face that she was aware of my shyness. "Dinner will be ready in about half an hour, so make sure all you boys are in your pajamas when I call you back for dinner."

"Yes, ma'am," I replied, hurrying around the large brick fire-place mantel that separated the large living area and led back to our bedroom and the bath quarters. Jimmy, Donald, and Michael had already taken their showers and had gathered in the area of the little foyer adjacent to the bedrooms to watch TV, but they paused briefly to look up at me in frustration, as if to say, "Better not make us late for dinner, Hershel!"

Our after-school routine was structured on the amount of homework each of us had, so we could allocate time to play outside. The kitchen was where Mama Hildebrand prepared our meals from the stove, which was separated by a large long bar with high wooden stools. The long bar doubled sometimes for eating and doing homework. On the stool side of the counter was a large formal dining table adjacent to the family room, where we all gathered during dinner. Mr. and Mrs. Hildebrand, as I said previously, were very caring foster parents and used these personal gatherings to teach all of us important moral and spiritual fundamentals of life. They were Christians, and before each meal, we took turns on different days to say individual prayers for our food, after which everybody could be heard saying in unison, "Amen." Mama and Papa Hildebrand were, in our eyes, very special people and sought to show us love, allowing all of us boys to show them love in return.

I believe, thinking back in my very pleasant memory, that they must have known how frightened and alone we felt because of all our individual traumatic experiences. I know that they tried lovingly to do everything in their power to make us feel that we were safe and under the atmosphere of a loving Christian family. I know that I so very much needed their soothing and loving parental ways toward me, and the others would help me make it through each day. Papa tried to instill the fundamentals of being a good, moral young man. Mama Hildebrand, I believe, having been a schoolteacher, tried to instill in us the proper use of the English language and grammar. There were times she would stop us in the middle of a conversation and immediately correct what we had said wrong, explaining the correct way we should have spoken and proper grammar and punctuation. These fundamentals of character building were the building blocks, hopefully, in our future adult lives.

After years with the Hildebrands and the loving devotion that they had shared with us in this special time in their lives, which I know now to be their retirement years, they reluctantly decided that it was time to leave and return to their own lives and home. They gathered all of us boys into the living room, as was the custom when there was to be a family meeting, to explain to each of us this decision for them to leave, but they reassured us that they would come back from time to time to visit. I remember that this separation, unlike the one that I had gone through with my real parents, was devastating. Trying desperately to hold back the tears but seemingly unable to, I began to cry, looking up at both Mama and Papa and pleading with them to please stay with us at least until our mama and daddy came to take me home. Mama looked down at all of us, and I could tell she was also saddened, because her eyes began to water, even though she somehow forced a smile. Mama jerked her head around, looking at all of us, and forced a smile.

Jokingly she said, "Oh, Hershel, after a little while you will forget all about me and this old man!" She looked over at and forced another laugh toward Papa.

"No! I'll never forget about you, and no matter what or where I am, I will always come see you!" I was looking back and forth at each of them, and I could see they were doing everything in their power to explain this sudden transition well, but I could also tell by the tears they were attempting to hold back that they loved us as they did their own children and grandchildren, and I knew, too, that they would miss us as much as we all would miss them.

Mama and Papa stood to their feet and walked toward where we were standing, with Mama reaching out to pull us all into her arms in an embrace. I looked up at Mama and could see tears flowing down her cheeks, and I could feel Papa's large hand on my shoulder squeeze me. With a quiver in his voice, he spoke the words that I have never forgotten since. "We love you, Hershel, and you're going to be a fine young man." And as he spoke, he also looked around at the other boys. "Now, you boys know that we will come visit you all from time to time." And with a loud clearing of his throat, he stepped back. "Now, Mama," he said, forcing a smile, "let those boys go. They've got to get in the bed. They'll have to be at school tomorrow."

The next morning was as usual as any other morning. As we got ready for school, Mama Hildebrand was, as she always did, preparing breakfast in the kitchen while we sat on our stools, facing her, looking across the counter and into the kitchen. Mama was her usual cheerful, smiling self, asking us questions. Did we have our books and homework ready to hand to our teachers? for instance. This morning, however, I could sense something in her personality that was different. Even though she tried to be her usual loving self, there was a sense of sadness in her voice.

"Mama," I asked, "is everything okay?"

She smiled as she usually did but looked down and slightly across the counter at each of us. "Yes, of course. You boys hurry up now and eat your breakfast. We can't miss that school bus now, can we?" I could see by the way her eyes looked that she was troubled and concerned about something, and I wondered, Was it what we had discussed the previous night about their leaving?

"Mama!" I attempted again and voiced my concern. "Are you sure there's nothing wrong?" I asked with a concerned look on my face.

"Now, Hershel, stop all that talking and finish your breakfast." She pointed toward the end of the counter at the bag lunches. "Don't any of you forget those before you go out to the school bus." She then briskly walked out of the kitchen and back toward her and Papa's bedroom.

After we had finished breakfast and gathered our packed lunches, I could hear Papa come from behind, saying, "Okay, boys, let's get out there to that bus stop." We all stood by the door, as was usual each morning, briefly waiting, expecting Mama and Papa to send us off and out the door. As if Papa knew what we were thinking, he began walking toward us, ushering us out the side door. "Okay, boys, Mama had to lie. Something about her head, I think." Papa slapped his hands together and rushed us out the door. "Get out there now. We don't want to miss that bus." I could see what seemed like a forced smile across his face as he waved us down the gravel drive and turned to walk back toward the house.

Glancing back over my shoulder toward the house, I could see Mama standing closely beside Papa outside on the porch as they both waved in our direction while we boarded the bus. Stepping up onto the bus and stumbling down the aisle and finally settling onto a seat, I hurriedly looked out the window and waved back at Mama and Papa as the bus pulled away from the driveway. I continued like that to not lose sight of them until eventually, the bus went over the hill and sight of the house and Mama and Papa were gone.

The reality of this day came to light later as I returned home. This would be the last time we would see Mama and Papa Hildebrand. Though it was discussed the night before that they would be leaving, we were unaware that they would be leaving that very day as we waved at them, getting on the bus that morning.

Stepping off the school bus and arriving back at the foster home on Hacks Cross Road, I felt deep inside of me that something was very different, and that feeling was realized when we entered the back door. As we took off our shoes, as was the custom before entering the laundry room, there was an unusual lack of aroma from the kitchen, which reinforced the suspicion that something was indeed different. We had been used to the aroma of Mama's cooking each day. Slowly we, Donald, Jimmy, Michael, and I, followed one another around the corner and down the small hallway that led to the dining area.

"Here they are!" The familiar voice of Mrs. Raines, the social worker, welcomed all of us, accompanied by her usual smiling face. As she stood up from the table to greet us, another couple, a man and a woman, also stood along with her, looking in our direction.

We stopped and stood in front of them and just looked with a confused expression.

"Boys," Mrs. Raines said, "these are Mr. and Mrs. Robertson. They are here to take over as your guardians in place of the Hildebrands, who, you boys do understand, have chosen to leave us and retire into their private lives."

The sudden realization of what Mrs. Raines said concerning Mama and Papa Hildebrand leaving us left me with a familiar emptiness, followed by the familiar traumatic depression that I had felt so many times before. I had learned to love Mama and Papa Hildebrand, to trust them as I would my biological parents. Even now, remembering back into those years, I know they were the building blocks of my personality and moral character. The years I spent with them showed how they were loving people, and I'm positive that all the other boys felt their love the same as I did. We would never see the Hildebrands return as promised. They were told, as they had explained to us at that time, that they would be allowed to visit us from time to time; however, the juvenile court system decided it would be too disruptive for us and for the adjustment of the new foster parents. I was devastated and believe I thought the other boys were also. I swore someday that I would find Mama and Papa Hildebrand and thank them and express in some way, if at all possible, how much their kindness and giving of themselves meant to me.

Adjusting to the new foster parents was difficult, and I thought how fortunate I was that it was the loving Hildebrands that preceded them.

One afternoon, while playing cowboys and riding my bike (pretending it was a horse) through the woods, weaving back and forth around large trees, I heard the voice of my foster mother from the house. "Hershel, come inside the house! You have visitors arriving shortly, and I know you will want to see them." Several years had passed and the only visitor I had had was an occasional social worker that drove me or the others either to the dentist or to medical appointments.

Pedaling faster and faster, I arrived in the open carport, then jumping off, I left my bike against the rack. Rushing inside, I excitedly asked, "Who is it, ma'am?"

"You'll see shortly. Now go into the bath and wash your face and hands. But you don't have to change clothes. Just ash that filthy face and those hands." She reached out, turning them over, then smiled at me, pointing to the direction of the bathroom.

I quickly washed my face and hands by splashing soapy water to the point I felt they were cleaned to her satisfaction. Grabbing the cloth with a blue stripe, which signified that it was mine, I hurriedly dried myself. Our bathroom was adjacent to the driveway and had small windows along the ceiling and walls, allowing light from the sun to shine through, and any car coming up the driveway would cast a shadow, and noise could be heard. I heard what I knew to be a car driving up the driveway, crunching the gravel. My first thought was that it was Mrs. Raines, the social worker, who was arriving to take me to some appointment. I always enjoyed going into the city of Memphis, and it didn't matter the reason, just so I could get out and see all the people in the big city and be mesmerized by all the traffic. I always had it in my mind, quietly praying, that hopefully, in the next car passing beside me, or wherever we traveled in the city, God would bless me by allowing me to see my daddy or mama.

Suddenly, I was brought out of my deep thoughts.

"Hershel?" my foster mother called, her voice coming from the front of the house. "Come here!"

"Yes, ma'am!" I replied and rushed into the direction of her voice, expecting to see Mrs. Raines standing next to her, but instead, she motioned for me to come toward her.

She grabbed me by both shoulders and excitedly looked into my eyes. "There is someone outside to see you that I know you haven't seen in quite some time," she told me, combing her fingers through my hair, and smiled, looking down at my face. "Now, you go out there and see who it is!" She turned me around and playfully swatted my behind.

"Yes, ma'am!" I said, then walked toward the side door of the house that led to the carport.

Arriving outside, I noticed parked on the driveway was a large car that I thought I recognized, but I just couldn't remember from when or from where. I knew, though, that I had not seen it anywhere in the area before, and I knew it was not one of the familiar cars driven by Mrs. Raines or any of the court's other social workers. No one was around the car, but I knew it had to belong to a guest that my new foster mother and Mrs. Raines had sent me out to meet. I began to search toward the front of the house and thought I heard voices as I walked around into the front yard. Looking up and in front of me, I began to scream out, "Daddy! Daddy!" Tears began to fall down my cheeks as I ran toward him, crying out with so much excitement I found it hard to catch my breath. Also, even in my excitement, I noticed standing next to him was my uncle William, his brother.

Uncle William pointed his large finger at me, saying with a big grin, "Hey, Bubba, remember your uncle William? And I bet you don't know who this is!" He put his hand on my dad's shoulder next to him.

I ran up to them as my daddy reached down and pulled me up into his arms in an embrace, tears streaming down both our cheeks. My daddy took a deep breath, then reared back, looking at and hefting me up and down. "My goodness, son," he said, laughing, "you sure have grown!" Then he lowered me back down to the ground.

"Oh! Daddy, Daddy, I'm so glad to see you! I missed you so much! I was so worried about you and Mama. I didn't know what happened to you," I said. "Do you know where my sisters are?"

"Yes, son," my father told me. "Now, calm down. I've seen your sisters, and they're okay. I know where they are."

"Please, Daddy, I missed you! Did you come to take me home? We can go now and get my sissies!" I said, with a pleading look, staring into his eyes.

"Your daddy's working on that. I don't want you to get a lot of your hopes up today, but I'm doing everything I can through the court system to make sure you come home soon. You just must be patient with your daddy for a little while longer. But I can promise you this, son, that it will be soon." Daddy smiled. "Son, let me ask you something else. Your daddy and uncle William have been talking to these people that take care of you earlier today, and they tell me you have a large wood-burning fireplace and they need some wood cut and stacked around back for winter."

"Yes, Daddy, and we usually stack it up around the side yard between those two large trees."

"Well, okay, son. How about you help me and your uncle William while we are here visiting? Wouldn't it be good to cut that wood and have it neatly stacked between those two big trees? I'm sure that they would like a little help and appreciate getting all this wood ready for winter."

I showed Daddy where the tool area was, and we gathered a chain saw and other tools. Daddy pointed to the far section of the yard, where lay a fallen tree that had been struck by lightning during a previous storm. "Let's start over there on that fallen tree," he said.

During the next several hours, my daddy and uncle William, along with my help, labored with cutting the tree to the size of logs that Daddy thought would be appropriate to fit and burn in the fireplace. That afternoon, I kept looking up over at my daddy while he worked, and thought that this was just a dream or my imagination and soon I would wake up in the usual cold sweat that I had felt so many times previously. I took a deep breath and looked around, smelling the air, rubbing my eyes, then looking in my daddy's direction. I knew it was not my imagination or some dream; it was, yes, reality. My daddy was truly here!

In the next several hours, we laughed together and at one another, then again, looking toward my daddy, I could see that he appeared happier and even healthier than the last time I had seen him. "Daddy," I asked, "is Mama okay? And how about sissy and Cynthia? The last time I saw them, they were in that large building those people took us to, where all the other kids stayed." I sighed at the memory. "Daddy, I was scared when I was in that place. I sure wanted you and Mama to come and get us and take us home, or anywhere else except there. There was a mean man there that hurt this other boy!"

"Well, son, let's not talk about that right now. Let us think and talk about happy things, okay?"

"Okay, Daddy. I just hope my sissies are okay. I miss them so much, and I worry about them all the time."

I must've had a pleading look on my face, because when I looked up into my daddy's eyes, he had sympathy in them, and patting me on the head, he told me, "Son, everything will be all right soon. I just have a few more meetings with those people at that building, and then if all goes well, I'll come and take you back home."

"Oh, but, Daddy, why can't I go home with you today?" I looked up into his face, pleading. "Daddy, oh, please, Daddy! You're here now. Please, Daddy, just go inside and tell them you're taking me home today! I know they don't mind if I go home with you today, Daddy!"

Looking down at me, he turned and stopped, sitting down on one of the round logs close by, then reached out and motioned for me. "Come here, son." I could tell by the shining and glistening in his eyes that I had made him sad and had upset him. "Son," he said with love and a quiver in his voice, pulling me up onto his lap and pressing my back to bring me close to his chest, "you've got to trust your daddy. I promise I'll be back soon, son. But you're going to have to stay here for just a short while longer. I have a meeting with the judge real soon, and when he says it's all right for you to come home with me, I'll be back to get you, okay?" He smiled at me then. "Now, let's you, me, and this big guy over there"—he pointed at Uncle William—"get cleaned up with that water hose around the back of the house, and then you can walk us back to the car."

I felt an emptiness fill my body, but I really didn't want to make my daddy sad anymore. I didn't want to let him go without me either. I held on to my daddy's large hand while we walked around to the carport, slowly washing my hands and face off all the sweat that had collected flecks of sawdust, as my daddy reached over, grabbing my head and shaking it, saying, "I think you're all cleaned up," as if he knew I was moving slowly on purpose. "Now, come on, son. Let's go tell the people in the house that you all have got plenty of wood for the winter and we're finished."

Daddy slowly walked toward the side door, saying he needed to say goodbye to and thank my foster parents for their politeness in allowing them to visit. The walk seemed as though I was going through a long dark tunnel, and holding on to my daddy's hand, I was unaware if I said anything or noticed anything around me; it was just me and my daddy, no one and nothing else.

When Daddy spoke, it was as though he did in slow motion, then suddenly, Daddy knocked loudly on the side door and I was suddenly brought back to reality again. My foster dad was opening the door, looking down off the stoop at my dad and me. He smiled, saying, "I know that Hershel enjoyed your visit today." He looked at me, my daddy, and Uncle William.

Uncle William then spoke. "I'm the boy's uncle." Then he reached out his hand as if to shake my foster father's. "Pleased to meet you," he said.

"We think a lot of our little Hershel," my foster father said. "He's quiet and shy, but I'm sure he will grow out of that soon." And they all laughed. Reaching out and presenting his hand a second time, he said, "Thank you so much, Mr. Marise. This wood, I'm sure, will last all winter." Then also reaching next to him, he shook Uncle William's hand. "And thank you also, little Hershel's uncle, sir, for your help. I can see the resemblance between you and your brother and little Hershel here," he said, putting his hand on top of my head, smiling politely down at me. "Mr. Marise?" He looked over at my dad. "You can sure tell that this is your boy. Thanks again for all your hard work. Now, I'm going to leave you three alone for a few minutes so you can say your goodbyes." Looking down at me, he smiled, then turned and walked inside the house, briefly turning to add, "Now, after Daddy leaves, Hershel, you come inside and wash up for dinner," as if to tell us to hurry with the time we took to say our goodbyes. "Mama," he said, talking about my foster mother, "should be almost finished with our dinner."

After we walked back toward their car, I noticed that Uncle William was walking farther behind, as if to allow me and Daddy our last moments together. "Daddy," I said, with a pleading look on my face, as we slowly walked back the agonizing few yards to their car. "I wish I could go home with you now!"

"I know, son, but it won't be long and you'll be home, where you belong," Dad said. "Now, I don't want to hear another word about it. I don't want to make our visit sad, and we sure don't want to upset anyone. That might make it difficult for me to come to visit again." He smiled at me. "Now, listen to your daddy and do what I tell you."

"Yes, Daddy," I responded. "Okay, I will." But the tears began to fill my eyes and run down my cheeks.

"Son, I love you, and you must trust me." He reached down with his hand, and with his thumbs, he wiped both cheeks of my wet tears. My daddy knelt on one knee and brought me forward into his arms and chest, squeezing me in a powerful embrace. "You stop that crying, and right now," he told me, pushing me back and away from his chest. He then looked deeply into my eyes, and I could also see that he was doing all that he could within his power and for my benefit to fight back his own tears. I could see the redness and the glistening shine in his eyes, which made me feel sorry for my poor daddy. I surely didn't want to make him cry. I loved him so and had missed him so much, so I attempted to do like he asked and stopped the flow of tears.

Giving me another hug, he rose up and motioned for Uncle William, who had been standing at the other end of the car. "Come on, Bill, we need to let Bubba get inside and cleaned up for dinner." He placed his large hands on top of my head and smiled. "Now, get inside," he told me with a slight push, and reluctantly I began to walk toward the house.

I turned around and stumbled backward as I watched Daddy and Uncle William get into their car. Then, hearing the rumble of the motor, I saw Daddy wave as the car backed out of the drive and into the road. I continued to watch Daddy's arm as my uncle William steered the car down the road, where it eventually disappeared out of sight over a slight hill, going behind the forest of trees that lined the road. I ran down the driveway toward where the car was last seen, waving one last time into nothingness down the road.

Going Home with Daddy

———————— ❧ ————————

The day had finally come, the day that my daddy was finally going to take me home with him. I had been here in this Germantown foster home just off Hacks Cross Road south of Memphis, Tennessee, for several years now, and I wondered why I had the sickening, frightening feeling in the pit of my stomach. I'd been so disappointed before on so many different occasions, so was it because of the many days and nights that I'd prayed and cried out to God, pleading for him to reunite me with my dad and mom, my sissy Pat, and our baby sister, Cynthia?

Was it finally that my prayers were being answered after all this time?

As I looked around, there were several brown grocery sacks packed, in place of traditional luggage, containing all my clothes and belongings. They were stacked inside the house and next to the back porch, ready to leave whenever my dad arrived in that old Buick he had driven when he visited previously with my uncle William. I was pacing back and forth, going from the front door to the back, looking at and peeking out of each window. I had a deep thrill that soon I would see that old Buick come around the trees, proceeding on the blacktop road that was Hacks Cross Road and eventually into the driveway that adjoined the house. Soon my hopes and prayers were answered with the familiar sight of that old Buick I knew was my dad's beginning to travel up the driveway and toward the rear of the house.

I excitedly started yelling throughout the house, "My daddy's here! Hey, Michael, Jimmy, Donald, my dad's here, and I'm finally going to go home!" Running into the other room, I excitedly screamed toward all the other boys, but the excitement I thought I would see on their faces was not there; instead, there was sadness. I looked back and forth at each of them, wondering why they were not happy for me. Wasn't this what we all wanted? To be reunited with our real families? But then, sadly I began to understand. This had been our family, mine and theirs, and suddenly, like all of them, I, too, was filled with emptiness. Looking back and forth at each of them, I could feel my eyes begin to tear up. "I'm so sorry!" I said. "I'll miss all of you too, but my daddy's here. Don't you understand? I'm finally going to go home to be with my daddy and mama. That's my real family! But I'll be back to visit and see everybody real soon, I promise." And again, reaching out, I grabbed each of them, looking up into their faces. I attempted to smile at each as if pleading with them to understand and be happy for me.

"Your mommies and daddies will come real soon and take you all home, just like my daddy is today," I told them. A great sadness filled my heart, and with an attempt not to cry, I turned and rushed out the side door where I knew and expected my daddy's car to pull up close to the carport.

"Daddy!" I was screaming and rushing toward the car with my arms reaching out toward him.

He opened the door and squatted down, scooping me up and embracing me tightly. "I told you your daddy would be back to get you!" he told me as he placed me back on the ground.

"Yes, Daddy, I knew you would!"

We gathered up all my clothes and placed them in the car and said our goodbyes to my foster parents and all the only other family I had known. Then, we finally pulled out of the driveway. I was so excited as if I were in some sort of dream that had come true. But this was not a dream. No, God had answered my prayers as Mr. Gabe said he would. I don't think I heard anything that my daddy was telling me for the next several minutes.

I looked over toward him as if in a daze, then said, "Daddy?" I caught my breath through all the excitement. "I'm so glad to see you!"

"Yes, son," he said, "but we have an appointment this morning to go to the juvenile court and speak to the judge about taking you home with me. They wanted me to come by and bring you with me."

"Oh, Daddy, I thought we were going home to see my sissies and be a real family again!"

"Yes, son, but like I said, first, we need to go by the courthouse and make it official with the judge, then we'll be on our way home."

The next several hours were spent, as Daddy had said, sitting in the juvenile courtroom, speaking to the judge. I sat there on the edge of my seat as my daddy went forward toward the judge and was asked questions concerning his ability to provide for his family, and I was especially frightened as the judge pointed toward me as if to emphasize, "That young man, your son." I remember sitting there wondering if I had come this far, going home with my dad, only to be told that it would not be. Those traumatic moments and the answers Dad gave to this juvenile judge would make the difference. My dad spoke with authority, saying that he was a changed man and there was nothing as important as his family. He promised that he would not allow anyone or anything to stand in his way in providing a good and stable environment for his son and family. He also told the judge that he had become a Christian, having received a minister's license, did not drink alcoholic beverages, and attended church regularly with his family. With a final ounce of serious quiver in my daddy's voice and a glisten in his eye, he stoutly stood tall and told the judge that he intended to raise his family in a Christian home.

"Well, very good, Mr. Marise," the judge said, looking at my dad and then over at me. "Mr. Marise," he continued, "I can see the change in you since our last visit and don't see anything that should keep you away from your son, so I hereby decree that your boy be released in sole custody to you." He then looked to his left at a lady, his secretary. "Court secretary, have Mr. Marise sign the proper documents and this will be retired from the docket for today, and hopefully, this will put a finality to the separation of this young man from his family."

In the next several years, I would live with my dad and his new wife. My mother, who lived in Memphis, Tennessee, had remarried as well. My daddy's new wife had been married previously and had other children. Eventually, my dad had to go back to court and get custody of my sister Cynthia and a brother, who were also in the court's jurisdiction. My dad and his new wife were to have a son of their own too. My mom, with her new husband, would also have a son and gave him the name Edward.

I remember I was so happy finally going to live with my dad. It seemed like all the depressing days and nights in the juvenile court system, and even in the foster home in Germantown, Tennessee, were finally over. My dad drove to a small town outside of Memphis called Covington, Tennessee, driving up to a small house that seemed to be sitting off in some sort of flat field surrounded by a cotton crop. As we drove up, I could see the front door open and a lady and several small children come out, standing on the porch, smiling as they looked in our direction, where Daddy's car came to a stop. Daddy pointed toward the woman and the children on the front porch, then looked back at me, saying, "Son, that's your new family. That's my new wife and her children, and now we're going to be a family together." I felt a sinking in the pit of my stomach because this was not what I had expected, this was not what I wanted, but I did not voice my opinions, which was what I had learned to do in years before.

"Come on, son, get out and meet everybody," Dad said.

His new wife was Mary, which, I found out later, was what her friends and family called her. Mary Elizabeth was her birth name. My daddy and this strange woman met in the yard and embraced and kissed, then turning sideways, looking toward me, Dad said, "Son, this is my new wife and your stepmother, and these are her children." Then he pointed out each one. "This boy is Tommy," he started, then introduced the other children.

This was also a traumatic segment in my life story during my impressionable years, living with my dad and stepmother. The first place that we lived in was a small country town in western Tennessee named Covington. The house was a small white A-frame house that was positioned on what I could tell was the side of Highway 51 north of Covington and sat surrounded by large fields of cotton and corn on both sides of the highway. Off the road from there toward the town of Covington lived my stepmother's mother, sister, and nephew (whom I will not name for reasons of privacy), though I am sure that they've probably passed, all but the nephew.

I remember briefly, while visiting my stepmother's mother, the strong scent of what I thought were urine and other bodily odors. It was a small house but was the size of what we call now a box frame house, with a small kitchen in the back and barely enough room with all the clutter in the kitchen for anyone to sit down around the table, and if you did so, you had to go from underneath the table to squeeze between the wall and the table's edge. And vacating, that was the way you would do it.

On one occasion, while visiting, I could detect a strong odor coming from beneath the table, and while scooting back from my chair, I leaned over and looked underneath and spotted a cat that was ferociously eating a half-devoured rat. I immediately got up and ran into the other room, where this lady I now called my grandmother was, telling her about what I had seen in the kitchen underneath the table. She gave out a chuckle and said, "Old Young, that's our tom-cat. We keep him around for that very purpose, to keep the rats out of the bed while we sleep. You'll get used to it. We get a lot of rats around here with all these fields around us and the creek in the back of the house here." She then yelled out through the kitchen, "Get that thing out here!" And I could hear the scurrying of the cat and could see him grab the rat in his jaws, dragging it up on the table and pulling it through the window, dropping outside.

Her daughter, whom I'll call Aunt Sue, was sitting at her spot on the couch, which she did quite frequently because of her about 350- to 400-pound frame. She did get up on occasion, mainly to stagger, as if it were a drudgery to pull her massive size off from the couch, and wobble outside, where the toilet was. Each time she was to make this effort, it was followed by extreme body odor that I surmised came from the lack of bathing. At one point, she rose up and her mother let out a shriek of disbelief because sitting on the couch where she had risen was a suffocated, dead kitten that she had been sitting on. Granny, the name everybody called her, came over and, reaching down, picked up the dead kitten—we could tell by the stiffness of its small body. Then Granny, walking over to the screen door, slung it out into the front yard. Sometimes, Aunt Sue would sleep on the couch, so there was no clue how long the kitten had been dead.

I and my sister Cynthia and my brother were treated quite differently than they did our stepbrothers and stepsisters, I guess since we were not her blood grandchildren. The hostility and tone when she would call us by name was quite evident but would not be outwardly shown when my daddy was around. That's when Aunt Dot and Granny would then change their personalities to be quite the opposite and we would be treated like they did all the other children.

I remember one Sunday afternoon, my daddy and stepmother dropped us off after we had attended church and they went into town for some unknown reason, which was quite a thing that we did most Sundays. I remember the tragic events to this day and the terrible accusations that followed. My brother, my sister Cynthia, and I were told to immediately come inside Granny's house, then instructed to sit down on the couch as she stood in front of us with a stern, hateful look on her face. "What have you young'uns been up to? I'm not going to have you three heathens, especially you, young man," she said, looking hatefully at me, "come into this Christian home and behave in such a way!"

I looked, shocked, up into her face, completely bewildered at what she was talking about. This grandmother was very accusatory and sometimes would make up very severe things that would shock me, and I could not understand why she would be so evil with such shocking things that I choose not to even mention in this writing.

They, the other children, too, looked at us and looked up at Granny in disbelief at what she was saying. I sat in abject horror and disbelief as tears started to roll down my face at being accused of committing such an act. Later, when my dad and stepmother returned, she told them what she believed had happened and went into detail about the apparently horrible, illicit sexual acts that we supposedly did. For years later, I was traumatized from being accused of such a terrible thing. In fact, I was at the age that time when I believe I didn't have any idea of the difference between the body parts of a male and a female.

We were to stay in the small town of Covington, Tennessee, for several more years, and the next place we were to move to was close to a railroad track adjacent to Wooten Oil Company in Firestone, where they were said to make tires for different automobiles and trucks. All during the day and night, we could smell the rubber as it was molded into different shapes and sizes. This house was a fairly good-size house. It was an old high-ceiling farmhouse, and those of us that are old enough will remember that they were prevalent in the earlier years of the thirties, forties, and fifties. We were so close to the railroad tracks that when the train came from quite a distance down the tracks, we could hear its whistle, and as it approached our house and came so close, it would shake the old glass windowpanes throughout the boys' bedroom, which was on that side of the house. Also, on the other side of the track was the farmers' large silo, where grain was stored from the fields and off-loaded onto the open train cars that would steer off to the side and were positioned underneath a large silo tube.

There were also difficulties living in a house beside a railroad track, but because of the grain silos adjacent to them, I could see an abundance of rats. All during the night, I could hear the scurrying and chewing of wood in our bedroom walls. On one occasion, of which there were more, than I care to mention, I could hear the thump of something crawling through the broken windowpane and something else running along the hardwood floor. I would lie there with a cover pulled up to my neck, listening for the next sound, and suddenly, I could feel something jump from the floor and to my bed, running across my body. I'd immediately pull the covers over my head and kick the large rat that felt like an oversize kitten off my body and could hear it hit the floor and run across the room. This would happen throughout the night, and as soon as I would give in to my exhaustion and fall asleep, I would be awakened by another rat running across my body. Sometimes I would go into the very next room, which was a living room area, and try to fall asleep on the couch, pulling the door of the bedroom behind me. I would tell my stepmother about the rats in the room, only to be ignored or laughed at and told that I needed to grow up. "And I don't want you sleeping in the living room again," she would tell me. "We have a bedroom for all you boys back there. If the other boys can sleep back there, so can you, and I don't want to catch you back in the living room again, sleeping on my couch."

I would try to fix the hole in the window with some wood and cardboard, but to no avail, because it wouldn't take the rats very long to chew through what I had put up and enter the bedroom again. I assume that the rats were seeking refuge from the cold and/or possibly looking for something to eat. I did not want to be their meal for the night or get bitten, because I thought that any rat with teeth powerful enough to eat through solid, hard wood and enter the house had teeth powerful enough to eat through the soft flesh of a small boy like myself! I had seen those small beastly eyes glaring back at me when I would take my daddy's flashlight to bed with me at times, spotting them along the walls of the rooms late at night. The size of some of them was as large as a small cat or kitten, which told me that they were not afraid to defend themselves against anything or anyone that got into their way. Apparently, they had gotten that large feeding on the corn that was stored in the grain towers from the surrounding fields until the train off-loaded for shipment.

During the next several years, we were to move each year from town to town farther east in West Tennessee. From Covington, we moved to Brownsville, Tennessee, and then to the country outside of Milan, Tennessee, on a blacktop road called Grabal Road. I did not understand why we moved so often until I got older and thought maybe it was because we had so many in the family that we could not pay all the rent that was due. My daddy, without a doubt, did everything he could that once he had his family together, he did not want anything to break us up. I surmise that it took all that he made to supply food for our family of ten. We, at times with Mama's help, learned to grow a garden and supply different types of vegetables to have food to eat. Daddy did not have much left from his paycheck to pay for other things. The clothes we had were passed down from other relatives that we contacted from time to time, and it was an understanding that when relatives grew out of the clothes they had, they were passed down through other relatives that would fit them.

I remember that close to Jackson, Tennessee, we relocated to an old farmhouse that mostly had been an old slave dwelling from the Civil War. When we moved into the house, it had to be cleaned, but not the normal cleaning that one might think. The wall had to be stripped off all the old wallpaper due to age and peeling. When this was done, the old walls were revealed, along with everything that had made a home between the large wooden beams. The beams in this house were as large as or larger than a railroad crosstie, which told its age as what I suggested earlier. There were rat droppings and chewed-up old newspaper that the rats had dragged between the large crosstie walls to make themselves beds. As we cleaned between the beams, we also had to rid one section of a large black snake, which my mama and daddy thought about leaving where we had pulled it from because they said it was a good snake and ate all the rats that might come into the house or walls. After a lot of complaining, mostly from the girls, to Mama, fortunately, Daddy took the snake outside and left it in the barn that was across the field at the rear of this old house. I asked Daddy later in life why we moved to that old house, and he told me, "Son, with all we had in our family, we had to cut wherever we could when we could. And the man I rented the house from at first did not want to rent it because he insisted that it was not fit to live in and too old and would probably fall to the ground during the next lightning storm or high wind."

My daddy tried to explain further, saying, "Your mama and I were trying the best we could at that time to keep all you kids together, and one day, while driving, I noticed that old house off the road, and I just knew we needed to do something."

This old house also did not have a bathroom or running water inside, and during the winter, we burned wood from a cast-iron stove. When we bathed, there was a water pump out in the backyard, and this was where our drinking water came from as well. It had to be pumped by hand. In the wintertime, water had to be warmed up from inside on the wood-burning stove, as much water as we could and with as many pots from the kitchen as we could use. When we bathed, most of the time the bathwater had to be shared between as many kids as possible so we could conserve water and not have to keep pumping from the well. During the summertime, all we would do was pump a large long tub full of well water early in the morning and leave it out in the sun all day for it to warm. The only problem was that when it filled up, we could not move it and had to take our baths outside, with the possibility of all the other kids watching us when we bathed.

During the years I spent with my dad and stepmother, I probably saw my birth mother maybe once or twice in the early years. While we were living outside of Brownsville, Tennessee, my mother and my stepfather, Ed, showed up to visit and had brought us a small pony. My stepmother and my birth mother were not very friendly with each other, and I noticed—sensed, really—when the horse was delivered that my stepmother was not happy with the gift. After my mother left, I could hear my stepmother and my father having a loud discussion in the other room. "Your son Hershel should not have a gift if others in the family don't have the opportunity to have the same!" she was overheard stating. "Come in here!" she then yelled out to me, knowing that I was in the other room.

I saw my father on the other side of the room, looking out the window. She sternly looked from him toward me, saying, "That horse that your mother brought is your responsibility, young man, and you are the one that would take care of it and feed it. And you are to allow the other children to ride that animal too. And you better understand what I'm telling you, young man. Understood?"

"Yes, ma'am," I said, looking up at her, wondering why she was upset. "Everybody can ride it whenever they want to, and I have a place to store it up the road in old man Jones's place. He's got a barn up there."

"How do you know that he'll let you keep that pony in his barn or his field?"

"Well, sometimes I help them around the barn feeding the chickens, and I also help him with the other animals. And he's a really friendly man. I'll go up and talk to him first thing in the morning, but I'm sure he'll be okay with it."

"Okay, but if I hear any kind of complaining from any of the other children that you won't let them ride it, then we'll have to take a second look whether we can keep that pitiful thing."

"Oh, yes, ma'am," I told her. "Please, I'm sure everything is gonna be okay." Turning, I then left the room.

Each day before school, I went to the barn and Mr. Jones's house and fed the pony and did other chores around his barnyard to repay him for allowing me to keep our pony there.

Several months later, my dad got another job, as I mentioned earlier, close to Milan, Tennessee, just off Grabal Road. In this house, we had a barn close by in the back, and I was so happy that I had my own barn to keep my pony stabled in. But we couldn't afford to buy grain and hay to feed him, so I would take him out of the stall and tie him out where he could graze in the yard.

One day, before school, I tied my pony out in a good, high-grass section of the yard in front of the house, where I knew he'd have plenty to eat until I got back. Then later, like every day, coming home from school on the bus, I was excited to get back so I could brush down the pony and ride him through the fields, of which there was plenty—and woods too—where we lived. As the school bus approached the driveway where we lived, my eyes were on the yard. I could see my pony lying in the front yard, but he was not moving. Thinking that maybe he was just full and was resting, I ran off the bus and toward the front, where the pony was lying. Looking down, I noticed all four of his legs were stiff, and looking at his face, I could see that he wasn't breathing and both of his eyes were glazed over. I checked the rope around his neck, which I noticed had been tightened.

I quickly grabbed the rope, loosening it around his neck and pulling it over his head. Then I stood up, looking back down in utter shock. Tears began to flow as I jumped back to my feet and quickly started running toward the house. And as I approached, getting closer to the house, I looked and could see my stepmother standing on the porch, looking in my direction. I slowed my run down to a brisk walk as I approached the house, tears still flowing down my face, and began to run toward my stepmother, who was looking in my direction. Then I began to blubber out, "Our pony's dead! It looks like he had choked himself on the rope!" Looking up into her face, I asked, "Why couldn't you, Mama, have one of the others check on him and make sure this wouldn't happen? Or you could have loosened the rope!"

"Well, young man, I told you that horse was your responsibility and you were to take care of it!"

One of my stepbrothers came outside and said, "Bubba, I saw the horse was struggling, and I was going to go out there and loosen the rope around his neck because he was pulling against it, but Mama would not let me!"

I looked up into her face with anger and disbelief.

"Tommy! You get yourself back in that house! I'll take care of this out here," she said. "Bubba," she continued, looking down at me, "your daddy should be home here in a little bit, and then he'll deal with that pony. I want that dead thing out of my front yard before it starts to stink up the whole countryside!" Then, with an evil smirk of disgust on her face, she turned and went inside the house.

I slowly walked back toward my pony, retrieving the rope, and fell to my knees, crying, first looking up toward the sky, asking God to take my pony into animal heaven, and then down toward the ground where he lay. "God," I cried out, "he was such a beautiful pony, with those pretty blue glass eyes! God, he gave me over a year of companionship."

He was bothersome sometimes on numerous occasions. When I would tie him out, he would somehow break free of the rope, and when I came home, he would be nowhere to be found. But I would, in a nervous frenzy, track his prints across the road and down through the cornfields and cotton fields in what seemed like miles, continually tracing his prints until I would finally see him feeding on an ear of corn and then cautiously walk toward him with my open hand up toward him, slipping the rope that I had brought with me around his neck and trying to scold him on the way back home. Maybe, thinking back, I guess I was to blame. I didn't want to lose him, and maybe I tied the rope around his neck too tight for fear that he would get away again, which he had done on several occasions. I visualized him in my head in the final minutes of his life being frightened and pulling away, trying to get loose, but the rope tightened around his neck instead of slipping over his head like it had a few times before.

Going Home with Daddy

Part 2

My sister Cynthia was so sweet throughout her early years. She had fat cheeks, freckles, and piercing blue eyes that would light up the room when she came into it. She was a few years younger than I was, which made me her big brother, Bubba. My sister Pat, who was the eldest, apparently lived in Memphis with our mother Jeanette, who left Cynthia to be the only female sister of mine that lived with my dad and stepmother. However, I had three other sisters from my stepmother's first marriage, and they were the eldest. Now, on the other side, with us boys, there were me, my brother, my stepbrother Tommy, and another brother, who would be my half-brother from my dad and my stepmother's union.

During the first part of living with my dad and my stepmother, Mary Elizabeth, and all the other brothers and sisters, including my own brother and my sister Cynthia, I knew it was quite a change from the other places that we had stayed in through the years away from our parents. I could hear my sissy Cynthia in one part of the house. She was quietly whimpering. I leaned over, peering into the girls' bedroom, then I hurried into the room and around the bed, quickly kneeling. But I thought maybe I startled her, because she violently jerked her hand away from her face, looking in horror up into mine.

"Oh!" she said. "Bubba, where have you been? Why weren't you here to help me?"

"Sissy," I cried out to her, "what is wrong? Why are you crying?" It was obvious that she was emotionally traumatized. As I hugged her close to me, she began to cry into my chest, and I could feel her fingernails clawing into my chest. "Please, sissy, tell me what is wrong!"

She looked into my eyes and attempted to speak. "I've tried and tried, Bubba, I really have, not to make a mistake in the bed while I'm sleeping and have even tried to stay up all night, but sometimes I just can't stay awake, and then that is when I make the mistake and wet the bed again," she told me. "Bubba, I even tried to take all the sheets out and wash them before Mama gets home, but today she got home before I could finish all the sheets or make the bed with new ones. Mama whipped me real bad this time, and I tried to tell her that I have tried not to wet the bed and that I was sorry and was trying to wash them and would not do it again so she would stop hitting me…"

"Oh, sissy," I said. Looking down at her face, I could also see the red welts that covered her legs and arms. I hugged her close but tried not to touch any of the welts that covered her arms. I was so furious and tried not to cry with her, to not make the hurt any worse. I could see that she had on what appeared to be a large white cloth surrounding her bottom where her panties usually were. "What is that?" I asked, pointing at the cloth.

"Mama, after she whipped me, said that since I was acting like a baby, she was going to treat me like one. Mama said that my punishment was for the rest of the day, and through the night, I was to wear this diaper," she said. "Bubba, all the rest of the girls are laughing at me because Mama is making me wear this diaper around the house in front of them! They were all sitting in the kitchen earlier when I was washing the dishes, and Mama was allowing them to laugh at me. And then, when I looked around, Mama was sitting with a smile on her face.

"I cried and asked her, 'Please, don't allow them to laugh at me, and, Mama, don't laugh at me either, please.' I begged Mama.

"She replied sternly, 'Next time, I bet you will learn to get your-self out of that bed and go to the bathroom like you're supposed to. And stop being such a prissy baby! All these other girls are not as stupid as that, to just lie there and wet on themselves! I think maybe next time, if you keep acting that stupidly to wet on yourself, we will just have to make you a pallet over in one of those corners! That mattress costs a lot of money, and these other girls don't want to lie there in your stinky piss all night! Young lady, just shut your mouth and do not worry about what's going on over here and pay attention to how I taught you to do those dishes, or you might just have to do them over again. And don't you think I'm not going to check them after you're done either.' Mama pointed her shaking finger violently at me, motioning for me to turn toward the sink and finish the dishes."

"Bubba," she continued, "I love Mama and my other sisters, but she doesn't treat me the same way as she does all the others."

"Sissy," I said, "she does love you." But I couldn't force a believ-able facial expression to help her believe me.

"No, Bubba, she doesn't!" Cynthia said. "Last week, she made dresses for all my sisters and told me that she ran out of cloth to make me one. Bubba, I know that wasn't true because I looked in the cloth cabinet and there was still a whole half a bolt of cloth left. I asked her about it, and that was when she slapped me across the face, ask-ing why I was calling her a liar. Why does Mama hate me so much, Bubba? Why!" She looked desperately at me, her big brother, to give her an answer. "I try to do everything Mama needs for me to do, but she always beats me and hollers at me."

I pulled my sissy close to me in an attempt to soothe her. Holding her, I knew in my mind what she felt and why it was the way she did. Her grief at being separated from the other girls was justified. I, too, felt the same, but never to the extreme of physical and verbal abuse like my little sister, Cynthia, had gotten. I thought that Mama had to be jealous of our daddy and Cynthia, because when he came home, Cynthia would be so excited to see him, hugging on Daddy and lov-ing him so dearly, saying she missed him when he was away working. Or just maybe, while he was home, she felt safe. I knew that Mama treated her differently when Daddy was home, treating her as she did all the other girls. I felt it strange, not understanding the change in Mama's behavior toward Cynthia. When Daddy was home, instead of yelling as she did when he wasn't, she calmly spoke in what I thought was a normal tone. When Cynthia was disciplined when he was home, Mama would not beat her as she would all the other times; she instead sent Cynthia to a corner, where she would make her stay for what seemed like hours or until Daddy would finally say, "I think she has stood in that corner long enough, don't you?" Mama would look angrily toward Daddy, I guess because she didn't like it that he was concerned and taking up for Cynthia. She was the only one among the girls who was made to stand in the corner, and Mama blamed it on her taking after the disposition of my daddy's father, whom she claimed was called an ornery old man.

In one instance, Mama changed her expression of loving-kindness whenever she looked at Daddy to another one when she looked at the corner where Cynthia stood tiredly. "Okay, young lady, do you think you can do what you're told and behave yourself? If so, you can now join the rest of the family."

Daddy could see that most of the food that had been on the table was eaten by all the others. I, however, had thought ahead and had not eaten all that was on my plate. But as Cynthia sat down, Mama took my plate and the others on the table and started toward the garbage, where they were quickly crapped off. However, Daddy saw that everything was gone and asked Mama why she had emptied all the plates, including mine, when Cynthia had not eaten yet, and it was not necessary for her to throw all that food away, anyway. I was relieved that my daddy was complaining to Mama and was hoping that maybe, finally, he was noticing that Cynthia might not have been treated the same as all the other girls.

Mama looked up from the garbage and perhaps realized that without really meaning to, she might have accidentally revealed her true feelings toward my sister Cynthia to Daddy while he was home. With a lot of anger, she said, "If she wants more, there it is," pointing to the pile of good food she had discarded into the trash can.

"What in the world is wrong with you?" my dad said. "How can you treat that young-un that way? What has she done this time?"

Mama immediately saw that Daddy was getting very suspicious toward her, at the way she was suddenly acting toward Cynthia, and immediately changed her attitude. She told him that Cynthia had another accident in the girls' bed and that was what she was upset about. I knew that was not the entire truth, because that was not the only thing that caused Cynthia to keep getting brutal beatings. I think Mama was, in my opinion, making up excuses to Daddy to justify her anger and hatred toward my sissy.

Through the years, there were numerous times when I would come into the house and could hear my sissy suffering through a very violent beating. The majority of the time, Mama used to beat Cynthia with whatever she thought would bring the most suffering and cause Cynthia to scream the loudest. Numerous times throughout the years, before I eventually was forced to leave, I'd come into the house and plead with Mama to stop beating Cynthia.

"Mama, please stop!" I pleaded.

"She wants to do it again!"

Not knowing what it was that Cynthia was accused of doing, I screamed, "Please stop! Mama!"

That apparently caught her attention just briefly enough, and the look on her face was as though she was possessed by some sort of demon that I could only relate to one from a horror movie. She glared at me with what I could only describe as a demon-possessed smile upon her face and had slobber trickling down the sides of her mouth.

"Mama!" I again screamed because I could see that her eyes had that strange sort of glare that I had seen so many times before. I knew when that glare came, and if I had enough warning, I would take Cynthia and myself away from where she was. Mama would only then, if I screamed loud enough, suddenly act as though she would come back to herself. Her pupils would change to what I can only describe as normal, and her facial expression would also relax, changing back to her natural hue and color. Only then when Mama released her grip on her would Cynthia cower across the room, scooting on her behind until she thought she was far enough away that Mama could not swing at her with the switch she had been violently beating her with. The switch that I could also see had splintered on the end and broken into two pieces.

I raced over to my sister, falling onto the floor next to where she was crying. When I attempted to hug her, she grimaced, apparently because of all the lacerations she had received from the switching. I got her injuries and stains onto my clothes, but I did not worry or care about my clothes. I really wanted to hurt my stepmother for all the beating and hate she was inflicting on my sissy. I held Cynthia as I looked up at Mama. "Please, what did sissy do so bad that you had to whip her so hard?"

"Young man, the last thing you need to worry about is that 'heathen' there!" She pointed toward me at my sissy with her shaking finger and arm. "You need to mind your own business," she told me. "And what are you doing in here? I thought I had chores for you and the other boys? I know y'all couldn't have all of them done by now!"

I also thought that it was a good thing that I had come in early because she might have killed my sister if I hadn't. I always thought, with good reasoning and fear, that she hated my sister and secretly wanted to kill her because of her jealousy of Cynthia with the way our daddy showed what I thought was very little affection to my step-mother. I now believe he knew of Mama's jealousy and didn't want to make matters any worse than they were between him and her. I certainly did not want her to find another excuse to beat Cynthia any more than what she already did. I really did not think he was aware of how serious the hatred and jealousy were, though, and if so, she could have made it look like some sort of accident and my sister could have been seriously hurt or, yes, I thought of the extreme. These thoughts went through my mind all of our lives, especially my little sister, Cynthia's. The beating and emotional trauma had to be nothing short of what I now acknowledge would have to come from some sort of horror movie, one that only a demented horror movie director could conjure up.

This section of our lives was just one of many that had occurred, where I had to endure the physical abuse of my sissy that happened so many times, with her beaten with a large leather strap (belt). Or Mama would make her go out and get a switch from the brushes on the side of the house. Then I could see Mama take the switch from Cynthia while she was screaming and begging Mama to please not whip her. "Please, Mama!" she would scream. "I won't do it again! Please, I'm sorry!" And so many times I would also plead with Mama because I tried not to be too far away most of the time whenever Mama was around Cynthia, especially when she was tired from working all day in Milan, Tennessee, at the AT&T factory.

"Mama, what did sissy do?" I would ask as she started stripping the leaves off the long switch in an apparent attempt, in my opinion, to further intimidate and send more apparent horror into my little sister's mind.

"You get yourself outside. This is none of your business," she would say. "And if you give me any more trouble, I'll tell your dad when he gets home what you also did!"

"But, Mama, I did not do anything wrong! I just got home from school, and I and Danny and Gary did all our chores before we left this morning."

"You get yourself outside!" Mama screamed at me. "Right now! And don't you think I won't think of something that you should have done and tell your daddy. And don't you ever say that Danny did not help you with any of the chores, or your brother Gary!"

"Mama, I did not say that!" I told her, even though it was so true. There had been many times when our stepbrother Tommy knew that he could get away with just doing whatever he pleased while we did most of or all the work.

"Get your rear end out of here! I got your sister's discipline to take care of!"

This was so common, not only her making my stepsisters those dresses, but also with my stepbrother not sharing with most, if any, of the chores.

Tommy was crippled at birth and wore braces on both of his legs just below the knees. This handicap, however, did not interfere other than with walking normally as other boys. His upper-body strength was very strong because of his constantly falling and catching himself with his hands, which built up his arms and shoulders. We sometimes complained that he should help us with certain chores, but then quickly he would run after us, grabbing whoever he caught in those hands with their viselike grip, throwing them, and with his momentum, he would fall on top, giving those he caught a crushing blow. Then it was virtually impossible to break his grip, putting us at his mercy. Our only recourse from his assaults was to outrun him and to keep out of reach of those hands because if he got ahold of you, there would be no escape. We would outrun him by dodging back and forth, sometimes laughing as we did. Tommy would become furious, and I would see the rage and frustration on his face, which looked so familiar, like the look upon Mama's face when she became enraged. During these times, we made it a point to stay away from him, always looking to make sure he was not attempting to slip up on anyone he was mad with. During the day, we could find something to do for him to take his mind off getting even, and then eventually, he would forget and calm down. We did not want him to continue to think about revenge because we knew that if he got ahold of any of us, he would not let go until one of us or both got injured or terribly hurt from his assaults. Sometimes, one of us would slip into the house and try to find some leftover food that we could always use to calm him down.

From outside, I could hear the beating that Mama was giving my sissy, and it was all I could do to rush back inside and plead with Mama to please stop, but eventually, her screams quieted to a sucking of air from Cynthia, an attempt to stay quiet so as not to make Mama any madder than she already was. Then again, I painfully heard the switch whisk through the air, along with the continued screaming of Cynthia. And also the violence in Mama's voice as she screamed at sissy, "Next time, I guess you 'pee pot' baby will do what I tell you!"

"Mama, I'm sorry, I will. I promise I'll do anything that you want!"

By then what I was praying for would be one final wisp of air and the sound of loud screaming from sissy as the switch met her soft young flesh.

I got the impression when Cynthia got beatings that at times some were brief only because Mama might be just a little tired from work or maybe she thought that Daddy would be home soon and she didn't want Cynthia to be still crying when he got home. At those times, she would either send Cynthia to her room or find something for her to do outside, and mostly alone, without the other girls. Even though we were all packed into a small house, it was unavoidable that the other girls would spend all their time without meeting their sister. I noticed that there were times whenever the girls were doing what girls normally do when playing and/or living together that Mama would come around and separate them, calling her girls into another room, leaving Cynthia alone.

As I have said before, I, of course, loved my sister very dearly and felt so sorry for her and had such hatred and/or mixed feelings toward my stepmother, at the same time trying to understand why she felt the way she did toward my sister. I could see most of the time that Cynthia showed our stepmother so much love, and she probably felt that the punishment she had been receiving was, at that time, normal. Cynthia asked me constantly how she could do certain things that would please Mama, or what she could do before she got home to make her happy. There were times when I spotted Cynthia out in the outer field, stooping over, and I could tell that she was picking the wild dandelion flowers, gathering a large handful. Once, I ran out to meet her, asking, "Hey, sissy, what are you doing?" I could see exactly what it was in her hand and thought maybe she was gathering them for her and the other girls' bedroom.

"Oh, Bubba, look at what I got for Mama! Do you think she will just love what I have for her? Do you think she will love me?" Then she corrected what she said. "I mean, love these flowers?" She held them up with a precious smile on her pretty, freckled face. I felt so sorry for my sister, and at the same time, I felt anger, knowing that there wasn't anything as far as I was concerned to satisfy our stepmother or soothe the contempt she had toward the both of us, especially to my sister Cynthia.

Many times I spent out in the woods, looking up into the trees, asking God to please protect my baby sister. She wanted so much to please our stepmother. With tears streaming down my cheeks, I asked God to help my little sister, Cynthia, and did not want our mama to hurt her anymore. "God, she is trying so hard to not use

220

the bathroom in the bed. If you will, God, please help her. I think that Mama will probably not beat her anymore if you could and would help her control herself or wake her up so she can go before she makes that terrible mistake again. I know, God, that you love me and my sister as much as we love you." As I knelt there, I pleaded with God on the cold, damp wooded ground. "Please help my sissy! Dear God, I'm not asking for anything for myself." I shook my head violently, thinking it would look like a serious, sincere expression to God. "Just please, God, help my little sissy. I love her so much and worry about her. She loves you too. Please believe me, God, she really does, and she says her prayers each day. And I know that she loves our stepmama too." I raised my eyes toward the top of the trees, I think, in a gesture to look up, hoping that I would see and feel some sort of spiritual relief.

I thought at this time in my life what my grandmother had told me, that God hears his children always. I wanted to believe and feel a special feeling indicating that God was hearing my plea. Maybe it was just me, as a young child, needing to know that what my grandmother had said to me was true. "Bubba," she would say, lovingly squeezing my cheeks as she looked into my small face and blue eyes, "son, if you ask your heavenly Father for something with a faithful heart, he will fulfill all your needs."

I again closed my eyes, squeezing them tightly shut, clasping my fingers and hands together to make a tight fist. I started praying again with all my heart and spiritual strength. "Oh, thank you, God! I know you remember, God, what my grandmother told me, and I know how close she was to you, God, and how truly she believed that you hear me and love me and don't want any child as I and my sissy to be without being or feeling love! I know, God, that you don't want my little sister to be hurt anymore, do you, God? I am asking again, please, God, put kindness into our mama's heart so she will stop hurting her. God, I just don't know how much my little sissy can take. God, please, I love my little sissy, and if you will, Lord, please help her!" I screamed loud enough that even though I was deep into the woods, I was still afraid that my voice could be heard. But I really didn't care who heard me; I just wanted and pleaded for God to help her. "God, I can't take seeing Mama beating her anymore. Please, O God, please, help my little sissy."

After what I thought must seem like hours, I raised my eyes again to the sky, letting out a breath, then said, "Okay! God, thank you so much!" I took another deep breath and started to wipe back the tears that continued to run down my cheeks, then my nose, which had profusely started running to the extent that it had run into my mouth, and as I attempted to wipe it out of my mouth, I hacked and spit the excess over onto the ground. I wanted to stop the crying, and I felt such comfort, as though something deep inside of me was being relieved. "Okay, okay, okay, I'm so sorry, God, for all this crying! I just want you to please, God, hear me, but now I'll stop, okay, God?" I was continually trying to wipe the tears from my eyes, doing everything in my power to stop crying, because I was under the impression that God would be mad at me. "I know and believe, as my grandmother had said to me so many times, that if you ask with true faith, you can move mountains. God, I don't want that type of help, to move a mountain. I just want you to help me to help my little sister. And please tell me that everything will be okay now!" Then, as I got up from the damp ground filled with leaves, I felt a strange, wonderful feeling, as I usually did each time I spoke to God, and just knew that all would be all right.

It had started to get dusk, but I was not afraid of getting stuck in the wood when dark came, because I felt the presence of God's Spirit, and this kept me from worrying about anything. I felt a cool breeze blowing through my hair, and my cheeks, which had been wet with tears, now felt cooled from the flush that had covered my face and entire body, which must have come from the extreme passion of my prayer. Strangely, I thought I heard the crackle of leaves and limbs nearby, as though someone was walking. It might be possible, I thought, that one of my brothers had come out looking for me. In farms in this area of the country, people were usually very friendly, especially those on the adjacent lands, and didn't worry in those early days where their property lines ended or started. It was not uncommon to see another farmer either cutting timber or hunting nearby. I did, however, know that anything like that sound, especially the voice of someone speaking, had to be close by. As I stopped to listen, I turned my head to one side then the other to put each ear in several different directions, listening very closely and trying not to make a sound. I even tried to hush my heart, which was still beating rapidly because of my intense prayer and could be felt and, I thought, heard.

I could hear a faint whistle and humming, which I thought was familiar. I didn't know what it was; the sound of whistling just had the familiarity of something or someone. Suddenly, I knew why I felt this way. "Hey, mister!" I shouted. It was the old traveler that I first met at my grandparents' farm and then again years later at the foster home south of Memphis, in the township known as Germantown, Tennessee. It was Mr. Gabe, the traveling man. I always thought that Mr. Gabe had spirituality on him, as my grandmother had. "What a great surprise, Mr. Gabe. Wow!" I knew that I showed great excitement. "Strange that you just happen to be traveling through this area now." I really needed to see a friendly face and such a spiritual friend and thought at once that there truly was a God and he did hear my prayers. It seemed as though each time I reached such a desolate place in my thoughts, God sent me comfort in the form of a good friend like this good, spiritual traveler. Mr. Gabe always seemed to know just what to say to comfort me just when I needed it most. He, in this comforting way during our visits, would give me a message from the great Creator, God.

I stepped quickly toward Mr. Gabe to hug him or shake his hand, but when I reached out to where he was standing, or where I thought he was standing, I quickly stumbled to the ground and looked up only to see him a few feet away instead. "Oh! Mr. Gabe!" I said, getting myself up from the ground, again brushing the damp leaves off me. I then, again, walked toward where he was now standing.

As if he knew that I wanted to hug him, he quickly raised his arms toward me, telling me, "No, son! You must not get too close to this old man. I've been traveling quite a journey, and you don't need to get any of this road dirt on you."

"Oh, but, Mr. Gabe, you don't look dirty to me!" I said, looking up and down his body, at his clothes. I could not see any dirt at all on him.

Giving me that big bright smile I now remembered, he began to explain that he was on a spiritual journey that involved meditating and fasting. "I need not, at this moment in my journeys, come in physical contact with anyone or anything from this world."

I did not understand what he was trying to explain, so instead, quickly and excitedly, I said, "Oh! Mr. Gabe, I wish you had been here earlier. You could have helped me pray, as you did the last time."

"Well, okay, my child," he said with that warm smile of his. "Calm down now, my son, and tell Gabriel how you've been since the last time we've met." He seemed to be filling my entire body with that mesmerizing, illuminating glow that seemed to start from his face then flow downward throughout his entire body. This feeling seemed to flow through the very space that separated us, which felt as though an electric shock of static electricity was flowing throughout my body, followed by a cool, flowing breeze that seemed to rustle the leaves slightly on the trees just around the area I was standing. His beard was as white as first-fallen snow and looked short, close to the face. His hair was also white and flowed down to about his shoulders, as I would expect a traveling homeless hippie. *Hippie* was a term I heard grown people say that referred to travelers that resembled others like him in this era of the early sixties.

"My precious child, please tell me about that mule Old Blue. Is he still around, grazing out into the fields on your grandfather's farm?"

"Oh yes, I believe he is." But then I thought and answered, "I really don't know for sure, Mr. Gabe. I haven't lived with Grandpa or Grandma in a long time."

He seemed to be able to know what I was about to ask, as though he knew what I was thinking before I had the chance to say anything. "Yes, child, I know you are with your daddy, aren't you? It sure looks like you got your prayers answered the last time you asked our great Creator for help! Do you remember that we met each other around those two large lakes as I was traveling through?" He smiled with such pearly white teeth, showing me kindness, and I still felt that strange feeling that was coming from Mr. Gabe. I felt the great spirit of love that only I had known from my grandmother. "My precious child, I'm so glad to see your very own personal guardian angels still have kept you safe, which, of course, our heavenly Father has blessed you with. And I can see, by you being here, that you stayed away from the water's edge when you lived close to that lake not long ago. I can also see that you have not drowned or gotten bitten by any of the water creatures!" Then he reared back, letting out a loud chuckle.

"Yes, sir, Mr. Gabe," I replied with all sincerity. "I have tried to do what my foster parents told me. They were very strict, but that was because they loved us and were only concerned with our safety. The only time we could go near those lakes was when one of them was with us, either when we went fishing or went for a spiritual walk in nature, which we did mostly on Sundays. The Hildebrands called it a spiritual walk because as we walked, they would teach us about certain sections of the Bible, along with having us look throughout nature as we walked to notice God's little creatures like rabbits, squirrels and, sometimes if we were lucky, we might see a fox, or all kinds of other creatures that they would explain were the great Creator's handiwork."

"Yes, my precious child, these good people, the Hildebrands, were very special to have taken care of you and the other boys. That was your heavenly Father's plan for you at that very time in your life. As you grow older and go through your life, there will be things that might cause you to remember from this early time in life. Then a lot you'll understand, as things will be revealed, how the great Creator has protected you and shown his never-ending love to you. You must remember, my child, that you have been chosen by God to be here at this time and place. Your purpose throughout life is to serve the great Creator, our God. The great Creator, however, gave us all free will to make our own choices as we go throughout our lives, but we must remember to make the right ones. When you pray, your desire is to ask God to help you see with all your heart, to show you how you can serve him, asking God to show you how to be a good servant to him throughout your life."

"Yes, sir," I replied. "I was praying for my little sister, Cynthia, and asking God if he would please show her how to stop having those terrible accidents. Our mama we now have doesn't like it that my little sissy has these accidents while she is asleep, or any of the other bad things that upset our mama that my little sissy does sometimes. I think she misses our big sister, Patricia, and our real mother. Mr. Gabe, do you think this might be the reason she has these accidents at night while she's sleeping?" I asked with a sincere, desperate look as if pleading for Mr. Gabe to give me the answers that sought. "Mr. Gabe, I try to get up and slip into the girls' room, while trying not to wake up any of the other girls, so I can help my little sissy get to the bathroom. I do this because, Mr. Gabe, I love my little sissy and I don't like to see or hear our mama whip her as hard as she does. Oh, Mr. Gabe!"

I began to cry as I explained how much it hurt me.

"And I also cry a lot when I see Mama hurt her as bad as she does. Sometimes I beg for Mama to stop hurting her, then beg that she whip me instead. I scream at her, 'Please stop! Don't hurt her anymore!' I'm screaming at her, pleading with her, holding my head around the ears because I cannot bear to see or hear any more of her beating or hear sissy screaming for her to stop. Sissy is desperately trying to fend her off and defend herself from the violent assaults either by the belt or the switches that are cutting into her flesh. 'Please stop, Mama!' I scream. 'She won't do it again!'

"After Mama gets tired of whipping her, she says, 'Now, young lady, you take your little self into that bathroom and get that piss washed off you so you won't stink up all the other children in school. I sure don't want you to dare embarrass my other girls with your stink!'

"I try to wake her up, Mr. Gabe, several times during the night so she won't make our mama angry the next morning. Mama also checks each day the pallet she told Cynthia to place over in the corner of the bedroom and away from the other girls' beds. My poor sissy, if she does make another mistake, Mama will beat her, and, Mr. Gabe, she might even kill my little sissy! She won't allow her to wash her sheets and instead makes her sleep on them for several days. Mama will check her sheets with rubber gloves, I think, just to make my sissy feel ashamed. Mama makes her stand there while all the other girls giggle in the other room to see if there are any new wet spots, and if there is, Sissy will get another beating!

"So you see, Mr. Gabe, it is so important that you help me pray and ask God to help my sissy not to have these accidents. Mr. Gabe, please! Because…please! Don't you see? If I can't or am unable to get her up in time, Mama will beat her! Oh, please, Mr. Gabe!"

I continued to cry as I pleaded. "Mr. Gabe, I feel so awful and helpless at times that I could have done something to help her! If only I had gotten her up!"

"Now, my child," Mr. Gabe said, and his voice seemed to have a calming effect on me, as it had the last time we met. "God hears your cries, my son, and he will help you, as he always has and will continue to do." Mr. Gabe looked around and pointed. "You see that stump over there in the direction where a large oak had been cut down, leaving a flat smooth surface? Let's walk over there to that stump. That is going to be the place where you can come and pray. That tree stump will be your altar. Whenever you need to speak to our great Creator, that stump is where you will come. Of course, my child, you can always talk to God anytime and anyplace, but this will be the special place that only you, God, and I, Mr. Gabe, will know about," he said with a big smile. "Now, my child, let us go over there right now, and I'll follow, and we shall ask God for the things that you desire. I know and believe, my child, that you shall receive your every need."

Walking over to the tree stump, I turned to look around as I knelt to see Mr. Gabe's approval.

"Always remember, child, that our God is always here all around, and whenever you need him, he is always just a prayer away."

"Mr. Gabe, thank you so much! When I feel that all is lost, you seem to be passing through wherever I'm staying. I just don't know sometimes what I would have done without you helping me. And you seem to know all the ways to ask of our God."

"My child, God has revealed in the great book from the prophets, 'Suffer little children to come unto me,' and he will give them rest. You, my child, more than you know, are closer to God than any of all the other creatures of this world that have been created. When

I'm not around in this body, my child, all you need is to just focus on me and I will always be with you in spirit," Gabe said. "Now, my child, ask God all you desire and for his will to be done in your life, and you shall listen to, believe in, and feel the presence of the great Creator and receive his love."

I prayed again for what seemed like hours but must have only been moments, feeling such an overwhelming calmness as I did, asking God what he needed of me, as Mr. Gabe instructed. "Thank you, God, for all that you have done for me and my family. Thank you for sending your Son, Jesus, to give his life for all of humanity. I give my entire life for you to use in whatever way you need. I realize that the purpose of my life is, first, to serve you, then all that I desire will be given."

When I first knelt to pray, it was the early part of the afternoon, and after I finished and said to God, "I thank you and especially Mr. Gabe for always being there during the times in my life when it seems like I needed you most," it had gotten dark. I looked around me and wanted to say thank you to Mr. Gabe, but he was not there. I started getting to my feet and looking around, all the time yelling out Mr. Gabe's name. "Mr. Gabe, where are you?" Looking up at the sky, I also noticed that the stars had come out. *Oh, what a beautiful night!* I thought. I had realized that though I thought only just a short period of time had gone past, it must have been a lot longer. What had happened And where was Mr. Gabe? I felt such a peace within me, as though all my problems and fears had somehow been erased.

I looked up toward all the beautiful stars that were a part of God's creation. There was a gust of wind, and I imagined that I heard the faint voice of Mr. Gabe calling out from a distance, "Go home, my son. Your Father has heard your cries and will be with you always." I looked around me, but no one could be seen. I guessed it had to be my imagination.

When I got to the house, I could see my daddy standing out in the front yard, and he seemed to also be looking up at the sky. Looking in his direction brought a smile to my face, seeing my daddy standing there. "Daddy!" I hollered, increasing my pace, and when I reached him, I hugged him around the waist. Daddy brought one of his arms around my shoulders, which made me, as always, feel so safe, and I knew that now I could have a good night's sleep.

"Son, where have you been?"

"Oh, Daddy, I was just out in the woods over there," I said, pointing at the wooded area I had been in. "I think maybe I just lost track of what time it was and it got dark before I knew it."

Leaving McLemoresville for Memphis, Tennessee

———— ❀ ————

On a Friday night, as was the custom, my other siblings and I were enjoying the usual hamburgers and hot dogs, where were our delicacy once a week, after my dad and stepmother had gotten paid. Somehow during the night, there was a misunderstanding and I was accused of getting the last hamburger. I was on the table, but I did not take it and knew who did; it was her son. But to keep problems from getting any worse, I kept that to myself, as was the normal process of living for us.

She started fussing at me, calling me names. My dad at that time, after dinner, was over underneath the kitchen sink, trying to repair a leak. I was trying to defend myself, saying, "No, Mama, I did not get the last one!"

She was persistent, and she started teasing me, saying, "Yes, it was you, and you know it was you! You're always the one to think that you deserve more than anybody else. You should be ashamed of yourself!"

I continued to plead with her repeatedly, defending myself. And finally, I let it slip. I said, "Mama, it wasn't me. I saw Tommy reach for and get the last one off the plate!"

Her face began to turn red, and her eyes got a glazed-over look. "Now you're going to blame it on Tommy! And you know you're the one that got the last one. It was either you or Cynthia!" She walked over to where I was standing, between the kitchen and the dam, and started shaking her finger in my face, saying, "You know you're the one that got that. And now you're trying to blame it on poor Tommy!" Just the anger on her face not only scared me but also somewhat continued to frustrate me. No matter how long or how hard I denied it, she continued her badgering, shaking her finger in my face and screaming at me, "You're the one that took it! Admit it, you're the one that took it!" She continued shaking her finger in my face and yelling and screaming at me.

I began to cry, and she was so close, screaming at me, that the spit coming out of her mouth was covering my face. She kept insisting, repeatedly poking my cheek with her finger, saying, "Admit it, you're the one that took it!" She shoved her finger so hard into my cheek that it hurt me and pushed me back.

Then suddenly, I don't know what came over me, but when she shoved her finger into my forehead, I snapped my neck back and reached out, slapping her, which completely shocked and frightened me beyond anything I felt before. She ran toward my dad, who was still underneath the sink, lying on the floor, trying to fix the broken pipe, and I could see that he had sort of a smirk on his face.

"Son, you go outside and I'll be out there in a minute to talk to you."

This was the beginning of the end of my living with my dad and my stepmother. Shortly after that, I was asked to leave. Thankfully, there was a friend that took me off the road from my dad's house. This new place, I stayed at briefly for a while, and then I decided that I would go to Memphis, where my sister Pat and my mom lived.

I packed a small suitcase that I had gotten from my friend's house and proceeded up to the main highway in McLemoresville, Tennessee, and waited there for the Greyhound bus that I knew was traveling through from Huntington, Tennessee, en route to Memphis. Arriving in Memphis, Tennessee, about two o'clock in the afternoon, years after living with my dad and stepmother, I felt a deep-down thrill inside my inner being that I didn't know how to describe. I didn't know where to go. I did intend to go to my mother's house, but I didn't know where she lived. I did, however, remember my aunt Francis. I knew almost where she lived because of visiting her several times with my dad, who was her brother.

I walked through the terminal after retrieving my small suitcase from the underneath compartment of the bus. I knew that everything I had in the world was contained in that small suitcase. I didn't know what it was, but that bus terminal had a familiarity about it, with all the fumes and people rushing here and there, people sitting throughout, talking, watching small personal TVs that were attached to the same seats where they were sitting. I took a deep breath and pushed my shoulders back. Carrying my small suitcase, I walked out the front doors onto Madison Avenue, pausing briefly to look around, staring up at the tall buildings of the downtown area. There was nothing but asphalt and concrete, making me think this was a lot different from the small country town of McLemoresville, which I had become accustomed to after so many years. Memphis, Tennessee, had an extreme difference in size but was not an unfamiliar place to me due to relatives living in this area. I also thought briefly of my sister Pat, which somehow took a small piece of a frightening experience away, because I knew as soon as I found her, I would be okay.

So I started walking away from the downtown area southward, toward the location of Jackson Avenue, which was near where I knew my aunt Francis lived. I knew that if I could just get to my aunt Francis's house, then I could confide in her about my circumstances and that hopefully, she could help me find my sister Pat and my mother. I had just turned seventeen years old, and during all these years, I probably had not spent more than three years total with my mother. I had spent a lot of my childhood in and out of foster homes, state juvenile facilities, Catholic homes, etc. all my juvenile life. My dad, however, eventually went to court, as I mentioned earlier in my story, and obtained permission for me to live with him. That was when I was about nine. Again, because of hostilities with my stepmother, my dad was put in a very peculiar and awkward position with my other siblings, and as I was the eldest, the only alternative was for him to ask me to leave, which brings me to my present situation. I was excited to a certain degree and felt like this was going to be, whether good or bad, a new beginning in my life. I really didn't know much about my mother; I just knew that I loved her and had never been in any position during my life to either see her or live with her. And living with my stepmother, I had to suppress my feelings and never mentioned anything about my mother.

I continued walking, my suitcase seeming to get heavier and heavier, and began switching it from hand to hand, trying to pay special attention to the cars wheezing past me. I noticed it had begun to get dusk, and I decided to do what I did when I was living with my dad and I had to get from town to town, and that was hitchhiking.

I walked backward for a few steps, putting on my right hand and my thumb up, trying to catch a ride down Jackson Avenue. Then a car stopped. The driver, leaning over, asked where I was going. I leaned over to the passenger-side window and told him I was going to my aunt's house close to the national cemetery on Jackson Street. He said, "Okay, go ahead and hop in. I'm going that way." We drove down Jackson Avenue, and he carried on a general conversation, asking me where I was from and smiling over at me when he asked what problem I had gotten myself into with a smirk on his face. Looking puzzled over toward him, I asked why he thought I was in trouble. He answered, saying, "Well, you looked like you were lost, and you had that suitcase, hitchhiking in Memphis."

I began to explain to him, "I just caught a Greyhound bus from McLemoresville, and I was moving up here to stay with my mother until I found a job."

As he drove, he turned off Jackson Avenue onto another street, and I asked him why he was turning off Jackson. "Well, I got to go by a friend's house to pick up something." Then he reached over and put his hand on my shoulder, smiling and squeezing my shoulder. "It won't take a few minutes. Relax. I'll get you to your aunt's house in a while."

I began to feel very uneasy because of the way he looked at me and the way he was squeezing my shoulder. "Listen," I said, "my aunt Francis just lives down that street over there." I pointed to the direction I thought was close to the shopping mall that I was familiar with.

He continued to drive around different streets, talking to me about how old I was and that I was a really nice-looking guy. At one point, he reached over and put his hand on my leg, squeezing it, then I noticed he just turned onto another street that looked like had passed near my aunt's house. I yelled out, "That's my aunt's house, back over there! Let me out here. I'll walk from here!"

"No," he said in a calm voice. "Everything is going to be okay. I'll take you. Just relax."

"Now, please!" I said, feeling extremely uneasy. I was feeling afraid. My eyes began to water. It got to the point where I thought I was in fear for my life or whatever else this strange person had in mind. I was so close to my aunt's house, and I found myself riding in a car with some stranger that might be a killer and certainly had given me the impression that he had some sort of bad intentions.

"Just relax. You're making that handsome young face of yours look so good! I'll take you back in a few minutes."

"Now, please!" I began to plead. "Just let me out. I'll walk from here!"

He turned onto another street and drove down, circling back onto Jackson Avenue, then stopped. "Okay, young man. Here you are. Hoping to see you again!"

I opened the car door quickly, grabbed my suitcase, and started walking toward my aunt's house, which I knew was less than a block away. After taking several long strides, I briefly looked back to make sure he was pulling away from me. I made a mental note of what he looked like because I sure didn't want to run into him again. I noticed that he was in his late forties to early fifties, wore small-rimmed glasses, had short hair graying around the temples, and I certainly couldn't forget the smell of aftershave mixed with perspiration; that, along with the scared feeling, almost made me sick to my stomach. The street that I had gotten out onto was a large one, but I could see at the end, thank God, was the avenue that my aunt lived on.

I hurried up the concrete steps, reached her house, and knocked on the front door. The thought crossed my mind: What if no one was there? What would I do now? Where would I go? I thought, *Is there anyone else, a relative, I could call now?* I had come unprepared. I didn't have any numbers with me, and Memphis was such a big town. I looked around the side of the house, which had a driveway that went up into the backyard. My aunt's house was close to other houses, which was usually the case in large cities. I thought I heard the sound of a door slamming coming from the backyard area. I looked around at a clothesline with clothes hanging from it, and suddenly I heard someone walking from inside the house. I went to the back door, calling out loudly, "Aunt Francis, this is Bubba! Are you in there?"

"Well, I'll be! Bubba, what are you doing up here? And where's your dad?" She started looking around. "And Bonnie, your mom?"

"Aunt Francis, they're not here. I'm by myself. I hitched. Now, I took the bus. I am moving here!" I said. "Aunt Francis, I thought maybe I'd come by to see you and maybe see if you could help me find my mother."

"Son, come on in the house. I think I have some tea. Would you like some? You know your aunt Francis always has tea. Been doing some laundry, as you can see. With the clothes hanging outside, it sure makes everything smell better when they hang out in the air." She started rambling around in the kitchen. "Sit down over there," she said, pointing toward the table. "Bubba, you said you came up here to look for your mama and your sister Pat. I really don't know where your mom is. We really don't communicate that much. I have seen your sister Patricia, though. She comes by now and again. But I haven't seen her in going on two months now. I might have some phone numbers here. Let me look. I think she gave me her number the last time she came by to see me. She just stayed for a while. I think she had somebody outside in the car who didn't seem to have dropped her off because whoever it was waited in the car." She paused. "You want something to eat, young'un?"

She then began to name off country food that Southern women specialized in and then got up to get a plate out and began to dish out some beans and potatoes and corn bread onto a plate without waiting, really, for a response. She placed the plate in front of me and then a glass of tea. She again sat across from me. "So you're going to move to Memphis and stay with your mother?" she asked, giving me a strange look. "Does she know you're coming up here? I guess you're grown enough to decide what you want to do." She smiled at me.

"Yes, ma'am, Aunt Francis." And then I began to explain that while I was living with my dad, I had been asked to leave because Bonnie, whom I mentioned was my stepmother, and I had an argument and I just couldn't take it anymore. "She had gotten up in my face, accusing me of eating something, and followed me from room to room, fussing at me, getting up in my face," I began to explain. "I did try, Aunt Francis, to get away from her. But she followed me wherever I went like she wanted to cause a reaction."

Aunt Francis asked, "Where was your dad when this was going on?"

"He was doing his work under the sink, and I guess he wasn't doing anything or saying anything at that time." I began to tear up as I explained to Aunt Francis. "I guess I just lost control and slapped her without realizing what I was doing. She just kept accusing me of something I knew I hadn't done, then all of a sudden, I guess I couldn't take it anymore and slapped her."

"Well, son, what happened then?" my aunt asked.

"Mama looked over at Daddy, who was still under the sink, and said, 'Did you see what your son just did?' My dad answered, 'Well, yes,' and told me, 'Hershel, go outside,' with a slight grin on his face, and told my mama, 'Why were you badgering him, of all things, with food?' She answered, saying, 'He took the last hamburger, and I was saving one or two of those for my lunch for work tomorrow.' My sister Cynthia spoke up and said, 'Now, Mama, Hershel didn't eat it. I saw Tommy eating them behind the house just after we got home from school.' She interrupted Cynthia, saying, 'You are just taking up for your brother and blaming it on Tommy!'"

My aunt Francis was a precious human being and the sister of my dad. She had raised four sons and a daughter basically by herself on a farm that she sharecropped with the owner of the land, a Mr. Burns, if my memory serves me. Mr. Burns allowed her to live on the house that occupied part of the land he owned in exchange for part of the proceeds from the sales of the crops that she and her sons raised. My aunt Francis was also the mother figure in my life because she showed me and my sisters love while we also lived on this farm with her when we had no other place to live. This was during the time in our early childhood before we went to Memphis and got put into different foster homes and Catholic orphanages.

I and my aunt sat around the table and talked about the early times when we lived on the farm along with her children, my cousins, laughing and reminiscing about all the good times. We also had some bad times living on the farm because all of us had to do our own part helping in the fields and feeding all the farm animals because some of the animals were also used to working in the fields. We went to the fields early, and Aunt Francis would wake us before daylight and had something to eat on the table while she would be stationed up at the stove, looking back to make sure that we were eating. She would come around and place an egg on each of our plates, along with some gravy and biscuits, and whole hog sausage, which was well-known here in the Southern states. We had to eat in a hurry because we had to go to the field and work before catching the school bus.

Reminiscing about the early times on the Burns farm with my aunt Francis, I also remembered this was a good, loving, family-oriented environment that I really believed paved the way for my life. I wished later in my life that I had never left this lifestyle, but of course, life does not stand still.

"Bubba," my aunt said, "I don't know where your mother might be, but I can make a few phone calls and see what we can find out. I do have your sister Pat's number. The last time she visited, she left it with me. Let me look over here next to the telephone. I'm sure when we get in touch with her, she would know where your mother might be. She was here a few weeks ago, but she did not stay very long. I think she had someone down in the car and seemed to be in some sort of hurry, I guess to get back to whoever was waiting for her." She paused. "I'll also call Ruth Ann [who was her only daughter], and ask if she has heard from your sister."

I walked over to the big window that had a view of the street outside, worrying now if I would find my sister and thinking how I did not want to be a problem to my aunt. I noticed that this apartment that she now lived in was not like the large farmhouse in Ripley, Tennessee. Ruth Ann and my sister Pat were close to the same age and were inseparable when we lived on the farm. I began to walk around, looking at all the pictures on the wall of our relatives, some I remembered, and then others must have been old relatives from our past, because of the age of the photographs.

Going back to the living room window, I looked outside and began to wonder what the future was going to have for me. Then again, I didn't really care at this time; I just knew that God would take care of me and he was the one who had led me to this point in my life. My grandmother always told me to trust in the Lord and to ask and you shall receive the greatness that God has for you. I was finally here at a stage in my life where I could be with my mother and sister Patricia. I knew that I was old enough to get a job because I had worked during the summer at various farms. I was hoping, though, to find a job in one of the factories and possibly start a mature life in the big city of Memphis. First thing I needed to do when working was to get a car to get around, because I did not want the same thing that had just happened with that strange man to happen ever again.

I overheard my aunt talking to her daughter, Ruth Ann, and she explained to her, "Your cousin Bubba is over here at my house and had taken a Greyhound bus, saying that he is moving up here to live with his mother." As she spoke, she looked over toward me, smiling, saying, "Okay, I'll try that number if I can find it. If you hear of anything else, make sure that you call me right away, in case I can't find the number. Bye. Love you!" Turning toward me, she said, "Ruth Ann had this number." She looked down at her scratch pad. "But I think this is the same number that your sister gave me." She began dialing the number, and I could hear the ringing at the other end. Eventually, no one answered, and she hung up. "Guess we just have to keep trying this number, and Ruth Ann will also keep trying."

My aunt told me where her son Jerry worked. He was like a brother to me, and we had fond memories working, living, and playing on the Burns farm. I decided, being very nervous and fidgety, that I would walk up to the place she said that he worked at, which was a corner grocery store just a block away. As I walked toward the store, my mind began to think about finally getting the chance to spend some time with my mother, because in my earlier years, that wasn't possible because my sisters and I always got picked up by the police and taken to the juvenile court, or we were staying with relatives.

I remember, while we briefly stayed with my grandmother on my mother's side, my uncle Steven, who was just a year older than me due to my grandmother having him later in her life, was asked by my mother to take his bike and go to the corner store to get her cigarettes. I don't know why she did not go herself, as she often did while leaving us locked in the house alone. I think, looking back, that maybe she did not want to get into an argument with our grandmother, which she often did when she left us for long periods. Maybe it was also because Steven was there. Steven left with enough money for what Mama wanted, and a little extra for Steven to also get something for himself, and maybe for me and my sisters. A short while later, we could hear the awfully loud sound of what we knew to be fire trucks and police sirens. A short time later, a policeman came to the door; he was a familiar face from the times we had been taken to juvenile court for lack of parental supervision. He also knew my uncle and grandmother, which was why he was there. I could hear a mumble back and forth in their conversation, and suddenly my mother began to scream at the very top of her lungs. The policeman told my mother that Steven, her baby brother, was killed when a large truck collided with Steven as he crossed in front of it on Danny Thomas Boulevard. He had been dragged several hundred feet before other cars were able to notify the truck driver he had struck Steven and his bike.

I quickly shook my head and continued walking down the street toward where I knew my cousin Jerry to be. Entering the store at the corner, I just walked toward the back because my aunt told me that he worked in the meat department. I suddenly saw a familiar face, and both of us had a large smile on our faces. He took off the white apron from around his front and slung it on the freezer, then reached out. We embraced each other.

"Mother called and told me you were here and was walking up," he said.

We stood talking for a long while. He said that this was his break time, and so we went out the back of the store and spent time talking about our childhood on the farm.

I stayed the night at my aunt's and was later joined by her eldest son, James, whom I thought of as a father figure when on the farm and who ran most of all the farm business. James and Bobby, Aunt Francis's two eldest sons, were always good to us and went into the Marines while I still lived there on the farm.

The next morning, we finally reached my sister Pat, and of course, I was more than relieved. She said that she would come over to pick me up. I stood at the big bay window in great anticipation of my sister's arrival. When she finally arrived, I waved at her with an attempt to hold back tears of joy and was relieved to be able to do just that. After all, I was now a seventeen-year-old and needed to try to act like it. I ran out the door and got to the car, and she was just able to get out when we both hugged each other so tight I thought we were going to lose our breath. She quickly introduced me to her friend, who was driving, as I got into the back seat.

"Bubba, this is my friend Sherman, a good friend of mine, and, Sherman, this is my brother, Bubba." Then she laughed.

Sherman was a large Black man, at least 250 pounds. This was about 1970, but even then, I did not see color when I looked at a person; I looked at their personality and spirit.

For the next several weeks in Memphis, I stayed with my sister Pat and with other friends. The lifestyle of Memphis was somewhat different from the lifestyle that I was accustomed to in the small town. Of course, we had our share of bootleggers, and my best friend's mother was a bootlegger, so it was not that I hadn't ever drunk alcohol. In the small town, though, and being underage, you'd get it from the bootlegger and you'd go right down the country and drink from the tailgate of your pickup truck. But with my sister, we would go around to a lot of nightclubs and juke joints. I tried to put my big boy pants on and act like this was just another day.

I did eventually see my mother and my stepfather and the little brother whom they had together, Eddie. After a little while, it was arranged, and I moved in with my mother and got a job in a painting factory, from where I rode my little brother's bike back and forth each day. But eventually, my stepfather, not unlike my stepmother, felt that he did not want me there. After coming home from work one day, I was met at my mom's house by my sister Pat and was informed by her that I could no longer stay with Mama and would have to come with her. I was traumatized because I had been with my mom for several months now, had a job, and felt like everything was finally going well.

Eventually, I remembered I was interested in the United States Navy. While in school, I used to get the encyclopedias out and look at the pictures of the aircraft carriers, the section with the uniforms and the badges on the sleeves, and always had in the back of my mind that this would be my way to a better life. While staying with my sister and the lifestyle that it involved, I concluded I was even out of place with her. One day, I decided that I would walk myself into a naval recruiter's office and this would be my way out. I had just turned eighteen years of age in November.

Going to the recruiter's office in Memphis, Tennessee, I took all the tests, written, physical, and felt comfortable that I would be accepted. At first, I was worried about the written test, wondering if I could pass them. I really wasn't concerned with the physical part of it because I felt healthy. After all, I was eighteen years of age. This was about February after I had turned eighteen in November. I was taken into an office to review all the requirements that I had taken and was told, "Everything checked out okay on the written part of your required batteries, but there seems to be a problem with your blood pressure." I listened, and my heart just sank, thinking how I was worried about the written exams and now they were telling me that my blood pressure was going to disqualify me from enlistment.

I looked at the examiner, then the physician. "Listen," I said, "please, I have got to get into the Navy!" I was thinking silently to myself, *I am basically homeless, and I know that if I get in the Navy, I could somehow make a career of it and that would be my way out of living the lifestyle I have found myself in.*

The physician told me, "If you can get your blood pressure down to a normal level, then we can see what we can do." He also stated that because of my weight, which I had gained, I believe, from working on a riverboat, I was to refrain from taking any alcohol or having sex and come back in three days, and if my blood pressure was at the normal level, they would enlist me. I did this, and after three days, of course, the level did go down. I also pleaded again with the recruiter, and he said, "Come back in three months and get your weight down, because that's where your problem with your blood pressure is coming from, and then we will re-evaluate the situation." So for three months, I dieted and ran each day through the ghetto area of Memphis, where I lived, and lost thirty pounds by May 1. I was so desperate during this time I thought maybe I could go to a different town and enlist, so I went to Jackson, Tennessee, and of course, they were aware of my enlistment attempts at Memphis and sent me on my way.

Again, on May 1, 1972, I went back to the federal building recruitment office in downtown Memphis and approached the same recruiter, who met me in complete surprise and amazement at how much weight I had lost. He told me, "Son, you really want to get into the Navy, don't you?"

I responded, "Yes, sir. I have got to."

He said, "Come with me. Let's take that blood pressure, and if that turns out okay, we'll get you off to Orlando first thing in the morning." He walked me back to the hall toward the physician's office, calling his name. "Hey, Doc. You remember this young man back in January?"

"Well, I sure do! I believe your blood pressure was a problem, wasn't it? Let me check that. We still got your records from last time, and if your blood pressure checks are right, we'll take care of you." To finalize this dramatic and joyous accomplishment in my life, my blood pressure was normal, and I was put in one of the rooms of the Peabody Hotel, picked up by a government recruiter's car the next morning, was taken to the airport, and was flown out to Orlando, Florida, to begin my basic training in May 1972.

Now, I would like to briefly explain how I later in life attempted to cope with the traumas of my early childhood, which involved not only me personally but also my other siblings.

Survival Techniques Used with the Help of God

The world cannot be without stress. Since the beginning of the creation of the world, there have been various types of stressors. Throughout history, civilization has tried to develop different ways to treat the effects of the stressors of life. The world is full of nervous, tense, apprehensive, and worried people. Stress is an individual problem and thus needs to be managed on an individual basis. The environment in which people grow up relates to their tolerance to the type of stress they can endure. Several years ago, I began to write this biography of my life with the intention of helping people who have been in a similar disruptive lifestyle as me. Due to a dysfunctional and extremely emotional childhood, I have learned through various life challenges to handle stress and to live somewhat of a productive life.

In the next few segments, I would like to submit some ideas that I have used in an attempt to achieve this. I have chosen to be a survivor of dramatic childhood traumas, and in doing this, I have sought out different coping methods in order to find some sense of emotional stability.

Since I was a young child, my life has been out of the "norm," as our society would define as ordinary. My life was one of disruption and destruction because of the divorce of my parents and their inability to care or know where my two sisters or I would eat or sleep.

Most nights I had difficulty trying to sleep. I had frequent nightmares, where I would wake up screaming, shaking, and drenched in sweat. I began to have bad headaches, and my body would shake and quiver during and for several hours after violent arguments that we constantly had to endure. Depression and stress combined along with headaches and bleeding ulcers also brought on other sicknesses, such as pneumonia. My early childhood was filled with destruction and disruption for me and my entire family. Looking back on these difficult times and events in my life, I believe most of the problems were caused by the use of alcohol by my birth mother.

Her drinking alcoholic beverages, I believe now, created problems for my physical and emotional health at different times throughout my entire life.

I wanted to find a way to make my mother and father happy and stop their fighting and her drinking. I was constantly worried about my mother leaving and didn't know the people with whom she had left us most of the time. I had to find a way to stop worrying about my parents and/or the lifestyle we had to endure at such an early age. Later in life, I realized that eating healthy food and finding solitude was a way to calm the stress in my life. Walking in nature also helped me relax. Sometimes I would spend hours walking and talking to different animals throughout nature.

I also had a friend that would show up when I really needed him the most, at different times in my life, especially when praying to God about help in these bad situations! His name, he told me, was Mr. Gabe. He was a wanderer and said that he traveled throughout the world. I was so thankful that he would seem to show up just at the perfect time for me to have someone to talk to, and he seemed to always give me comfort with the things that he would say, especially about our heavenly Father.

My sisters were also a comfort to me with my physical and emotional health problems. We tried to spend as much time as we could together, talking and assuring one another that everything was going to be all right. My health and emotional problems began to get better with good food. I began to realize that eating the right foods and trying not to worry were effective to have better health. This attitude helped me learn what I needed to do to stay emotionally and physically strong. I also began to realize that bad emotional health sometimes leads to bad physical health. Both physical health and emotional health are connected, and one can affect the other. I have tried to keep my body healthy, which is a good principle. It has helped me set the foundation for my ability to train myself to handle the stressors of life.

Because of numerous other life experiences that were also very bad, I have had to continually study ways to manage stress and deal with depression throughout my life. I have read numerous books that specialized in ways to cope with stress. I am the second eldest of five siblings. Two of my siblings, a younger brother and a younger sister, died at an early age. My younger brother died at the age of forty-four and had already had two heart attacks and had acquired diabetes. At the age of fifty, my younger sister died just four months earlier than this brother. Her condition was alcoholism, emotional breakdowns, and liver damage, possibly brought on by the combination of pre-scription drugs and alcohol. The siblings had grown up around the same stressors. Another brother, who is forty-six, has diabetes and numerous other illnesses.

I have been fortunate enough to seek out numerous therapeutic books and lectures on emotional and physical health. I have survived and have the desire to continue to survive. I stay away from too much caffeine, watch my diet, exercise, and have stopped smoking years ago. I also avoid intoxicating beverages in excess.

In my early childhood, I did not want to face the realities of what was going on around me and what was hurting me either physi-cally or especially emotionally. I believe, subconsciously, I might have attempted to close myself off and deny what was happening in life. In this detachment style of denial, I protected myself from the reality of seeing and feeling physical or emotional things. This method of denial got me through safely when I had no other means of survival. However, as I grew older, I began to discover and realize I had lost touch with my true feelings emotionally. I had denied that my trau-matic past happened. Allowing this reality to surface at that time would probably have killed me from the shock. From an early age, I learned that in order to survive, I would have to find ways to deal with my traumatic past.

Conclusion

Stress is a condition or feeling experienced when a person perceives that "demands exceed the personal and social resources the individual is able to mobilize." In short, it is what we feel when we think we have lost control of events. What is confusing is that we think we know what stress is, because it is something we all have experienced. We must manage our stress levels according to our own personalities and vulnerabilities. Every person is different. What might work for one might not for someone else.

May God allow me to tell this story in the hopes and prayers that it will somehow help and bless others that have lived similar lives.

Your servant,
Hershel Marise

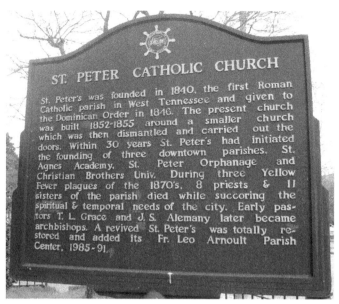

ST. PETER CATHOLIC CHURCH

St. Peter's was founded in 1840, the first Roman Catholic parish in West Tennessee and given to the Dominican Order in 1846. The present church was built 1852-1855 around a smaller church which was then dismantled and carried out the doors. Within 30 years St. Peter's had initiated the founding of three downtown parishes. St. Agnes Academy, St. Peter Orphanage and Christian Brothers Univ. During three Yellow Fever plagues of the 1870's, 8 priests & 11 sisters of the parish died while succoring the spiritual & temporal needs of the city. Early pastors T. L. Grace and J. S. Alemany later became archbishops. A revived St. Peter's was totally restored and added its Fr. Leo Arnoult Parish Center, 1985-91.

Saint Peter's Orphanage Plaque located in Memphis, TN where I was taken about 1959–1960.

Saint Peter's orphanage at the turn of the century. It has changed through time, but it was a frightening place for young orphans.

My mom, Juenette, her second husband, Edward
Crawford, and my brother, Eddie Crawford.

My mother's mom, my grandmother, Mrs. Carter.

In Columbus Ohio; little Hershel (Baba), and
my sister Patricia (Pat) middle 1950's.

My sister Cynthia and myself, Hershel (Baba), in Tennessee.

Hershel and big sister, Patricia. We were always close to each other.

Our mama, Juenette Marise, somewhere in Ohio 1950's.

My daddy in early 1950's the mid-south fair, Memphis, TN.
The date was covered up by his position in the photo.

Mama, Junette Marise, and little Hershel (Baba)
somewhere in time Columbus, OH.

My precious sister, Cynthia Jane (deceased at the early
age of fifty) sitting alongside my brother, Gary.

Hershel, Cynthia, and
Patricia visiting one of our
aunts on mama's side of
family in Muncie, IN.

Sister Pat, our loving daddy,
and myself, Hershel (Baba).

Our mama, Juenette, early 1950's.

About the Author

Several years ago, Hershel Marise began to write an autobiography of his life with the intention of helping people who have been in a similar disruptive lifestyle as him resolve their emotional past. Due to a dysfunctional and extremely emotional childhood, Hershel has learned through various life challenges to handle stress and to live a productive life. This biography has certain segments about the early part of Hershel Marise's life. It covers the adolescent ages of life. The traumatic childhood experiences that Hershel and his siblings endured, he wishes to share in this story. It tries to express to the reader that there is a great Creator, and this Creator has been sheltering and guiding Hershel throughout his life. Without this Creator, God, life probably would not have been possible for him. Hershel knows that God's DNA is, without a doubt, within him and that he did create all that we see, even when all of humankind gazes up at the sky at night and in awe of the universe and beyond. The greatest creation of all is the human body. Hershel does not believe he is a perfect man, and he does not think there is such a thing except one, and he is no longer here. Our great Creator is. Our Father is sometimes proud of his children, and sometimes not, but he loves everyone unconditionally. Hershel believes that as he goes through this life, he will, as the Father, give Hershel what he needs if he does his very best and asks the Lord to guide him through any trials that try to come between him and his love to the Father.

Printed in the USA
CPSIA information can be obtained
at www.ICGtesting.com
JSHW022109270723
45523JS00001B/48